Buddhist
Christianity

A Passionate Openness

Buddhist Christianity

A Passionate Openness

Ross Thompson

BOOKS

Winchester, UK
Washington, USA

First published by O-Books, 2010
O Books is an imprint of John Hunt Publishing Ltd., The Bothy, Deershot Lodge, Park Lane, Ropley,
Hants, SO24 0BE, UK
office1@o-books.net
www.o-books.com

For distributor details and how to order please visit the 'Ordering' section on our website.

Text copyright: Ross Thompson 2009

ISBN: 978 1 84694 336 2

A CIP catalogue record for this book is available from the British Library.

Design: Stuart Davies

Printed in the UK by CPI Antony Rowe
Printed in the USA by Offset Paperback Mfrs, Inc

We operate a distinctive and ethical publishing philosophy in all
areas of its business, from its global network of authors to
production and worldwide distribution.

CONTENTS

Acknowledgements

This book would never have been thought of without Andrew Morris who has been a companion in my journey in the borderlands between Buddhism and Christianity since our university days. It was he who planned and led the two courses at the Tibetan Buddhist World Peace Centre on Holy Island, off the coast of Arran in Scotland, where I reconnected with Buddhism and realized I had to write this book. On a more academic level thanks are due especially to Paul Williams and Gavin D'Costa with whom I discussed my original ideas. Though they won't agree with the position I come to in this book, their constructive criticisms helped me avoid some pitfalls and create a much sounder basis for it. I am likewise grateful to all who kindly read the typescript and made the positive comments that appear on the cover and elsewhere; and to my Sri Lankan friends Niwantha and Athiene, who gave me a sense of how Buddhism works for ordinary believers, and introduced me to temple worship. Finally as always I thank Judith, my wife, who read the drafts and suggested some valuable improvements to both style and content.

All You Need to Know

This book presupposes no detailed knowledge of either Buddhism or Christianity, and ideas are explained as they arise. Those who have not encountered Buddhism at all need to know that in the centuries before Christ it divided into two forms:

The **Theravada** or 'Way of the Elders' aims to be close to the original teachings of the Buddha as expressed in the texts written in the Pali Language. This form predominates today in Sri Lanka, Myanmar, Thailand, Laos and Kampuchea.

The **Mahayana** or 'Great Vehicle' adopts a more speculative approach with more tolerance for ideas from different traditions, based on innumerable texts written in Sanskrit, as well as the languages of the lands to which it spread: China, Korea, Japan and Vietnam. Zen Buddhism is the best known form of Mahayana Buddhism in the West, but equally prevalent is Shin Buddhism, about which more is found in Chapter 5.

In the early centuries after Christ, Buddhism in India incorporated Tantric techniques, that is a variety of 'skillful means' – phrases, gestures, rituals, even sexual practices – thought to assist liberation, as well as a very rich mythology of Buddhas and deities. In Tibet this was further mixed with the local shamanism to produce a variety of Mahayana Buddhism that is so distinctive that it is often called the **Vajrayana** or 'diamond vehicle'. Along with Zen this is probably the best known form of Buddhism in the West.

As for Christianity, most but not all readers will be aware that it also takes three main forms.

Eastern Orthodoxy claims to be faithful to the teachings of the early theologians and the councils of the Church up until the eighth century. It involves intricate worship including the veneration of icons, and an emphasis on the universal Christ and the mystery of God, and is the predominant form in Greece, the

Balkans and Russia. In the book 'Orthodox' with a capital 'O' means this form of Christianity.

Roman Catholicism also claims this basis but adds to it the authority of the Pope and the later councils of the Western Church. It divided from Orthodoxy in 1054 and predominates in the western Mediterranean, Poland, Ireland and Latin America, having a foothold in many lands colonized by France, Spain and Portugal.

Protestantism broke from Catholicism in the early sixteenth century, rejects all authority other than the Bible and (in varying degrees) human reason, and asserts that salvation comes not through the Church but directly to the believer through faith. It predominates in Northern Europe, North America and Australasia and has a foothold in many lands colonized by Britain.

The **basic beliefs** common to all Buddhists, and those common to all Christians, are summarized at the end of the Introduction.

Buddhism expresses itself across many **languages**. I use the terms most familiar in the West, which is most often Sanskrit, sometimes Pali or Japanese, and occasionally Tibetan or Chinese. Where the term has become part of Western vocabulary – like 'karma' and 'Nirvana' – I do not italicize; otherwise I italicize all words from non-English languages, but avoid the use of phonetic markings. They are obviously not integral to the original languages, nor do they contribute to correct pronunciation or correct understanding of the terms. For the same reason Tibetan terms are transcribed phonetically, so as to be easily readable.

Bible references are from the New Revised Standard Version, unless otherwise stated.

Autobiographical Prelude:
The Twice-Shattered Pot

I am there and I am here
I am away and I am home,
I am never again and not yet
and what is here dissolves:
a space to imagine, a place to be.
Here is where it happens,
There is where it rests.
There is where it happens,
Here is where it rests.

I wrote this little ditty while looking across the waters on a warm, hazy day from the Tibetan Buddhist World Peace Centre to the coast of Arran in Scotland. It means many different things to me, but right now it refers to the 'here' and 'there' of the Buddhism and Christianity that (I now think) have always been there in my life, sometimes changing places. For a long time my Christian faith was where it all happened for me, but even then there was an unconscious Buddhist in me where all that activity implicitly came to rest.

What I am exploring in this book is the possibility for me now to affirm equally the here and the there of my life, and profess an explicitly Buddhist Christianity.

So though this book is not a spiritual autobiography, my reasons for writing it are very autobiographical. So to provide the best way in to the book, I begin with my own life. I sense that my own journey through the two faiths is important not because it is special, but on the contrary, because it is becoming quite common in a world where people are inevitably increasingly eclectic, choosing a faith not because of their origins and roots in a society, but because it rings true at a certain point of their life journey.

I write because I have come to a point in my life where I feel I owe both faiths a kind of unconditional allegiance. Faiths do have a habit of generating unconditional allegiance in some people, which is one of the reasons why some other people fear and avoid them. What makes for this kind of allegiance, and what makes it healthy or dangerous, is one of the things this book will touch on. But my specific dilemma comes from believing I have an absolute allegiance to both Buddhism and Christianity, without denying the real differences between them. How can I avoid being torn apart by serving two masters, or if I am torn apart in some way, how can I live with that with integrity, and even make spiritual use of it? These are the kinds of question I have in mind as I write this book, and I have no doubt that they are not questions for me alone.

So let's take a brief look at this little life of mine, and how it has been at different stages Buddhist and Christian. I find myself best able to do this by focusing on certain 'snapshots' just as one might do when thumbing through a photograph album. Certain memories stand out as somehow significant in they way they were forming me as a Christian or a Buddhist.

Two Childhoods

One of the earliest snapshots is of my sister and me together with our mother attending the Eucharist at St. Andrew's, Surbiton. I was then about six or seven, and my sister two years younger. Two or so years earlier we had both been baptized in that Church, but my father had not attended because of his agnosticism. The Church was a 'shrine' of the then strong Anglo-Catholic tradition. I remember a dark, tall, austere, empty space, which the rich tapestry of the vestments, the smell of incense and the chanting of the liturgy filled. The service was in Prayer-Book English, not Latin, but that made little difference to a schoolboy of six or so; the worship left me with an atmosphere, not concepts. Above all

4

I remember going up to the altar and kneeling with mother, and that expression of devotion on her face, as she received something I did not know about, but could tell was very special – Holy Communion. In a sense I then knew what 'mystery' was – a bodily act that went beyond what words could say – and this has become more and more vital to my faith, both as a Christian, and as a Buddhist.

The next snapshot at first sight has nothing to do with 'religion'. I was at infant school, around the same stage in life. It was playtime and outside the gate a large crowd of children had gathered, screaming and shouting. I went to see what was going on, and saw the children had discovered a large stag beetle. A big American boy whom I was very afraid of was whipping the beetle to death with a skipping rope. As far as I could tell most of the children were egging the boy on; perhaps for them the black little monster was an epitome of evil, or perhaps watching cruelty happen was just fun. I don't know, but all my sympathies were with the beetle as it lay on its back waving its legs in a futile attempt to ward off the rope. There was nothing I could do – the boy with the whip was far too big and menacing, and seemed to have the support of everyone else – so I just watched helplessly. This feeling of helpless sympathy has stayed with me; it epitomized feelings I have always had when the weak have been made to suffer by the strong and we can do nothing about it. Looking back I think there was something Christian in this sympathy for the underdog (even if the 'dog' in question was a beetle!), and something Buddhist about the way it extended to beings not on account of their humanity, but their sentience. The fact that this superficially ugly (but actually very beautiful) creature evoked these feelings, not because it was like me, but simply because (so far as I could tell) it was suffering, is very Buddhist, I think, related to an ethic of *ahimsa*, not-harming, which perhaps predisposed me to embrace Buddhism when I later came to know about it.

The third snapshot relates to the first time I talked with my father about religion. I was about eight, and we were in the kitchen, and he was explaining that he thought we could not know whether or not God existed, and that he believed Jesus was a great teacher, but not the Son of God. It may have been at this stage, or maybe later, that he explained that as a child he had worried deeply about whether God existed. But it suddenly dawned on him – almost as a revelation – that if God existed, in his infinite goodness he would not mind whether we believed in him or not, and certainly would not punish us for not doing so. So whether he existed of not was not something to worry about.

Suddenly it all made sense to me. Though I had a strong feeling for what I have called mystery, I had never formed a very clear idea of God. I was a little bit dyslexic at that stage, and confused the terms 'God' and 'dog', which did not help clarify anything! Altogether, God for me then was a bit like England – everybody seemed to believe in it, so it must exist, but I had no idea what it was. So when it emerged that someone as worthy of respect as my father was not concerned about God's existence, it suddenly became obvious to me that there was no God at all.

Looking back I suppose my age was significant: the time when boys turn from their mothers and start to model themselves on their fathers. Be that as it may, I rapidly out-trumped my father by becoming a strict and dogmatic atheist. My world view became something very familiar these days, scientific rationalism with a slightly pantheistic edge. I remember failing to console my mother and sister on my grandfather's death by explaining that he would be eaten by worms and become part of the whole wonderful cycle of nature! But at the time this really did console me. And I loved classifying and organizing the world, devising little tables of the different classes, orders and families of animals, based on the Encyclopaedia Britannica, all beautifully illustrated with little pictures. This love of classifying has never left me and sometimes I do take it too far!

A Teenage Buddhist – of Sorts

My encounter with Buddhism began when I was about 13. There was at that time, in the middle to late 1960s, a turning in youth culture to the East, pioneered by my pop idols, the Beatles, and others. We had in the town of Godalming, where our family now lived, a beautiful new library set by the river, where I loved to browse and read. I discovered a book (which I cannot now trace) relating Buddhism to the ideas of the 18th century philosopher, David Hume. It was dry and academic and there must have been lots in it I did not understand, but I got the gist. Both Buddha and Hume taught that the world was an impermanent flux, and that ideas of self and substantial reality were illusions. It was just the right thing to open the mind of a dogmatic atheist towards a kind of religion.

My imagination was being opened at that time, too, to poetry and drama – as well as female beauty – by a new English teacher, so I began to move beyond the narrow literalism of my boyhood. You could say the feminine or the mother was becoming the dominant force in my life again, after my period of father-dominated rationalism.

So I devoured many books on Buddhism by Ananda Comaraswami, Christmas Humphreys, D.T. Suzuki, Alan Watts and others. I told my parents, to their alarm, that I wanted to be a Buddhist monk when I grew up. At around 16 I wrote a long essay on Buddhism in which all the different schools were classified with my usual systematic neatness. It opened:

Buddhism is the religion of the Buddha, or 'Enlightened One,' who lived from 563 to 483 BC in North-Eastern India, and who preached that a state of being called Nirvana could be reached, after many lives of suffering, by anyone who led a life of good action and thought, and meditation. This was taught in the 'Four Noble Truths,' the 'Eightfold Path' and the 'Three Signs of Being' (suffering, impermanence and no-self),

7

and in other sermons and parables.

As the style here suggests, my Buddhism was of the head rather than the heart, and a matter of beliefs rather than practice, the latter being limited to a few attempts at meditation. In many ways Buddhism went with the grain of the introverted, solitary nature of my personality, just as, later, Christianity would go against and challenge it.

Two Conversions

In my later school years the Christian Union grew strong, preaching an uncompromising Evangelical Christianity, eagerly seeking conversions, and getting people very worried about hellfire. My friends and I held fast to our skepticism in our school days, but as we went our separate ways to university, one by one we succumbed. Before I converted to Christianity, however, I had an experience which was almost a reconversion to a kind of faith that combined – as I now see – my youthful poetic romanticism and the Tibetan form of Buddhism I had been learning about and moving towards.

I was walking back in my hometown in the Christmas holidays in one of the long winter evenings, feeling rootless and disoriented, not knowing whether I belonged here in this place I loved with my school friends and my memories, or at university where an exciting new world was opening up. I wrote:

I came upon a silent space. It was the war memorial, half-built, with the still fish-pond and the moon in it, in the moonlight. And the trees toward the west were towering, and the sky above them still lit, deep blue and silver, with stars, stars just beginning to show as lighter silver. I felt I had come upon somewhere in my mind, to one of those distant projections of our heart that we imagine, but never imagine realized. The perfection. The motionlessness... I moved, only I...

Something in all this made the questions my Christian Union friends raised seem limited and pointless:

> Why was the vision so Christless? Why was it that now the question of salvation seemed so petty? Because, damned or saved, it made no difference... Christ is specific, something to cling to. And it is, at bottom, the desire that one should individually continue, that makes one cling. But here it was not I, it was all around me... that existed, in that long moment, generously prolonged. That I should make an act, for this piece of flesh and mind alone, is... ludicrous.

But the issue went deeper, I felt.

> A sense of deep ecstasy entered through my heart like an icicle, the pond and moon were icicles mirroring a beyond. That was the ecstasy, the standing outside oneself, the 'turning about in the deepest seat of consciousness', the conversion inward towards the universe as it thrives within you as everywhere.... That the moon was just matter and the mists a dispersion of water; all this made for the intensity, the beauty, the truth. And it is Buddhism that could be my only companion in these truths, because it tells me about the impermanence and the round of suffering, and the terrible, beautiful Emptiness of things. [At the touch of Christ the Savior this beauty and truth is destroyed.]

The brackets represent deletion by a later editor, the me that a couple of months later had converted to Christianity. That conversion was absolutely different, as much to do with other people as this was an affair of my solitary self and the universe. After withstanding the dogmatic approaches of the university Christian Union – which horrified me, yet which I could not tear myself away from – I met two American students who had left their university and joined the Children of God. This sect has become rather notorious because of its combination of Evangelical Christianity and free love, which inevitably led to divisions and scandals, but this hippy-looking couple seemed to possess an innocence and freedom that contrasted with the straight-laced Puritanism of the Christian Union. I gave myself to the happily defenseless Christ I glimpsed in them.

Though I had been fighting against this fate for some time, at some level I obviously felt the need for it. Buddhism, as I said, had encouraged me in my solitude, and paradoxically – for this is obviously quite contrary to the intention of Buddhism – allowed me to become quite 'ego-bound' in the sense I shall explain. Christianity, by challenging my isolation and breaking by egocentric shell, opened me to others. Somebody commented that I was smiling and laughing much more.

Priesthood and After

After that I did not tarry long with the Evangelicals, but made my way slowly towards an Eastern Orthodox spirituality which seemed the best way of combining my new faith with the Buddhism that had mattered so much before. In rapid succession I met, fell in love with, and married Judith, who was a committed Anglican, then a lay worker. I settled on the Anglican variant of Christianity. It was not the form I was closest to spiritually, but in those days it had a humility about it, and a reserve about speaking too confidently about matters of faith, epitomized by Michael Ramsay who had recently been Archbishop. Anglicanism echoed my earliest experiences of the faith, and enabled Judith and me to be pilgrims together on the journey that led first me, and then when it became possible, Judith, to priesthood.

This led to 20 years of ministry in Bristol, and later as a theological lecturer in Cardiff. In many ways this was a very creative, successful and happy time of my life. I saw myself at that stage as a staunch though imaginative defender of Christian orthodoxy. But it all unraveled, as desires which my Christian faith had left untouched surfaced in a personal crisis. I think I had entered priesthood for authentic reasons, but it is hard for a priest not to become a little bit 'ego-bound'. In Christian terms, the hand of God was shown even in my sinfulness, thrusting me out into a bleak but transforming wilderness; in Buddhist terms, my own karma resulting from ego-bound desire had created, by the law of cause and effect, its own destructive consequences.

After my crisis, I began to publish, writing books on the sacraments and on Christian spirituality. My research for the latter deepened my knowledge of what I had already known; the incredible richness of that tradition, and the way it uses language in a paradoxical and poetic way that runs contrary to the objectifying rationalism that from the Middle Ages on increasingly became the norm in theology: reaching beyond words into the 'apophatic' indescribable depths of the divine mystery.

On travels in 1998 across the Himalayas into the Tibetan part of Nepal, as well as the Buddhist worship around the great stupas in Kathmandu and Sarnath, near Varanasi, I had already had my first real experience of living contact with Buddhist people practicing their faith. Then in 2007 on Holy Island, off the coast of Arran in Scotland, I connected with a living Tibetan Buddhist community, not only in dialogue, but in the sharing of worship and meditation in Christian and Tibetan Buddhist traditions, as well as offering reflections based on my work on Christian spirituality. Then a week later, at a Christian conference about forgiveness, I found myself – without really intending to – coming out with related Buddhist insights. What was going on?

I realize now that my two 'conversions' are as it were juxtaposed in my life. Both were intensely real, but whereas I have lived out a loyalty to the latter, I have yet really to explore the space the former opened up. The experience of Nepal and Holy

Island opened the space again, but the agenda of exploring the relation between my two 'conversions', and how I can be loyal to both, remains.

Making the Sky My Own

I guess a superficial look at part of my life could lead someone to describe me as a Christian who converted to Buddhism, and a similar look at a later part could lead another person to describe me as a Buddhist who converted to Christianity. The latter is how for a long time I described myself. It was after all a good and interesting way for a liberal Anglican priest to see himself. I did not claim that I had forsaken my Buddhist 'errors' for the Christian truth, for I always acknowledged that I had learned a lot from Buddhism. But I believed I had taken the Buddhist 'insights' into the ultimate truth, which was the Christian Gospel.

My crisis taught me that it was not enough to take on board spiritual insights from Buddhism. I actually needed some Buddhist practices, and more precisely some ways of feeling and being I had known in my Buddhist days, in order to come to healing, wholeness, salvation, liberation – or whatever one calls it. It has become clear to me that though in the Christian tradition there is plenty of talk about the need for humility, there is a lot in the practice that encourages one not to tackle the core task of freeing oneself from being 'ego-bound'. This is my term for the basically Buddhist idea that suffering comes from desire, and in particular the need, of the ego to hold onto things in order to hold onto itself. We define ourselves by desires that do not in fact originate in us, but as it were work their own way through us. Buddhism explains these desires as the result of past karma, past grasping that has built up a strongly defended ego.

Later on this book will explore the deep roots of clinging and desire. What is relevant now is that at an early stage my introverted Buddhism, and at a later stage my public Christianity, had in different ways failed to confront me with the fundamental problem that 'I' was. This was even more apparent when I became a priest, which offered me a strong, respected ego on the condition that I acted in certain loving, loyal and 'sacrificial' ways. Before I was a priest, and again now, I did not and do not think that priests are special people, but when I was one I subscribed to a 'high' view of priesthood that made us 'ontologically distinct' from lay people. Now priests sometimes (not always) seem to me to be trapped by their ego-needs into trying to make a success of churches that in our secular age are almost bound to decline. In my time I had been trapped in that way.

Being ego-bound is like a plant being pot-bound. At first the plant is protected and grows well, but after a time the roots exhaust the nourishment that is available in the container, and the pot, containing all root and no soil, cannot even soak up the rain that falls from above. A wise counselor whose job was the care of the clergy once told me that he found a majority of priests had 'dried up' after twenty years of parish ministry, but sadly, in many cases, their own and other people's expectations can lead them into denial of this condition. A pot-bound plant will die unless the pot is broken open so the roots can grow into the wider soil. In the same way the ego-bound priest will die spirituality unless something breaks and he or she is forced to find a new and broader way of being a priest. Thankfully, in me something had broken.

This image of the pot, however, needs an image to counterbalance it. As well as being more free, I was in obvious ways more limited now. The loss of the practice of priesthood concentrated my energies into the writing of books. I had always wanted to write, but previously my energies had been too dispersed for the sustained concentration required. My counselor asked me to focus on the Taoist image of the waterfall, which, the more it is channeled, the faster it flows and the deeper the ravine it carves. So my constraints could enable me to be more creative.

And there is a third image that comes to mind, different again, which comes from one of Anthony de Mello's wonderful parables:

> A crow once flew into the sky with a piece of meat in its beak. Twenty crows set out in pursuit of it and attacked it viciously. The crow finally let the piece of meat drop. Its pursuers then left it alone and flew shrieking after the piece of meat. Said the crow: "It is peaceful up here now. The whole sky belongs to me." (1983, p.178-9)

This is an excellent portrayal of desire, combining the notions of Buddhism with the mimetic theory explored in Chapter 4. The crows chase the one piece of meat rather than looking for their own, because the others are chasing that one piece of meat. By relinquishing that kind of desire, the first crow finds that he possesses much more – the whole empty sky. When Mahayana Buddhists speak of 'emptiness', they are surely describing something like this openness that is free from desire. It was what I had found by the memorial pond, I think. There is plenty in the Christian spiritual tradition from the Gospels onward, through Meister Eckhart and most of the mystical tradition, about the need for 'detachment'. But on the whole this tradition does not seem to be alive in our churches today. And when you speak of it, people look puzzled, and think you must be a Buddhist!

Jesus in a Buddhist Frame?

Now in my most recent crisis, the person of Jesus has become more important to me than he ever was before. Though being 'born again' is supposed to bring you into a loving relationship with Jesus, that did not happen to me at my conversion from Buddhism to Christianity. It is my recent crisis, which has led me away from active ministry in the Church, that has brought me close to Christ, as the one who befriends sinners and in his passion shares not only pain and death, but also and perhaps most importantly of all, shame. Or more precisely he shared in the experience of being shamed without actually becoming ashamed. In the face of torture and torment, he is recorded as holding quietly and non-violently to his human and perhaps divine dignity. He has shown me a way to do the same, and paradoxically I know that to become non-violent without being crushed and self-abasing is hard indeed, and needs all the disciplines of becoming free of ego. For both retaliatory 'fight' and self-humiliating 'flight' are ways of preserving the ego. Jesus teaches us to stand there without ego in the fullness of our humanity – in what made Pilate exclaim, seeing him in the purple robe and crown of thorns, "*Ecce homo*", 'Look at the human being', 'behold humanity'. As so often in the Gospels, this is at once irony, and revelation.

But where do I find the disciplines of ego-loss? More, certainly, in Buddhism than Christianity. Of course there is much in monastic and other Christian tradition about self-denial and mortification of the self. But a lot of it makes me uneasy. It seems to be more about humiliation – creating a sense of intense guilt that is in fact very egocentric, very obsessed with *my own* sins – than finding the kind of freedom from the ego and its desires that is symbolized in the story of the crow. To follow Christ in his journey through crisis, I need to look again at Buddhist practice.

In this sense I wonder if Jesus Christ can be loved and understood more fully if we make deep connections with crucial aspects of Buddhism. So, paradoxically, perhaps, what Christians need to do in order to be (in Christian terms) 'saved' is to believe in Christ in a much more Buddhist way, and let go of some of the ego-bound ways of believing in him that have become endemic and second nature to us in the West.

Two Masters – or Two Parents?
I can think of two kinds of objection to the line of exploration I

am suggesting. First, some might regard the very attempt to hold together Christian and Buddhist loyalties as fundamentally confused. In this connection, some might point to Jesus' saying, 'you can't serve two masters' (Matt. 6.24; Luke 16.13). But that saying is warning of the dangers, not of having two teachers of faith, but of being divided between the teacher of faith and something else, namely 'mammon' or money. Jesus was making the point that would be obvious to any Buddhist that you will not progress very far spiritually if you remain attached to material possessions. What he was clearly *not* saying was anything like, 'You must have me, Jesus, as your spiritual master and nobody else.' Jesus seems to have decisively rejected that kind of exclusive role, disparaging titles like 'rabbi', 'father' and 'master' (Matt.23.8-10) – though his followers were quick to forget that. The Buddha likewise comes across in the sutras as a tender and tolerant guide, not an exclusive tyrant.

My life, therefore, does not have to be torn between two absolute allegiances. It feels more positive – like having both a mother and a father. Genetically and in my upbringing I have gained a tremendous amount of different things – mostly but of course not all positive – from both my parents, and there is no sense in which they compete for my soul. If I were forced to specify, I would say that the Buddha is my spiritual father and Jesus my spiritual mother. Perhaps the reasons why are obvious from my biography: I learned Jesus in a tender, mystical way through Church and my mother, and from my father I learned a critical reflectiveness about the universe that fed into my Buddhism.

That is not to say that Jesus is all about emotion and Buddhism an entirely intellectual philosophy. I learned the profound rationality of the Christian tradition, and the affective devotion of many forms of Buddhism, later on. There may be some who would call Buddha their mother and Jesus their father. My point is not about who is mother and father but that both have been parents to me, gaining authority not through claiming it but through the good things they have given me and the way they have shaped me into the person I am.

The other objection is that I could be basing too much on 'my own' Christianity and 'my own' Buddhism. The flaws I have found, leading me from one faith to the other and back again, were after all my own flaws, deriving from my own ego-bound way of using these faiths, and perhaps I should not be questioning the truths of those faiths in themselves on the basis of what is questionable about me!

But we do not know a faith at all until we start trying to practice it in our lives. There is something absent-minded (as well as old-fashioned) in the kinds of 'comparative religion' which treat the different religions as thought systems – sets of propositions dangling in mid air – without enquiring deeply into what roots those systems in the lives of believers. So it has to be my Christianity and my Buddhism that I have to begin with, simply because in the deepest sense I know no other Christianity and no other Buddhism.

Passionate Openness

The experiment that proves a spirituality valid – if anything does – must be a whole life wholly committed to it. But if it is an experiment that is involved, a readiness to be found wrong and to seek deeper is also required. Can one be passionately committed to one's ideal and yet ready to let it go? ... Only a spirituality like that stands a chance of relating to reality. (Thompson and Williams, 2008, p.132)

This book's subtitle is designed to express the spirit in which it is written, which these words of mine express. But it also is meant to express what the 'Buddhist Christianity' of the title takes from each faith. From my 'father' Buddhism I have learned the openness represented for me in the concept of Emptiness and the image of the open sky: the state beyond ego-full desire, the freedom that comes from the radical renunciation which can give up even spiritual treasures when they constrain and delude us. And from my 'mother' Christianity I take the thrust towards passionate offering of life in love embodied in the passion of Jesus. I am of course totally unworthy of both ideals, but they are the ideals I would like to profess, and I hope this book will show that though there is a real tension between them, they are not in the end incompatible.

My Story – Your Story – History?

To show this I need to move on to explore Christian and Buddhist 'truths', and what the faiths might learn from one another. And though my initial intention was much more modest and personal, the experience of researching, thinking and feeling through, and writing this book has enabled me to see a convergence between my own search and other people's search and even the broader sweep of history.

This convergence has emboldened me to advocate quite a bold and distinctive standpoint, namely that to be both Christian and Buddhist is both legitimate and beneficial. Where I have come to on my journey is not only 'all right,' but has something to offer to others.

Aloysius Pieris claims that 'deep within each of us there is a Buddhist and a Christian engaged in a profound encounter' (1988, p.113). If this rings true for you (and I suspect you would not be looking at this book if it did not do so in some way) then this offering of my personal explorations may be more than a narcissistic enterprise! Meanwhile according to another inter-faith scholar Heinrich Dumoulin (1974, p.31), historian Arnold Toynbee has remarked that future historians might see more significance in the first interpenetration of Buddhism and Christianity than in the conflict between capitalism and communism.

Since he wrote, violent conflicts between the three Abrahamic faiths – Judaism, Christianity and Islam – has been one factor that has caused dialogue between them to eclipse, to some extent, the Christian-Buddhist dialogue. I know there are those who would style themselves Jewish Christians, or Christian Muslims, just as I have come to call myself a Buddhist Christian, and I empathize with those sorts of bridge-building positions. But such standpoints will be very different from a Christian-Buddhist one. And it would be a disaster, I think, if the three Abrahamic faiths drew together in a way that divided them more deeply from the Eastern half of humanity, as represented in the Oriental faiths of which Buddhism is one.

In that sense it seems to me all the more urgent at this stage in history to move forward the Christian Buddhist dialogue. Because of Buddhism's affinity and co-evolution with the other oriental faiths, and Christianity's belonging to the Abrahamic faiths, Christian-Buddhist dialogue may form the bridge that can one day bring all the faiths together, not I hope into one universal faith, but into the deep solidarity and mutual enrichment that seems so unachievable today.

So in the Introduction that follows I set my personal journey within its wider historical context. I will define the kind of Buddhist Christianity I will be exploring, say how it differs from other versions, and try to placate those who urge that the very idea of Buddhist Christianity is pernicious or impossible.

Introduction

Ways of Being a Buddhist Christian

Do not try to find pleasure by making a name for yourself through good deeds. Practice instead universal loving kindness that is directed toward everyone. Never seek praise for what you do. Consider the earth. It produces and nurtures a multitude of creatures, each receiving what it needs. Words cannot express the benefits the earth provides. Like the earth, you are at one with Peace and Joy when you practice the laws and save living creatures. But do it without acclaim. This is the law of no virtue.

(cited in Riegert and Moore, 2003, p.82.)

Probably you are unable to decide whether this saying comes from a Christian, a Buddhist or some other source. It contains elements of well-known sayings of Jesus about not parading your piety before people but seeking only the reward that comes from God (Matt. 6.1-4) and about learning from the way God provides for nature (Matt. 6.25-33). But it also contains elements – 'universal loving kindness that is directed toward everyone' and 'save living creatures' – that while not un-Christian in content suggest Buddhist concepts, as well as others – 'practice the laws' – that sound Confucian (though in another context they could be Judaic). But paradoxically the result of this fusion is not to obscure Christian teaching but to set it in a new context and enable us to grasp it afresh.

The First Buddhist Christianity

In fact the words come from an imaginative – if not always accurate – translation of 'Jesus sutras' composed by Christian monks from a monastery at Da Qin along the Silk Road into

China. The monks had arrived as missionaries invited by the Chinese Emperor and founded the monastery in about 635 onwards. But later imperial hostility and the rise of Islam isolated and destroyed the little known community of Christians in China, and the sutras were hidden in a cave, where they were accidentally rediscovered in 1907. They represent an old and rare attempt to see the world with both Buddhist and Christian eyes. Perhaps the recovery of the texts betokens the opening up of a possibility that has a fragmentary past and has long laid dormant.

For in many ways I see a deep continuity between this early Buddhist expression of Christianity and what this book is attempting. The synthesis that – so far as we can tell from a few manuscripts – was developed then is closer than anything else to the kind of view I wish to explore. The monks were Nestorian Christians. They saw Jesus a fully human person indwelt by the divine – rather than, as in what became orthodox Christianity, being the Son of God in person. That may have made it easier for them to accept other mediators like the Buddha. However, Chapter 1 will argue that this is possible even from the orthodox point of view.

At the same time, the Nestorians shared the (then) orthodox understanding of God as wholly beyond words and concepts and even beyond being itself. So they were readily able to identify God with the *Sunyata* or emptiness described by the Mahayana Buddhists in their surrounding culture, in a way that can sound strange to our ears, but which Chapter 8 will develop.

Many of the quotations with which the chapters of this book begin are taken from this early tradition, but on the whole I will leave it to you, the reader, to make the connections between the quotation and the chapter.

From Separation to Encounter to Transformation

Excellent histories of the encounter between Christianity and

Buddhism have been written and it would be fruitless to try and repeat that work in this book. What concerns me now are the relatively rare times when there has been movement beyond encounter to interaction and mutual transformation. In this introduction I offer a very short outline of this encounter, then describe the philosophical questions that have recently cast doubt on the basic principles of inter-faith dialogue. After dealing with those questions – which would have invalidated the whole idea of this book – I discuss some notions of 'Christian Buddhism' that seem to me too distantly related to either faith, before proposing my own stricter criteria for the kind of Buddhist Christianity this book seeks.

The similarities in many Buddhist and Christian teachings have led to speculations (e.g. Bruns, 1971, and Amore, 1978) that the very beginnings of the latter were marked by deep inter-action. It has been suggested that Jesus or the early Church – or perhaps the ascetic Jewish sect known as the Therapeutae which may have had an effect on Jesus – may have been influenced by Buddhism. But long ago Richard Garbe (1914) argued convinc-ingly that the only real candidates in the Gospels for imitating Buddhist sources are Simeon's prophecy (Luke 2.22-35), Jesus' temptation in the wilderness (Mat 4.1-11 et al.), Peter walking on the water (Matt. 14.22-33 et. al.), the feeding of the crowds (Mark 6.30-44), and the mention of the wheel of births in James 3.6.

Conversely, certain similarities between Christianity and Mahayana Buddhism have not convincingly been explained by any historically traceable influence of the former on the latter. So Perry Schmidt-Leukel, a leading recent authority in Christian-Buddhist dialogue, writes 'we must conclude that, for all practical purposes, Buddhism and Christianity developed without taking any notice of each other' (2005, p.2).

The Chinese Nestorians apart, encounter between the two faiths only got underway when the Christian colonial empires began to expand from the fifteen century onward. But this encounter was marked on the one hand by empire-based mission, and on the other by resistance and occasionally, as in 16th and 17th century Japan, fierce persecution. The nineteenth century, however, saw the development in the West of a Romantic idealism that was very attracted to aspects of Buddhism and the other oriental faiths. The first societies dedicated to dialogue, and the first Buddhist missions in the West, developed in the late 19th century, though it has been convincingly argued (e.g. Lopez, 1995, and Sharf, 1995) Buddhism began to change its face to provide what the West felt it needed. There developed what the Buddhist scholar Bernard Faure describes as 'neo-Buddhism' and others have termed the Navayana or 'new vehicle':

> a "pure" Buddhism, devoid of any 'superstition', which was miraculously transmitted through various cultures over the centuries to reach the modern Western world. In fact, this Buddhism is a relatively recent invention, the result of a series of reforms in various Asian countries and of increased contact with the West. It has developed in response to colonization, the requirement to modernize, and the influence of Protestantism. (Faure, 2009, p.3-4)

Many in the West responded eagerly. Disillusioned with Christian dogmatism, we found ourselves attracted to what Stephen Batchelor commends as *Buddhism without Beliefs* (1997), in which the rational, meditative and mystical aspects are emphasized at the expense of the popular and liturgical. This is certainly the kind of Buddhism that attracted me in my teens, and though it has much to commend it as a philosophy of life in its own right, its relationship to Buddhism as practiced down the centuries in the East is more tenuous than is sometimes realized.

After the Second World War and the ensuing dismantling of the colonial empires, 'dialogue' became a much more real possibility for both sides. In the 1950s Buddhist and Christian monks began corresponding and visiting one another. The Zen Buddhist D.T. Suzuki and the American Episcopal Priest Alan Watts both helped the West understand Zen in many publications from 1957 onward. The Vatican II reform in the Roman Catholic Church beginning in 1963 replaced the older Catholic exclusivity with a new openness to dialogue with other faiths. In the wake of this monks Dom Aelred Graham (1963) and Thomas Merton wrote books exploring the relation between Zen and Catholicism. Meanwhile the Kyoto School – already an ecumenical venture within Buddhism involving dialogue between Zen and Pure Land sects – began to venture into dialogue with Christian Faith; the writings of Keiji Nishitani (1982) and Masao Abe (1995) explored the relationship between Buddhist Emptiness, post-Christian Western nihilism, and the Christian emphasis on transcendence and self-emptying in God, which Chapter 8 will develop.

On a less academic level, the Vietnamese monk Thich Nhat Hanh (1995) explored the relation between Buddhism and politics as well as Christianity. The Tibetan or 'Vajrayana' tradition became better known through the teaching and publications of H.H. the Dalai Lama, Tenzin Gyatzo, (e.g. 1996), as well as Chogyam Trungpa (1995) and Lama Anagarika Govinda (1969). Several individuals are now both Christian (generally Roman Catholic) priests and Buddhist monks, and many strive to combine the practice of Buddhist mediation with Christian acts of worship and prayer in their life – possibilities explored in Chapter 6.

For many Christians and Buddhists, dialogue remains anathema, but many now believe the dialogue between the two faiths is entering a new stage, in which the aim is not merely to learn about one another, but be transformed by the encounter, hopefully deepening one's own faith in the process.

The Language-Game Game

In the 1960s and 70s, when I moved to Buddhism and then to Christianity, this mutually transforming dialogue had a lot going for it. The world had moved beyond colonial empires and resistance toward great movements of populations, leading to multi-cultural societies, a genuine determination to overcome parochial and racist perspectives, and a real fascination with one another's religions and cultures. And yet there was a sense in which the hegemony of Western liberalism and rationalism still prevailed, sufficiently at least to provide a common language in which different faith members could listen to one another's arguments and evaluate them within a shared sense of what counted as reasonable. Despite our differences in religious tradition and culture, it was felt we could still find common ground in terms of ideas, experiences and values that transcended religious difference.

However, from the 1970s onward this rational hegemony has been shattered, making inter-faith dialogue a more difficult and problematic exercise, even as in view of religious-based conflict it becomes more urgent. What broke the hegemony was a growing sense that ideas, arguments, experiences and values cannot be separated from the culture and the religious language in which they are expressed. Both are, therefore, embedded in what the philosopher Ludwig Wittgenstein termed 'forms of life', in that they cannot be understood apart from the ritual and ethical practices the religion encourages. Religions and cultures are what he termed 'language games'; just as you can only learn a game by playing it and following its rules, so you can only understand a religion by following it according to its rules.

This was often taken to mean that we have to treat each religion as its own self-interpreting system, so that comparisons between them are impossible. For example you cannot know what a Mahayana Buddhist means by, say, 'emptiness' except by living the Buddhist way of life in which that term functions, or what 'the Holy Spirit' means for a Christian except by living the life committed to Christ. You simply have to choose your faith and live within it; but there is no reason, external to any faith, which we could have for choosing one faith rather than another.

Absolute Relativism?

This resulted in a dramatic polarization. On the one hand, it led to the closely related theories of pluralism and relativism. Faiths had no common denominator. There was no more point in trying to build common ground between say Christianity and Buddhism than trying to breed a new species from a turkey and a crocodile! So a laissez-faire tolerance of all religions, cultures and ideologies prevailed. But the other side of this total tolerance was a total intransigence. If my faith is a closed system, nobody can argue me out of it, and I am utterly safe in my convictions. So in the case of Christianity, post-liberal and radical orthodox theologies have wasted no time in welcoming the demise of the old liberal consensus – the move from modern rationalism to what has come to be styled 'postmodernism'.

The combination of total tolerance and total exclusivity sounds paradoxical, but the Catholic theologian Gavin D'Costa (1990, 2000) has discussed the religious pluralism advocated by Christians John Hick and Paul Knitter, the Jewish Dan Cohn-Sherbok, the Hindu Radhakrishnan and the Dalai Lama. He shows convincingly that behind every kind of tolerant pluralism there lurk presuppositions that are regarded as beyond challenge. And this seems inherent in the logic of pluralism and relativism. In a paradoxical way, relativism leads to absolute, unassailable positions, while it is the belief in absolute truth and justice that relativizes different standpoints and renders them accountable to wider humanity.

If relativism is true, this book is futile, so I need to say a bit about why I do not believe it. The first thing to say is that very few pluralists take their tolerance to its logical conclusion. If there is no shared court of appeal by which we can assess different cultural and ideological systems, tolerance ought to be our attitude to fascism, slavery, and views advocating violence against women. Appeals to universal reason, justice and humanity should be dismissed as simply asserting the old Western liberal hegemony. In a relativist framework nothing can be said against Nazism when it describes Jews as vermin that need to be eliminated. At this point, most relativists stop short and allow some kind of appeal to a justice and humanity that applies universally across cultures and religions. But that concession sells the relativist pass. If a minimal appeal to universal justice and humanity is allowed, why not expand this into a generous and maximal possibility of appeal to such good things?

Secondly, it is acknowledged to be far from clear that when Wittgenstein wrote about language games, he had anything as big as a religion or a culture in mind. To apply his concept to religions takes to extremes a 19th century notion of faiths as self-contained systems. But this notion needs to be challenged. Whenever it has been geographically possible, faiths have exchanged ideas and practice, even when their official teaching has said that this should not happen. Karen Armstrong for example (1999) has shown how much the idea of God has evolved from the interaction between Jewish, Greek, Christian and Islamic ideas. Religions are much more open to one another, and more capable of recognizing truth as well as error in one another than they might like to think.

Finally, I have argued elsewhere (1989) at a length I cannot go into now that relativists often rely on a confusion that enables them to assert something very obvious and uncontentious, and treat this as proving something much more extreme and counter-intuitive. Few would doubt the obvious point that different cultures use terms in different ways. As the radical theologian Don Cupitt points out, "when we use biblical signifiers such as

'God' or 'the Son of God' nothing can guarantee, and there are many reasons for doubting, the truth of the assumption that the signified must be identically the same for us as it was for [the biblical writers]'. (1986, p.365). In the same way when Christians affirm the existence of God, and Buddhists deny it, it is far from clear that they mean the same thing by 'God'. However, differences about meaning are not a deep problem, so long as we are sensitive to them and do not always assume writers must mean what we would mean by a term. It is usually possible to get a good idea of what a writer means by studying the context in which a term is used, in her own writing and the wider culture in which she wrote.

But the point about meanings is often treated as if it were a point about truth or reality. It is concluded from a statement like Cupitt's either that there is no such thing as God or the Son of God, or that God and the Son of God are 'constructed' by the culture that describes them. But this confuses the issue of meaning with the issue of being. It is true that our language, culture, ritual and so forth evoke meanings and conjure up a vision of the world. But whether that world 'exists', whether the vision is a good guide to how things are or a delusion that will deceive us is another issue, and not one that can be settled within the culture itself.

So on the one hand it is important to respect a foreign culture or religion and enter sensitively and imaginatively into the way it evokes a vision that is other than our own. And again, when it comes to evaluating the truth of the vision, we should not assume our own culture has all the necessary criteria. That was the problem with the old liberal hegemony; it assumed Western rationalism had the final criteria for evaluating whether other cultures were in tune with reality or deluded.

Relativism would suggest that the most meaningful discourse would be that employed by tight elites following their own esoteric jargon-rich language-game. All authentic religions would be esoteric, comprehended only by the initiated. Esoteric discourse that prides itself on its unintelligibility to the uninitiated takes place, of course, both in the academic world and in religions. The participants can enjoy a sense of bathing in rich meanings denied to the 'outsider'. But as far as the real world goes, this is an excellent way to talk nonsense. It is only when we try to exchange our ideas with people who do not understand or accept our presuppositions that we really begin to know what – if anything – we are talking about.

The Inter-Faith Imperative

It is here that inter-faith dialogue – of a kind – becomes essential. I boldly suggest that it is absolutely the only way we can begin to assess the truth, not only of another religion, but of our own. How can this happen; how can two faiths come together and find a way of assessing themselves and the other that is not an imposition of their own tradition on the other? It may help to tackle this big and difficult question with an analogy I have used before (1989).

Imagine two cultures. One has the concept of a circle as a geometric construction, a locus of points equidistant from a center; but like the Aztecs it has not discovered the wheel, its coins are oblong, and it regards the circle as a purely theoretical idea never instanced in the real world. The other is more practical; it has no geometry, but has the idea of a circle as the shape it carves its wheels to make its vehicles run smoothly. Here seems a clear case where the term 'circle' has different meanings in the different cultures.

But along comes the latter culture in its smooth-wheeled chariots and 'discovers' the former. When the battles subside, it learns the reason why its wheels run smooth – because the circumference stays equidistant to the axle at the 'center'. And the other culture learns that its geometrical constructions have technological applications. Each society has learned something, and has had to stretch its concept of circle to do so.

Both cultures have been able to expand their concepts to include the reality the other culture is talking about and to grasp how it relates to the reality described by their own. It is in the same way that when religions engage with each other – especially religions as different in their basic concepts and presuppositions as Buddhism and Christianity – they are forced to discover the spiritual reality they are talking about. They may not end up agreeing in everything they say about that reality. But they will have had to stretch their own concepts, and may well have gained a deeper understanding of the reality they are engaged with, through having to go beyond their words and concepts to what lies behind them.

The aim of inter-faith dialogue, then, should not be agreement, but insight. The best way to engage in it is not to sit eyeball to eyeball, as it were, teasing out comparisons and contrasts between beliefs, but to sit together looking out on the human world we share, describing it to each other in our different ways, and see what truths we can learn from each other. This is what this book will try to do.

To anticipate a possible criticism, there is no overall world view I am trying to impose on the two faiths. A vision of the world whereby we can 'stretch' the two faiths has to emerge from the dialogue between the two faiths, and their interaction with other thought that makes sense of the world. In this book two areas of current thought in particular are brought into a kind of 'trialogue' with Buddhism and Christianity: the psychology of desire in Chapter 4, and current science in Chapter 7. Elsewhere there is an implicit 'trialogue' between the two faiths and our perceptions and intuitions, in which none is allowed to define the framework for the others. The exercise is a bit precarious, like sewing together one's parachute out of different materials while in free fall! But that is safer than imagining we already have a hole-free parachute of our own when we have not!

So this book, after looking in the first two chapters at the teachings of the two faiths and their founders, explores through the faiths the things we all experience, suffer from and wonder about. Chapter 3 looks at what is wrong with the world, what makes us unhappy or dissatisfied, exploring Buddhist and Christian understandings of suffering and sin and their origins. Chapter 4 takes a deep look at desire, obsession and ego-centeredness, not only as a personal phenomenon but as built into our society. Chapter 5 looks at our experience of being transformed and liberated, and in particular, whether we find we can do this by our own efforts or need help that comes from beyond us. Chapter 6 looks at specific acts of devotion and meditation in both traditions, while Chapter 7 broadens the perspective to look at the cosmos we encounter through science, and Chapter 8 'grasps the nettle' of how each faith understands the ultimate ground and goal of life.

Christian Buddhisms

Despite the criticisms just explored, many have argued that the insights of Christianity and Buddhism can be combined. Don Cupitt was the first to popularize the term 'Christian Buddhist', and looking at what he means is a good way to understanding the rather different approach I shall take.

Cupitt invites us to

Imagine a person who is skeptical or at any rate agnostic about all the metaphysical and doctrinal aspects of traditional Christian belief but who very much wants to cultivate the ethics, the inwardness, the spirituality and many of the ritual practices of Christianity. He speaks of God... as... a jewel, diamond or pearl; that is, as that infinitely precious indescribable secret which is the goal of the spiritual life...

Furthermore, our Christian Buddhist speaks also of Jesus, but he does not think of Jesus as the divine Christ of the Church who lives and reigns in a higher world, because he has no reason to think there is such a higher world. Instead he studies the tradition of the words of that neglected spiritual master, the historical Jesus. (1980, p.83)

Cupitt says of the faith of his Christian Buddhist that "the content, the spirituality and the values are Christian; the form is Buddhist" (p.xii). There is no doubt that Christian Buddhism of this sort is very attractive to many Christians who are disillusioned with the narrow ethics and dogma of the established churches, but wish to follow Jesus in some way. I do not wish to decry it, but my search leads me somewhere different, for two reasons

First, the principal source of the Christian Buddhist's faith is clearly his own vision and judgment. It is his confidence in this that enables him to sit light to the Buddhist and Christian traditions, and as it were go direct to the 'original teachers'. Don Cupitt – at least in the period in which he developed his Christian Buddhism – very much believed that the individual had to piece together his own religion for himself. But this implies a higher estimate of the self than we find in either faith. And (see Chapter 2) I think it is very hard to get to the original Jesus or the original Buddha apart from the traditions and writings about them that have come down to us through the Church or *Sangha*.

That does not mean we need to follow the convert from Buddhism to Catholicism, Paul Williams, when he asks the Church to 'tell me what to think' (2002, p.137ff). Even the person who lets the Church do all his thinking for him has decided to take this option among the many available in our multicultural world. These days, none of us can delegate our accountability for what we believe. But it seems foolish to prefer the insight of one person – me – to the generations that have helped form a whole tradition of deep spiritual enquiry and reflection – and that of course is Williams' main point.

And this brings me to my second point. Attractive as Cupitt's 'Christian Buddhist' is, I am not sure of the sense in which either the 'form' of his belief is Buddhist, or the 'content, spirituality and values' Christian. There is little evidence of any specific Buddhist belief or practice. And if the belief in the Christ of incarnation and resurrection and the Church's sacraments are gone, to what degree does the saint's admiration for the historical Jesus make him Christian rather than say Moslem or Hindu? Faure writes acerbically of the '"Neo-Buddhism" that 'Neo-Christianity' comes up against during 'religious dialogues' which sometimes lead to 'Zen Masses' that have little to do with either Zen or Christianity. This is what happens when you put too much water in your holy wine or tea.' (p.140) Is Cupitt's saint perhaps really a 'Neo-Christian Neo-Buddhist'?

I have a liking for strong wine, strong tea, and traditional belief and practice. My own biography, at least, has led me to take especially seriously the aspects of each faith that seem incompatible with the other – no God and no soul in Buddhism, for example, and the need for grace and the historical atonement on the cross in Christianity. Hence my Buddhist Christianity can be no bland blend of the tamer aspects of both faiths, but must result from a wrestling of the seeming incompatibles, allowing each faith to shake the other to its very foundations.

The 'Mahayana Theology' of the American Episcopalian theologian John Keenan (1989) seems to represent another, more carefully worked out form of Christian Buddhism. Keenan adopts a much more precise form of Buddhism than Cupitt, specifically the Yogacara school. But the Christian doctrines of Trinity and incarnation are in the end dissolved into the ineffable mystical consciousness that is ultimate reality for the Yogacara. The Christian doctrines seem to me to lose focus through being defined in entirely mystical terms. The realism and challenge of

Christian faith evaporates, it seems to me, into a position more Buddhist than Christian.

The same seems to be true of the several variations of 'Zen Christianity' which have been suggested, from Dom Aelred Graham (1963) onward (e.g. Kennedy, 1995; Leong, 2000); the iconoclastic, and anti-doctrinal emphasis of Zen serves to soften the edges of Christian doctrine and so create a variant of Cupitt's Christian Buddhism. Not that I would deny the strange affinity between Jesus and Zen which these writers have suggested (see Chapter 2). And it is actually a Zen Buddhist writer, Masao Abe, who develops something more like what I term Buddhist Christianity – he will be crucial to the thoughts developed in Chapter 8.

What makes for Buddhist Christianity?

If I follow those who reverse the terms of Cupitt's 'Christian Buddhism' it is partly to distinguish what I am seeking from the (perfectly respectable, but different) positions of Cupitt and Keenan. And it is partly to express my hunch that Christianity offers us a lot of beautiful content for faith, while Buddhism offers many good ways of understanding, holding and practicing that content. By the end of the book it will be clear why I seek to 'be a Christian in a Buddhist way'. In that sense it is fitting that Christianity should be the noun, and Buddhism the qualifying adjective. I believe this sets me in continuity with the old Chinese Nestorians, who could be regarded as the first Buddhist Christians.

What might it mean to be a Buddhist Christian? From my autobiography I hope it is clear why both Christianity and Buddhism specifically are more important to me than they seem to be to Cupitt's Christian Buddhism. There is an orthodox Christian in me – which could be described as Anglican with a strong leaning towards Eastern Orthodoxy – and a specific Buddhist leaning – definitely Mahayana, with strong empathy with the Vajrayana. Though I share with Cupitt and with many a fascination for and love of Jesus and the Buddha, I have found that what brings me closer to them is not detachment from tradition, but the kind of mutual interrogation of traditions that this book is about.

So in this book what I will be trying to explore and defend can now be stated in two theses:

1. It is possible to be a Buddhist Christian in the sense of holding a religious commitment that is both within the range of legitimate Christian commitments and within the range of legitimate Buddhist ones.

2. This Buddhist Christian commitment will involve changes in the ways in which most Christians and most Buddhists have interpreted their faiths, but the changes will be good ones in the sense of offering a deep understanding of the world we are in and our possibilities of transformation into a better life.

I avoid the competitiveness that would be involved in terms like 'better', 'deeper' – still more 'best' and 'deepest'. I am not trying to offer something better than before, but something different you may like to consider for yourself. I guess what is distinctive in the position I am arguing for is that most previous dialogue has mostly been either more tentative and respectful of each tradition as it stands, or more bold in constructing a 'Neo' Christian Buddhism that sits relatively light to both traditions.

Immediately the first thesis invites us to ask how we assess what is 'within the range' of 'legitimate' Buddhism and Christianity. It is important to find ordinary, uncontentious criteria on which a majority of Buddhist and Christians would agree.

Buddhist Commitment

One becomes a Buddhist by reciting the triple refuge, which I quote in the Pali version of the Theravada tradition.

Buddham saranam gacchami (to the Buddha for refuge I go)
Dhammam saranam gacchami (to the Dharma – the Teaching – for refuge I go)
Sangham saranam gacchami (to the *Sangha* – the Community of those on the way to Enlightenment – for refuge I go)

And though Buddhism is very varied, all would assent to the Four Noble Truths:

This is the noble truth of suffering: birth is suffering, aging is suffering, illness is suffering, death is suffering; sorrow, lamentation, pain, grief and despair are suffering; union with what is displeasing is suffering; separation from what is pleasing is suffering; not to get what one wants is suffering; in brief, the five aggregates subject to clinging are suffering.

This is the noble truth of the origin of suffering: it is this craving which leads to renewed existence, accompanied by delight and lust, seeking delight here and there, that is, craving for sensual pleasures, craving for existence, craving for extermination.

This is the noble truth of the cessation of suffering: it is the remainderless fading away and cessation of that same craving, the giving up and relinquishing of it, freedom from it, nonreliance on it.

This is the noble truth of the way leading to the cessation of suffering: it is the Noble Eightfold Path; that is, right view, right intention, right speech, right action, right livelihood, right effort, right mindfulness, right concentration.

(*Samyutta Nikaya* 56.11, tr.. Bodhi, 2000, p.1844.)

The fourth Noble Truth comprises the Eightfold Path. And the suffering described the Second arises because of the Three Marks of Being: 'all formations... are transient (*anicca*); all formations are subject to suffering (*dukkha*); all phenomena are without an ego-entity (*anatta*)' (tr. Nyanatiloka, cited in Humphreys, 1970, p.59). The Buddha's final words are said to be, "All things are subject to change. Practice with diligence."

These teachings – as my school essay identified – are universal to Buddhism. In the Mahayana the Eightfold Path is generally interpreted in terms of the six perfections of the Bodhisattva – giving, morality, patience, energy, meditation and wisdom. But the Path itself has not been and could not be replaced or rejected by any position that regarded itself as Buddhist.

Christian Commitment

Christianity has been as varied as Buddhism, but all mainstream Christians have begun their Christian lives in baptism, when a threefold commitment was made by them or on their behalf. In many denominations this commitment is renewed every Easter. It involves a threefold renunciation of what were traditionally called 'the world, the flesh and the devil'. I print the modern Anglican version here:

Do you reject the devil and all proud rebellion against God?
– I reject them.
Do you renounce the deceit and corruption of evil?
– I renounce them.
Do you repent of the sins that separate us from God and neighbor?
– I repent of them.

The candidate for baptism then 'turns to Christ' and affirms a threefold commitment, which in the oldest version is the basis of the so-called Apostolic Creed.

> Do you believe and trust in God the Father?
> – I believe in God, the Father Almighty, creator of heaven and
> earth.
> Do you believe and trust in God the Son?
> – I believe in Jesus Christ, God's only Son, our Lord, who was
> conceived by the Holy Spirit, born of the Virgin Mary,
> suffered under Pontius Pilate, was crucified, died, and was
> buried; he descended to the dead. On the third day he rose
> again; he ascended into heaven, he is seated at the right
> hand of the Father, and he will come again to judge the
> living and the dead.
> Do you believe and trust in God the Holy Spirit?
> – I believe in the Holy Spirit, the holy catholic Church, the
> communion of saints, the forgiveness of sins, the resur-
> rection of the body, and the life everlasting. Amen.

The Nicene Creed of 325, recited in churches to this day, is a
development from this early commitment, with extra clauses
added to emphasize the divine birth of Jesus Christ and his
equality with the Father, matters to which I also feel myself
committed.

Many Christians specify their commitment in yet greater
detail, including, for Catholics, the 'infallible' papal pronounce-
ments, and for many Protestants, specific affirmations about the
infallibility of the Bible and the nature of the atonement by Christ
on the cross. But those varied commitments are not believed by
all Christian denominations. I think it is enough to take the
baptismal commitment – with its affirmation of God as Trinity,
and Christ as incarnate Lord who has saved humankind by his
cross and resurrection – as our standard for what counts as
Christian. What matters to me is to show that in making a
Buddhist commitment, Christians need not be rejecting their

baptismal Christian commitment.

The Challenge

So the basic position of the book is – as it needs to be – bold but simple, and with fairly conventional criteria for assessment which most Buddhists and Christians will, I hope, understand and assent to.

But the means of getting to that position will involve some challenging stretching of ideas and spiritual intuitions, which will not only open up members of both faiths to each other, but render them more open to those who hold neither faith, at least in the sense in which I have defined them. In other words, this is a book not only for those who feel they can make either the Christian or the Buddhist commitment their own, but also for those who find those commitments baffling or stultifying, and prefer to live their lives without commitment or creed. If you are part of that great and honorable company, I offer this book to you also, because I think the effort of unraveling the Buddhist and Christian commitments in the light of each other will serve to open up their meaning, making it perhaps easier for you to make them your own.

For reasons that will become clear especially in Chapters 5 and 6, I think faith commitments do need to be lived out in the context of traditions and communities, not in isolation. So if this book can help you find your way to a Christian or Buddhist commitment (or both) I will be very glad. But I do not mind which.

Chapter 1

Dharma Embodied? The Buddha and the Christ

The plateau of the temple area [is] a wide plain of shining polished stone offering a marvelous view over Chiang Mai and the whole valley below. If you turn around, you find yourself surrounded by several smaller and bigger stupas, all covered with gold, dazzlingly reflecting and radiating Thailand's bright sunlight. Due to the enormous height, the temple plateau is at times hemmed with tattered clouds, and so you can't help thinking that you stand in the middle of a celestial palace... No doubt everything in this place proclaims the supra-mundane, not to say 'divine' nature of the Buddha.
(Perry Schmidt-Leukel, 2005, p.152)

Few Buddhist temples are quite as glorious as those at the North Thai capital, Chiang Mai, here described. But anyone who has experienced Buddhism as practiced in its native lands will notice the degree to which the Buddha, like Christ, is a religious figure, adored and worshipped. As Schmidt-Leukel goes on to argue, there is a sense in which the Buddha participates in and mediates the faith he preached, as surely as Jesus Christ does, though in a different way.

This may come as a surprise to those acquainted with the stereotype that prevails in the West, which contrasts Jesus, worshipped as God incarnate, with Buddha as a purely human teacher who points to the way beyond him. Of course the beliefs that surround the Buddha are by no means identical to those that surround Christ. There is a clear sense in which Jesus in Christian beliefs is more 'divine' than the Buddha. This is hardly surprising, since the divine is not a decisive category in

Buddhism. But this chapter will also clarify a sense in which Jesus is more human too.

I thought long and hard over which this book should tackle first: Jesus and Gautama, the original teachers, or Christ and Buddha, the central figures of the Christian and Buddhist faiths. Historically, I can imagine you protesting, the chapter looking at the key figures of Christianity and Buddhism should surely precede discussion of the religions to which they gave rise? And for teaching purposes is it not important to establish the clarity of the 'original message' before we look at the complex ways in which those original teachings of the Buddha and Jesus Christ have been built on, and often distorted?

But in the end it became clear to me that where we all start from is not 'the original' Gautama or Jesus, but the Buddha or Christ as a figure of faith. It is through the art and culture they have inspired, through the experience of worship and meditation, and through encounters with people formed by the respective faiths that Christianity and Buddhism have moved me and challenged me to look at the original teachers. Insofar as I can be said to have a personal relationship with either Jesus or Gautama – and one can only have a very metaphorical kind of friendship with a person who lived so long ago and who is so largely mysterious and unknown – it is one that has been shaped and formed by the experience of countless others in the faith traditions they each inspired.

Starting from Actual Belief

Approximately 1.9 billion people describe themselves as, or practice as, followers of just one person Jesus, while probably well over 350 million are followers of another, the Buddha. Another 1.1 billion follow Mohammed, so close on 60% of the world's people build their lives on what they understand to be the teachings of just three people. That is an amazing fact, though some would see it as a regrettable one.

Certainly the attempts to build whole cultures and societies around these figures has led to many distortions, and strange anomalies like the warrior-monks of Japan and the Christian crusaders; so much violence justified by reference to those who taught peace and non-harming! It is understandable that many today prefer to separate politics from religion and pursue a private spirituality, basing themselves on what they see as original teachings and distancing themselves from the mainstream religions. But I am not among them.

I for one am grateful that the attempt was made to build a society around Jesus, and a society around Buddha. Had the attempt not been made, those teachers would have been unlikely to impact on me, and might have been largely forgotten as just one more obscure Jewish and Hindu teacher respectively. It may well be true that neither Jesus nor Gautama desired to found a new religion or faith community, separate from the traditions they were trying to reform. Nevertheless I am grateful that history has done more than either probably intended, enabling me and many others to learn from them some two millennia later.

For these reasons I start by considering Buddha and Christ as we experience them through their faith communities now – in spirituality, doctrine and art – as glorious mediators of faith adored by their followers, and lying at the heart of cultures that may be disappearing (as cultures, as distinct from the faith communities that survive) only in our own time. I will look at the way the Buddha is seen, often, as an embodiment of the Dharma, and see how close this is to the early understanding of Christ as the Word and Wisdom of God. But we will note how those early Christian understandings became eclipsed by the Nicene doctrine of Christ as the incarnate divine Son within the Christian Trinity. I will investigate the exclusiveness associated with this doctrine, and see how the Buddhist notion of no-self, as well as the teachings of the early Christian 'fathers' themselves, may suggest that Christ, if he is really divine, should not be reduced to a particular historical individual. I will look at the Buddhist 'Trinity', and see how it is quite different from the Christian Trinity, but in a very significant way.

Only then will we be in a position to move from the well known – what Buddha and Christ are in the faith of their followers today – to the obscure – what the original Jesus and Gautama did and taught. The traditions will have given us frames with which to view both teachers clearly. But we may find that the teachers are not static objects sitting in the center of the frames – as the traditions might like to think – but in many respects more like quarry that leaps across the frame and beyond, encouraging us to move the traditional frameworks a little so as to see them better.

Buddha as Dharma and Christ as Wisdom
The opening quotation of this chapter illustrates how highly the Buddha is revered even in the Theravada Buddhism of Thailand. What is implicit in this simpler Buddhism becomes explicit in the Mahayana, where the concept of the Buddha reaches far beyond the historical figure of Gautama. Whereas the Pali texts used by the Theravada treat the Buddha as a human being involved in very human situations, in the Sanskrit, Mahayana texts he seems to inhabit a fantastic, mythological realm, rather like those we see depicted in the Tibetan *tankas*.

> The Buddha was once staying at Rajagriha, on the Gridhrakuta mountain... He was surrounded by a hundred thousand monks and Bodhisattvas and Mahasattvas numbering sixty times as many as the sands of the Ganges. All of them were in possession of the greatest spiritual energy; they had paid homage to thousands of hundred millions of billions of Buddhas... All these were accompanied by innumerable [mythological creatures including various kinds of demons, dragons and winged beasts]. This great

assembly all joined in revering, paying homage to [the Buddha,] the World-Honored One. (Opening of the *Mahavaipulya-Tathagatagarbha Sutra*, cited in Suzuki, 1963, p243-4)

Clearly the idea of the Buddha had grown well beyond the historical human individual. For the Mahayana, every sentient being is said to be endowed with 'Buddha Nature'. 'Buddha Mind' – symbolized by the great stupas erected over the relics of the Buddha's body – is the key to all knowledge and all reality, since all reality is ultimately – in the Mahayana tradition – mind.

Meanwhile the body of the Buddha also gained a mystical significance. In the Pali Canon, the earliest Buddhist scriptures, the Buddha contrasts his physical body with the Dhamma or Dharma, the teaching or truth that can be seen through him. 'Why do you want to see this filthy body? Whoever sees the Dhamma sees me; whoever sees me sees the Dhamma' (*Samyutta Nikaya* 22.87).

By 400AD the Mahayana tradition had expanded on words like these to form the doctrine of the Trikaya, the three bodies of the Buddha. The body that was manifest in and changed through the course of space-time was termed the *Nirmanakaya*, or 'body of change'. More refined and more all-pervasive was the *Sambhogakaya*, the 'body of mutual enjoyment', which devout followers of the Buddha begin to experience within themselves. And most remote and absolute of all was the *Dharmakaya*, the body of teaching, truth or law, which transcends space and time and is related in Mahayana thought to the *Tathata* or 'just-so-ness', the interdependent co-arising of all things, and the rich *Sunyata* or emptiness of things – concepts to be explored in Chapters 7 and 8. The wonderful miracle of the way the world is just as it is, is ultimately identified with the Buddha and his teaching.

Comparisons with the Christian view of Christ suggest

themselves. The saying about seeing the *Dhamma* is reminiscent of the words in the Gospel of John. 'Whoever has seen me has seen the Father' (14.9). There is similarity in difference here: both Buddha and Jesus offer a vision of something beyond themselves, but in the case of the Buddha this something beyond is impersonal, the Dharma, while in Jesus it is personal, the Father.

Meanwhile the concept of Buddha Mind reminds a Christian of Paul's language about 'the mind of Christ' (1 Cor 2.16). Buddha Mind is more omnipresent than the mind of Christ, which in Paul appears to be attributed to the Church rather than the whole cosmos. However, well known lines in the Gospel of Thomas (v.77) ascribe these words to Jesus:

> I am the light that is above them all. I am all things: all things came forth from me, and all things attained to me. Split a piece of wood, I am there; lift up the stone, and you will find me there.

Behind such sayings probably lies an early identification – perhaps even a self-identification – of Jesus with the Wisdom of God, which Hebrew writings had tended to personify as a female figure accompanying God in his work of creation. By the late New Testament, the prologue of John's Gospel (1.1-14) had replaced Wisdom with the similar, but less feminine notion of the Word of God, which incorporated both the prophetic Word of God's judgment and the Greek stoic understanding of the Logos, the ordered structure of the universe that makes it intelligible to human 'logic' or reason (Thompson, 2009, p.33-7). Buddhist *Dharmakaya* does indeed sound very like Hebrew Wisdom.

> She is a breath of the power of God, and a pure emanation of the glory of the Almighty; therefore nothing defiled gains entrance into her. She is a reflection of eternal light, a spotless

mirror of the working of God, and an image of his goodness. Though she is but one, she can do all things, and while remaining in herself, she renews all things; in every generation she passes into holy souls and makes them friends of God, and prophets... She reaches mightily from one end of the earth to the other, and she orders all things well.' (from Wisdom 7.22b-8.2)

Compare this with the *Dharmakaya*

It is not an individual reality, it is not a false existence, but is universal and pure. It comes from nowhere, it goes to nowhere; it does not assert itself, nor is it subject to annihilation. It is forever serene and eternal... [It] has no boundary, no quarters, but is embodied in all bodies.... There is no place in the universe where this Body does not prevail. The universe becomes, but this Body forever remains. It is free from all opposites and contraries, yet it is working in all things to lead them to Nirvana. (Avatamsaka Sutra, tr. Buddhabhadra, 34. Cited in Suzuki, 1963, p.223-4)

So the Logos which Christ embodies can be compared with the *Dharmakaya* which Buddha embodies, though again there is difference as well as likeness. For the Logos arises through God's ordered and rational making of the world, while the *Dharmakaya* in a sense is the world just as it is, there being no concept of a deliberate act of creation. But there is enough likeness here, perhaps, to justify the Korean Buddhist, Bokin Kim's remark:

When I read the description of Christ as the Truth, Light and Life in the Gospel according to John, I feel a strong urge to replace *Christ* with the term *Buddha* – not Gautama Buddha but Dharmakaya Buddha. Here Christ refers to the source of the historical Christ just as Dharmakaya Buddha is the source

of historical Buddha... Christ only is the Truth, Light and Life.
Similarly there is a Zen *koan* saying, 'Buddha alone exists'.
(Gross and Muck, p.53)

Jesus' Uniqueness and No-Self

It might seem, so far, that Buddhists need have no problems with
the Christian doctrines of the incarnation – the embodiment of
God in Christ – and the Trinity – the three persons of God. There
is a sense in which Mahayana Buddhists explicitly, and
Theravada Buddhists implicitly, already see the Buddha as a
kind of incarnation of the Dharma, and already, in the Trikaya,
have a kind of equivalent of the Christian Trinity. But this may be
jumping too far too fast.

Taking up the incarnation first, José Ignacio Cabezón – a
convert from Catholicism to the Vajrayana Buddhism of Tibet –
remarks that Tibetan Buddhists at least have no problems with
the idea of the divinity of Jesus, because their universe is full of
beings that incarnate divinity. We might add that the virginal
conception of Jesus – often contested by liberal Christians – is
paralleled in the Buddha's own conception from Maya without
any father. Miracles are ascribed to the Buddha and his
followers. Even resurrection is, I am told, regarded as happening
on occasion in Vajrayana Buddhism. No, according to Cabezón,
"what Buddhists find objectionable is (a) the Christian character-
ization of the deity whose manifestation Jesus is said to be, and
(b) the claim that Jesus is unique in being such a manifestation"
(Gross and Muck, p.24). Hindus might echo both objections, of
course. The objection is the opposite of that of Muslims and Jews,
who share (a) the God of Abraham with Christians and agree as
to the divine nature, but object to (b) not that God should have
many incarnations, but that God can have no incarnation at all.

Regarding (a), Cabezón sees the God whom Jesus is said to
incarnate as an amalgam of two elements, the God of Abraham
and the Old Testament, and the God of Greek neo-Platonic

philosophy. Chapter 8 will look more closely at these elements of the Christian God and why Buddhists find them problematic. It is mainly (b) that concerns us now: the idea that Christ is the one and only mediator, and the one and only incarnation of the one and only God.

This, of course, is something that offends not only Buddhists, but those of all other religions, as well as some Christians. But throughout its history mainstream Christianity has claimed that its own scriptures commit it to such a belief. In John's Gospel, Jesus is said to claim (14.6), 'I am the way and the truth and the life. No-one comes to the Father except through me'. By the fourth century the idea of Jesus as the incarnate Wisdom or Word of God had grown into the faith expressed in the councils of Nicea (325) and Chalcedon (451) according to which Jesus Christ in his own person united the human nature we all share with the divine nature of God the Son. Soon the Church was proclaiming that there was 'no salvation outside the Church' in which this belief in Christ was taught.

Now in an early essay I remember defending the widespread belief that such an understanding made Christ unique, rendering any other incarnation of the divine impossible. My argument – like many, perhaps all such arguments – rested on the idea that each human person was unique; no two human individuals are the same. It seemed to follow that only one human person could also be the person of the Son of God. Any other person – like the Buddha – would be a different person, and as there were not two Sons of God, but only one, only one person could incarnate him.

No-self, Jesus and Christened Humanity

Many Christian writers (e.g. Samartha, 1991) argue that, in view of such conclusions, we need to rewrite the doctrine of the incarnation in less exclusive terms. But I now see that my argument actually misrepresents the traditional doctrine as clarified, both by many Eastern 'fathers', and by Thomas Aquinas in the West.

According to them, though Jesus Christ was human through and through, it was not his human personhood or individuality that represented the divine, but rather the humanity he shares with all people. As a human being Jesus Christ was 'personless' – the beautiful Greek word for this is *anhypostasia*. The person of Jesus Christ, according to this understanding, is not a human individual, but the Son, Word or Wisdom of God. In the thought of early theologians like Justin Martyr, Irenaeus, Alexandria, Origen, the Cappadocean fathers and Maximus the Confessor, though only one person, Jesus Christ, incarnated the Word of God, the incarnation 'christened' the whole of humankind so that all human nature participated in the divine. "Through the incarnation the divine Logos incorporates himself not in the body of a single human being alone, but in the totality of human nature, in humankind as a whole, in creation as a whole" (Sherrard, 1998, p.58).

In the story of Philip's conversion of the Ethiopian eunuch (Acts 8.26-40) there is a very significant late addition. In the earliest texts, the eunuch is reading about the suffering servant in the prophecies of Isaiah. The apostle Philip explains to him that the passages refer to Jesus' death and resurrection, which he goes on to describe. The eunuch's response is immediate: "What is there to prevent me from being baptized?" Philip's response is equally immediate: as soon as they find some water, he baptizes the eunuch without more ado. Baptism is a spontaneous and natural response to what Jesus has done for humanity. But verse 37 – an addition present only in late, probably second century manuscripts – corrects this spontaneity. In this verse, in response to the eunuch's question, Philip replies, "If you believe with all your heart, you may." And the eunuch replies with a little creed:

"I believe that Jesus Christ is the Son of God." The implicit change is momentous. Baptism is no longer a response to the wonderful change that Jesus has achieved for all humanity; it is now the profession of faith that enables one to receive – in contrast with sinful humanity at large – the benefits of what he has done. Christianity changes from a joyous trust in which one opts into redeemed humanity to a self-interested creed in which one opts out of a condemned humanity, to follow the Son of God.

The Sixth Zen patriarch declared

> Deluded, a Buddha is an individual being;
> Awakened, an individual being is a Buddha.
> Ignorant, a Buddha is an individual being;
> With wisdom, an individual being is a Buddha.
> (Platform Sutra, cited in Kennedy, 1995, p.124)

The Zen-practicing Jesuit priest, Robert Kennedy, asks can we not say the same about Christ? When we are deluded, we see Christ as an individual being, but when we awaken, we see every individual being as Christ.

If that is so (and I recognize conservative Christians will contest it, and resent being thought 'deluded') then (at least in principle) another human life, with a different human history and psychology, might also incarnate the divine nature in our human nature. But such a person would be the same person as Jesus Christ, namely, also the Son, Word and Wisdom of God. Or as Buddhists might term it, the Dharma. Jesus and the Buddha on this view would be the same person, expressing the same divinity (since there is only one divinity) through the same humanity (which is my humanity and yours) though in a different individual with a different history and culture. And though Jesus and the Buddha are historically different, and even have a different role in our liberation, it is hardly possible to distinguish between the Buddha nature all beings share and the light of Christ that enlightens everyone (John 1.9).

Such ideas are easy for many Buddhists to grasp. D. T. Suzuki writes, "Christ is conceived by Buddhists also as a manifestation of the *Dharmakaya* in a human form. He is a Buddha and as such not essentially different from Shakyamuni [Buddha]. The *Dharmakaya* revealed itself as Shakyamuni to the Indian mind, because that was in harmony with its needs. The *Dharmakaya* appeared in the person of Christ on the Semitic stage, because it suited their taste best in this way" (1963, p.259). He goes on to say how the *Dharmakaya* manifests itself even in the spirits and 'demons' of animists and polytheists. Here Suzuki shows an extremely different (though still a little patronizing) attitude to 'primitive religion' from that shown by monotheists, Christians included, for whom the objects of animist and polytheistic belief have long been seen as either idolatrous delusions or else 'demonic' in the sense of evil.

The Human Being

If these ideas are much harder for many Christians to accept, it is perhaps because we have become so individualist in the modern West. We have a radically different understanding of the 'person' from the Greek Fathers, who could be claimed to have invented the concept specifically to make sense of the Trinity and the incarnation. It is hard for us to see a person except in terms of their unique, distinctive individuality, in terms of what makes them different and separate from other individuals. Chapter 4 will clarify how this view is created ultimately by the workings of human desire. We shall see how liberation or salvation involves the stilling of individual-centered desire, such that we cease to see other humans as alien, and begin to see them all as Christ.

In lectures and conversations, the Greek Orthodox theologian, Maximus Lavriotes has expressed this very radically. Humanity is not, for him, a collection of separate individuals but one interdependent unity. Christ is not a separate unique person, but the whole of this humanity taken into unity with God. The early 'fathers' who worked out the doctrine of the incarnation did not see it in terms of an achievement by a unique individual, Jesus of Nazareth, but rather as the taking up, in Jesus, of human nature into the divine nature. So it is not as special individuals that we are redeemed, but as belonging to a humanity that has become (in the Orthodox sense) 'divinized', transformed into the divine through Christ, without losing any of our earthy humanity.

So – argues Lavriotes – when people ask me at a party (as they are wont to do) who I am, I should not say with pride, "I am a priest"... "a theologian"... "a writer", but with far greater pride, "I am a human being", knowing that this means, at the deepest level, I am that which Christ has taken into the divine. And when someone approaches, I should not say, "Hello Fred!", but with far greater insight, "Hello me!" knowing – again – that 'me' names Christ, who we both are.

The incarnation in Christ then does not arise as something that makes him unique and special and distinctive. Or rather, his uniqueness lies in his having overcome uniqueness, overcoming those desires that proceed from the competitive, separate ego, and becoming, as he called himself, simply 'Son of Man' – which many scholars interpret as meaning, simply but profoundly, 'the human being' (cf Wink, 2001). So perhaps those Eastern theologians like Katzumi Takizawa and Seiichi Yagi, who build a Christology on the notion of no-self and the overcoming of self in Christ, are actually recalling us to an aspect of the original doctrine of incarnation which we modern Westerners have lost, in the process becoming highly competitive in our advocacy of the special uniqueness of Jesus as Savior.

I do not, in any case, know what it would mean to be 'saved' by or come to the Father 'through' an individual man. The 'I' of the great sayings ascribed to Jesus in the Gospel of John, like 'I am the way, the truth and the life' (quoted above) can be interpreted in two ways. Jesus could be referring to himself as an individual man, in which case he is either deluded or arrogant.

Or it could be that he had so lost the sense of a separate ego that the 'I' he refers to is identical to the way of life he taught, and reality itself, and the life of all things, through which all beings come to God. That is what Buddhists would term the *Dharmakaya*.

Robert Elinor in his beautifully illustrated *Buddha and Christ* (2000) offers images that "invite the viewer and reader to see Buddha and Christ as local inflections of a universal archetype: the cosmic Person imaging wholeness. It nevertheless celebrates the distinctive character of the face of the Buddha and the face of Christ, the incredible variety of their forms" (p.15-16). In Chapter 2 we will see there are many differences between the Buddha and Jesus, and in Chapter 5 we shall see that their roles in the liberation of the world may be quite different too. But they could both have roles that are decisive, unique and indispensable. In that sense they could be distinct 'inflections' of the one Person who shows forth in our human nature what Christians call the divine.

If both Christ and Buddha are genuine incarnations of the divine or the *Dharmakaya*, we would expect that their different historical situations would inevitably 'inflect' and limit the way they refract the divine life into human life. They would not be identical because they were different human beings with different personalities and histories, but behind the difference would lay a similitude in their inner persons. What is explicit in the one would be implicit in the other; what is light in the one is dark in the other; but it would be there. The Buddha would have a 'Christic' shadow, and Jesus a 'Buddhic' shadow. We shall see how the history of the two faiths, for all their distortions, has served in many ways to liberate this shadow, and so confirm its existence.

Trikaya and Trinity

I move quickly to territory to which Chapter 8 will return in more depth, to look at another central Christian doctrine, the Trinity, in relation to the Buddhist Trikaya, which is sometimes offered as a kind of 'Buddhist Trinity'. John Keenan (1989), for example, relates the Father to the *Dharmakaya*, Jesus Christ to the Body of Bliss, and the Holy Spirit to the Body of Change. I think such moves are regrettable, partly because they distort the Christian Trinity, and partly because they limit the immense richness of the Trikaya.

Taking up the last point first, the Trikaya has been used as a model in many suggestive ways. The Dalai Lama (1996, p.118) compares the Body of Change very convincingly with the earthly body of Jesus of Nazareth; the Body of Bliss with the risen Christ, with whom believers enjoy a personal friendship through the Holy Spirit; and the Dharma Body with the Logos, the eternal Word that Jesus incarnated.

This suggests a viable interpretation of the saying just noted, 'I am the Way, the Truth and the Life'. Jesus could here be saying that he is (in Buddhist terms!) *Nirmanakaya*, a *way* of transformation mapped out in his historical path; *Sambhogakaya*, a *life* of bliss in the Holy Spirit he would send, expressed in the 'body' of the Church; and *Dharmakaya*, the ultimate *truth* of all things. Does Christianity not in fact imply the three bodies of Christ – the historical, material body, the spiritual body that is the Church, and the cosmic body that is the Logos or divine Wisdom?

Radical Equality

In Christianity, however, something quite radical happens. If the doctrine of the Trinity is taken seriously, the levels are equalized. For the bodies of the Buddha, however interpreted, exist on different levels, descending from the most refined to the most material. Christians developed their doctrine of the Trinity from neo-Platonic triads which were hierarchical in the same way as the Buddhist Trikaya. For the neo-Platonist philosopher Plotinus (204-70CE), for example, the ineffable One emanated the Logos, who in turn emanated the 'World Soul' or Spirit. But after much thought and fierce debate, Christians resisted the temptation to see Christ as an emanation inferior to the Father from whom he came. They began to insist that the three 'persons' of the Trinity were equally divine. The expressions of God in history came to be seen as not inferior shadows of the ultimate, but as identical in being with their ultimate source.

This had two radical results. On the one hand the figure of Christ, as well as the Spirit that animates the cosmos and the Church, were exalted to divine status. This undoubtedly created one pressure towards seeing Christ as the one and only Savior, divine above all others. But we have seen that there is a contrary aspect of this. Christ is fully human too. The Trinity exalts the lowly, earthy factors of our history and our humanity to equality with the divine. Though Christian faith and spirituality did not always grasp this, Christian art steadily came to do so.

In the Middle Ages, in the East but more especially in the West, depictions of Christ acquired a warm, human quality. The three illustrations on my web page www.holydust.org/christand-buddhapics.htm reflect this humanity in different ways, and show divinity reflected in the glory of the humanity. Likewise, popular piety came to emphasize – in Catholic devotion to the cross, and in Protestant pietism and evangelicalism – relationship with a very human Jesus. As Terry Muck writes, "The popular Buddhist approach to the Buddha tends to produce a godlike Buddha in a religious tradition that insists on his humanity, and the popular Christian approach to Jesus tends to produce a very human Jesus in a religion that insists on Jesus' divinity" (Gross and Muck p.98).

However, I am suggesting that there are aspects of Buddhist and Christian doctrine that actually underwrite these popular trends, even if they are not always the most emphasized aspects. Indeed in Mahayana Buddhist doctrine the *Nirmanakaya* is a projection of the dharma-body of the ultimate Buddha-nature into space and time rather than a real human body of flesh and blood. According to the Third Great Council at which the Mahayana tradition separated from the Theravada, the Buddha was free from birth from all passions and defilements, never said a word that was not intended to enlighten, was in a state of perpetual meditation, and his body was without limits, never tired, slept nor dreamed. So Mahayana doctrine tends toward the equivalent of Docetism, the Gnostic Christian view that Jesus was human in appearance only, but in reality purely divine.

The Buddha was never of course seen as 'wholly divine', but in Mahayana Buddhist thought "the Buddha's human form was now little more than a white lie intended to gradually guide people toward the truth" (Faure, 2009, p.9). As described in the *Mahavaipulya-Tathagatagarbha Sutra* quoted near the start of this chapter, he seems to inhabit realms of exuberant fantasy rather than this solid earth. However, the Elders who originated the Theravada tradition opposed the Great Council on most of the above counts, regarding the Buddha as a more human figure, though the art and religious practice, as noted, also tends to suggest a serene godlikeness that is remote from human suffering.

Conclusion

This chapter has suggested that the Christian understanding of Christ may not be as distant as is commonly supposed from the Buddhist understanding of the Buddha. It is possible to see both figures as embodiments of the ultimate wisdom or law of the universe.

However, critics might object that such connections do violence to both traditions. The teachings considered in this chapter are not stand-alone edifices but integral parts of the inter-locking network of ideas and practices that make up each faith. When one doctrine is interpreted in the context of another faith, it can suffer a kind of violent overturning.

We have seen that if Buddha and Christ are to be identified as incarnations of the Logos or Dharma, then their separate identity is lost, and individualistic understandings of Jesus' and our own identity have to be challenged by the Buddhist idea of no-self. And if a correlation is to be made between the Trikaya and the Trinity, the equality of the latter has to be allowed to challenge the hierarchy of the former, and suggest that embodiment in human flesh is in no way 'inferior' to the ineffable ultimate. This is something only the Vajrayana form of Buddhism seems able to affirm. All in all, Jesus Christ has to become less uniquely and individually divine than a lot of Christian doctrine claims, while the Buddha has to become more earthy and human than a great deal of Buddhist devotion and practice suggest he is.

The crucial question is whether such challenges and changes would represent, for the faiths concerned, violence or healing. But to answer that requires a careful attention, first (in Chapter 2) to the historical figures who have been affirmed as mediators, and what in them might have given rise to such description; and second, to the complex sets of beliefs within which the idea of mediator has been developed. We need to consider what the central figure in those sets of beliefs is seen as liberating us from (Chapters 3 and 4), what his role in the liberation is (Chapter 5) and how our own practices engage with liberation he has made possible (Chapter 6). Only then, having explored some very real differences, will the book be able to develop a clearer idea of the world (Chapter 7) and the liberating reality these two figures embody and open up for us within it (Chapter 8).

Summary

1. Our investigations need to start from the Buddha and Christ that people actually believe in. Only through them will we be able to discern anything of the 'original' Gautama and Jesus.

2. There is a parallel between the way the Buddha is seen as

embodying the Dharma and the way Jesus is seen as the incarnation of the Word and Wisdom of God.

3. The Buddha is not claimed to be a unique incarnation, as Christ often is.

4. However, the traditional teaching held that Christ's incarnation 'christens' the whole of humanity, not just a particular individual.

5. If Jesus incarnates the divine then he transcends the individual self.

6. Parallels between the Trinity and the three bodies of the Buddha are weak, because the significant thing about the Christian Trinity is the equality of the persons.

7. The Buddha is often imagined as not quite human, whereas Jesus, though fully divine, is fully human too.

8. The similarities between the Buddhist understanding of the Buddha and the Christian understanding of Jesus Christ are sufficient to invite us to investigate whether each might learn from the differences.

Chapter 2

Was Jesus a Buddhist? The Teachers and Their Teachings

Love your enemies, do good to those who hate you, bless those who curse you, pray for those who abuse you. From anyone who takes away your coat do not withhold even your shirt.

Hatreds do not ever cease in this world by hating, but by love... Overcome anger by love, overcome evil by good. Overcome the miser by giving, overcome the liar by truth.

Your father in heaven... makes his sun rise upon the evil and on the good, and sends rain on the righteous and the unrighteous... Be perfect, therefore, as your Father in heaven is perfect.

That great cloud rains down on all whether their nature is superior or inferior. The light of the sun and moon illuminates the whole world, both him who does well and him who does ill, both him who stands high and him who stands low.

Blessed are you who are poor, for yours is the kingdom of God.

Let us live most happily, possessing nothing; let us feed on joy, like radiant Gods.

The kingdom of God is as someone who would scatter seed on the ground, and would sleep and rise night and day, and the seed would sprout and grow, he does not know how. The earth produces of itself,

The yeoman farmer gets his field well ploughed and harrowed. But that farmer has no magic power to say, 'Let my crops spring up today. Tomorrow let them ear. On the following day let them ripen'.

first the stalk, then the head, then the full grain in the head.	No! It is just the due season that makes them do this.
Truly I say to you, if you have faith the size of a mustard seed, you will say to this mountain, 'Move from here to there,' and it will move; nothing will be impossible for you.	A monk who is skilled in concentration can cut the Himalayas

These pairs of quotations, alternately from the Gospels and from Buddhist scriptures, represent a small sample of a great collection the Biblical scholar Marcus Borg has gathered together in *Jesus and the Buddha: the Parallel Sayings* (1997) – a classic that ought to be on the shelf of everyone interested in the relation between these two faiths. (The sayings are taken respectively from Luke 6.27-30; Dhammapada 1.5 and 17.3; Matthew 5.45, 48; Saddharmapundarika Sutra 5; Luke 6.20; Dhammapada 15.4; Mark 4.26-9; Anguttara Nikaya 3.91; Matthew 17.20; Anguttara Nikaya 6.24.)

The sayings are not identical, and do not seem to be copied from each other; there is a subtle but definite difference in the style that betokens a difference of original context and different manners of speaking in different cultures. This fact underlines what we have already remarked: the different histories and cultures of the two faiths, and the fact that no definite influence either way can be firmly established prior to the Nestorian arrival in Mongolia and Northern China in the seventh century onward, far later than all the above sayings were written down. There is no evidence that the sayings were copied or transferred from one tradition to the other.

A Universal Ethic – or a Radical Challenge?
Given that difference, the similarities of these sayings and so

many like them is all the more striking, all the more in need of explanation. One kind of explanation often advanced is that the likeness arises from a basic human ethic shared by all humanity. They taught similar things because they taught what all great ethical teachers teach. But it has to be said that what these two teachers teach in many ways contradicts the common human understanding and practice – including of course the understanding and practice of many of their professed followers! Taking up the themes of each of our pairs of sayings in turn, it has to be said:

- Love of enemies is a very exceptional ethic. The duty of vengeance for attacks on one's kin, and the support of one's own people and one's own side in any conflict, represent a far more widespread and, many would say, a far more realistic approach.

- The indifference of God or the forces of the cosmos to the moral stature of the individual is most often associated with an atheistic or a despairing ethic. Belief in a God or a karma that rewards the good is far more common, even among the followers of Christ and the Buddha. People very often shorten the saying of Jesus to 'the sun shines upon the righteous' – thereby neatly reversing the meaning of the original saying to express the more widely shared belief! The notion that there us something exemplary and even benevolent about the divine or cosmic indifference is seldom found, but it seems to be there in those sayings.

- The notion that poverty is of value goes against an almost universal and natural human valuing of wealth, as something good in itself and as something that proves either good karma or the reward of a just God. Both Buddhism and Christianity spawned movements that embraced poverty, though (historically speaking) the embrace was often a little tentative, as monasteries often acquired great wealth in both traditions. Such movements exist at the periphery of several faiths – the Essenes of Judaism, for example – but cannot be said to be mainstream in any other faith except Taoism (under Buddhist influence)

- Trust in the ways of nature rather than human timescales and plans is admittedly quite a widespread tendency in human ethics. It goes against the grain of the expansionist, nature-conquering West, but is of course again coming into vogue as we realize the damage we may be doing to the natural world, and thereby to ourselves, by our human triumphalism. There is, however, something characteristic to the Buddha and Christ in their use of homely analogies from the world of nature – a feature they share, again, with Taoism.
- The power of the spiritual (in the one case, 'faith', in the other, 'concentration') over matter is again a common feature in religions, though it goes against the grain of our science-dominated age. But there is, again, something distinctive in the bold, counter-intuitive and startling simplicity of the way the Buddha and Christ express this.

All this suggests to me, at least, that there is something in the interillumination between the teachings of these two traditions that is not explicable in terms of common-sense universal human morality (even if there is such a thing). Of course, culturally Jesus is a recognizable Jew, and Buddha is recognizable as belonging to the Hindu tradition; neither is a weird alien from their culture dropping like a thunderbolt from heaven. But there is, in what is common to them, something that is also distinct from their preceding culture, distinct from common-sense morality, and distinct too, it has to be said, from much of the way their followers have actually behaved. This distinctive likeness to each other appeals to us, not as common sense, but arguably because it resonates with something deeper than our or any other human culture. Perhaps the affirmations of the previous chapter begin to make sense, as we are invited to see both teachers as embodiments of the dharma, the wisdom, the deep logos-logic of being itself? Somewhere in us we know that where these two voices unite, we need to listen to what they say, contrary and challenging though it always was, and still is.

How do we know what they taught?

Now some readers will by this point be objecting that I am writing as if I know the teaching of these two teachers. Many scholars would ascribe at least some of the above sayings, not to Jesus, but to the Gospel writers. A huge academic industry has developed in modern times devoted to discerning the 'authentic' sayings of Jesus, that is, those that can be ascribed to Jesus himself rather than the tradition that arose from him. There is no equivalent industry in Buddhism.

The sayings ascribed to Jesus can be found in four very short gospels, plus several apocryphal gospels and a scattering of quotes through the rest of the New Testament. All of them are in Greek, not the Aramaic which Jesus himself would have spoken. All of these writings (except some of the apocryphal gospels) are generally agreed to have been composed within a lifespan of Jesus' teaching ministry, that is, by around 100AD. Teachings ascribed to the Buddha are by contrast immense, spanning several cultures and languages, and mostly written several centuries after the death of the Buddha. It would be impossible to discern which of these sayings are 'authentic' to the Buddha.

Nor have Buddhists found it necessary to do so. Mahayana Buddhists tend to view Buddha as "a model and ideal to be followed", a "timeless paradigm" (Faure, 2009, p.17). And while the historical figure is more important in the Theravada tradition, the search for the "historical Buddha" is largely the invention of Western "Orientalist scholars who... wanted to see [Buddhism] as a religion which would tie in with their own views: rather than being a religion revealed by a transcendent God, this was seen to be a human, moral, and rational religion founded by an extremely wise individual" (p.16-17). Meanwhile the practical core of the Buddha's teaching, expressed in the Four Noble Truths and the Eightfold Path (cited in the Introduction) is universal to Buddhism and uncontroversial.

A lot of 'Jesus scholarship', in any case, is based on Western assumptions and priorities. The aim is to construct a coherent history of the evolution of Christianity out of Judaism, including in this history an account of the role of Jesus in this process. In the interests of historical continuity two kinds of discontinuity are ruled out: miraculous events like the resurrection that cannot be squared with a modern Western understanding of the way the world works; and more generally, accounts that might involve the disruption of history by divine intervention 'from outside'. Now Buddhists (except westernized ones) have much less of a problem with the miraculous, so to follow the main agenda of the scholars would be to enter territory which, however relevant it may be in the dialogue between Christianity and modern skepticism, is hardly a priority for dialogue between Christians and Buddhists.

Furthermore, there is an extraordinary tension in the criteria for reconstructing the 'authentic' Jesus. By one set of criteria we seek to reconstruct a history that is as 'smooth' as possible. Jesus has to be in maximal continuity with his background and culture, and yet also (along with other factors) to account for the arising of the sect that became Christianity. So for some scholars Jesus becomes a very ordinary Jewish rabbi, while for others he becomes something closer to what Christian tradition ascribes to him; and the features that loom large, inevitably, fall into the overlap between Christianity and Judaism. This process tends to distance Jesus from any wider links such as interilluminations with Buddhism.

But by another set of criteria, however, teachings that merely repeat either Jewish or later Christian tradition can be ascribed to those traditions. Jesus is therefore found in the kinds of saying that cannot be ascribed either to his Jewish context or to later Church teaching. And as we shall later see, that inevitably makes him an un-Jewish and even un-Christian figure, a sage who leaps out of his context with a wisdom that may indeed look rather Buddhist.

So for various reasons it would not further our aims to apply to the Gospels criteria for discerning which sayings are 'authentic'. That would be to apply to Jesus criteria we cannot apply to the Buddha, making our results lopsided; it would apply to Jesus modern Western historical criteria that are not of great interest to Buddhists, making him a tamer and more 'modern' figure than we need to. And it would yield very few results that all scholars could agree on anyway. We are left with the simpler project of comparing the teachings ascribed to each teacher in the tradition, whether 'validly' or not. Even that, we will see, yields a lot that is of interest, and a lot that liberates both teachers from the traditions that arise from them, and surprises us.

The Teachings

Despite their similarity in content, it is quite easy for anyone at all familiar with Buddhist and Christian scriptures to discern which source each of the opening quotes comes from. The Buddhist sayings are more philosophical, and spell themselves out more. They tend to be in the indicative, describing how things ought to be. The vivid, down-to-earth style of Jesus with its pithy imperatives is instantly recognizable, addressing us with a challenge as to what to do.

These differences, however, mainly concern style and context. Though of course we cannot always separate 'the medium from the message', many of the parallel sayings in Borg's collection look uncannily like translations of the same fundamental idea into two different contexts and ways of speaking.

Many authors have explored the startling likeness-in-difference between the teachings of Jesus and the Buddha. I shall consider the Christian scholar Marcus Borg and the Zen teacher Kenneth Leong. Their approaches are different in starting point and approach, but convergent.

Jesus and the Buddha: Borg's Summary

Borg groups his parallel sayings – sampled above – under nine main chapter headings. The headings in themselves suggest nothing remarkable: most teachers of most faiths would have things to say in most if not all the areas. What is remarkable is the degree to which the teachings in each section build up into a coherent vision. Allowing for differences in style, if we did not know otherwise we might assume these two teachers represented the same faith.

1. **Compassion:** be generous with others as with yourself; love even enemies; take no life – be pacifist; do not avenge evil deeds, but seek the sinner's repentance.
2. **Wisdom:** open your eyes to the light; let wisdom grow gradually; give unselfconsciously and indiscriminately, like the sun and rain, and without thought of gain.
3. **Materialism:** do not worry about material needs, poverty is a blessing, and the storing of wealth an impediment; the poor who give all are more generous than the rich who give their surplus.
4. **The inner life:** worry about the impurity that comes from within, not outside; build your soul like a good solid house, but have no material home; be fearless, and free from the cravings that control people; lose your self.
5. **Temptation:** both teachers were suspect for their associ-

ation with sinners; both were tempted in three ways by the Evil One; both at some stage fasted, at another enjoyed the good things of life; both led notorious sinners to new life.

6. **Salvation** is based on truth and vision, and on faith and love for the Teacher, who wills it for everyone, though only a few attain it; it cannot be forced but comes in its own time, like the harvest.

7. **The future**: all that exists will perish; heaven and earth will pass away. The world will stray far from the teaching, but the teacher will come again to restore the world. (There is an unresolved tension between optimism and pessimism in both teachings.)

8. **Miracles**: both teachers were described as having healed people, walked on water and through walls, and controlled the elements; both were seen to radiate light, and at the end of their lives ascended.

9. **Discipleship**: both gathered a group of committed followers, including (though reluctantly in the case of the Buddha) women, who were detached from worldly goods and represented a new 'family' supplanting their original family ties; both chose a specific leader for this group.

This is an impressive list, but is there a unity or a unifying set of themes behind these various interilluminating teachings? Do Jesus and Buddha just say and do similar things, or is it possible to discern a Buddha-Mind / Mind of Christ as a deep vein running through all the teaching?

Jesus and Zen: the Reflections of Leong

I for one think so, and here I turn for help to Kenneth Leong, who argues that Jesus is best understood as something akin to a Zen master or a Taoist sage. (Taoism was a huge influence on Zen Buddhism.) He introduces his book with an autobiographical comment: "I left Jesus to search for the Tao when I was sixteen.

Now I am forty, and I realize that I could have found the Tao in Jesus" (1995, p.11). Leong does not, like Borg, bring Jesus into direct relation to the Buddha; but he opens our eyes to what might be called the Buddhist (and Taoist) in Jesus.

Leong points first to a vein of humor and exaggeration. As argued later in this chapter, these elements are abundant in Jesus, but alas rather rare in religion generally, which often encourages a deadly seriousness. For Leong, however, "what most people refer to as 'seriousness' is actually a sign of the ego. Most of us are 'serious' because we are too self-obsessed – obsessed by our own self-importance and our notions of what is good, what is right, what is true" (p.12), while humor represents "the mental ability to discover, express or appreciate what is ludicrous, incongruous or absurd" (p.13) – something essential if we are to grow beyond the bounds of our egos. Zen is full of humor with its zany *koans* which are not unlike jokes which we have to 'get'; enlightenment can be signaled by a roar of laughter. But Christian discourse and (see later) depictions of Christ often seem deadly serious and without a trace of humor.

Leong describes Zen as a learning of the art of living our ordinary lives with an eye to beauty in the detail, as in the Japanese Zen tea ceremony or the art of trout fishing (see the quote at the end of Chapter 5). It involves renouncing any dreams of another world and a different future, and creating in the here and now an "ordinary magic":

> To live in the present means, for me, taking delight in the day's magic moments, from morning tea, hunched over a manuscript, to the day's last moments, snuggling and talking with my wife. Happiness isn't somewhere off in the future, but in the morning's phone conversation with someone seeking advice, in this noon meal with a friend, in the evening's bedtime story with a child, in tonight's curling up with a good book. (p.67)

And as the Zen poet Mumon put it

> The flower blossom in spring; the bright moon in autumn;
> The cool breeze in summer; the white snow in winter –
> When the mind is not obstructed by anything,
> Every season is a good season. (cited on p.120)

Leong sees this emphasis on the present as reflected in Jesus' teaching of the kingdom not as a political realm coming in the future, but within hand's reach, present here and now (Mark 1.15).

Scholars would vary in this assessment of Jesus' kingdom teaching, but it is certainly true that Jesus describes this kingdom in ways that make it sound like a 'looking glass world' profoundly different from any conventional political order. Just as Taoists speak of *wu-wei*, working without effort, so the kingdom arrives among us not by our putting up a resistance to evil (Matt. 6.39), but by our trusting and yoking ourselves with a master who said, "my yoke is easy and my burden is light" (Matt.11.30). At the same time the coming of the kingdom in our midst involves watchfulness, diligence and a willingness to give up what stands in the way. It requires what T.S. Eliot described in *Little Gidding* as "a condition of complete simplicity, costing not less than everything."

Liberation

The Buddha is cited as saying, "My teaching is like the sea. It is wide and deep but it has only one taste. The taste of the sea is salt. The taste of my teaching is freedom," (cited by Corless, 1989, p.26.) That freedom seems to be at the core of both Jesus and the Buddha's teaching; it is, as Eliot says, both simple and costly, and it is what holds together the themes discerned by both Borg and Leong. It is what makes me feel justified in using a single term, 'liberation', to describe what Buddhism describes as

'Nirvana' or 'Release', and Christianity 'Salvation', 'Eternal Life', 'The Kingdom of God' and 'The Kingdom of the Skies'. This last is most often rendered as 'heaven', which is a standard circumlocution for 'God', but evokes something of the freedom de Mello's crow found in the whole sky.

Such a move can only be assessed as this book proceeds, exploring the different conceptual systems within which this original goal came to be expressed and changed.

The Teachers

> In a country such as Sri Lanka... the average pedestrian who sees the statues of the meditating Buddha and of the crucified Christ erected on our roadsides has learned to distinguish at least intuitively, if not articulately, between... the tree beneath which Gautama the Indian *mystic* sits in a posture of contemplative calm, and the tree upon which Jesus the Hebrew *prophet* hangs in a gesture of painful protest; in short, between the tree that *bears* the *fruit of wisdom,* and the tree that *bares* the *cost of love.*
>
> (Pieris, 1988, p.111)

Aloysius Pieris here draws a twofold contrast: between Gautama the mystic or sage and Jesus the prophet, and between the serenity of Gautama and the suffering of Jesus. The contrasts are connected: it is the wisdom of the one that makes him serene, and the prophetic challenge of the other that gets him crucified.

Both contrasts are undeniably true of a lot of the art created by the two traditions and the perceptions it embodies and instills. But are they true to the original people, Gautama and Jesus themselves? Are there a prophetic passion in the Buddha and a mystical bliss in Jesus that tradition obscures?

Prophet Versus Mystic?

Taking up the first contrast, it is easy to draw a sharp dichotomy between, on the one hand, wisdom and mysticism – as the contemplation of the timeless realities embodied in nature, in order to learn general ethical insights – and on the other hand, prophecy, as focused on the specific acts and judgments of God in human history and the political struggle against injustice. And at first sight the Buddha falls much more easily into the first category and Jesus in to the second. But this categorization is only half valid.

Back in the 19th century the German atheistic philosopher, Friedrich Nietzsche urged concerning Jesus that "there yawns a contradiction between the mountain, lake and field preacher, whose appearance strikes one as that of a Buddha on soil very little like that of India, and the aggressive fanatic, the mortal enemy of theologian and priest" (1968, p.143). This old and controversial estimate has been given new impetus, as a group of scholars including John Dominic Crossan and Marcus Borg have argued that we should see Jesus primarily as a wandering sage or wisdom teacher. Though such an emphasis would indeed bring Jesus closer to teachers like the Buddha, it would not mean that we had to see Jesus as Nietzsche did, as a kind of oriental guru born in the wrong place. Wandering sages and philosophers were familiar throughout the Mediterranean world of Jesus' time. Typically they combined – as Jesus did – an eccentric asceticism (the Greek 'cynic' Diogenes, for example, lived in a barrel) with an appetite for life and a flouting of polite convention. They would travel with just a simple tunic and a cloak, sandals, a staff, and a bag or purse for all their belongings. Significantly in the gospels Jesus tells his disciples to do even without some of these seemingly minimal requirements (compare Matt. 10.9-10; Mark 3.8-9; Luke 9.3).

However, an amazing variety of incompatible scholarly conclusions have been drawn about Jesus. This variety has been captured in a verse alleged to go to the rhyme, 'Tinker, tailor...'

Wandering preacher, zealot, activist, magician,
Cynic peasant, prophet, wisdom-logician.

If Crossan, Borg and others emphasize the second line, there has been no shortage of scholars emphasizing the first, so presenting a Jesus very different – at first sight – from the Buddha, and much more at home in his Jewish context. So in their different ways John Meier, E.P. Sanders and N.T. Wright see Jesus as the last and greatest of a line of Jewish prophets, challenging people and especially the authorities to change their ways in the light of a coming Messianic reign and/or the judgment of God.

It seems to me that this prophetic dimension in Jesus is undeniable, but that there is no reason why it should not be combined with the wisdom dimension. Judaism, as noted in the previous chapter, has a wisdom tradition of its own, and Jesus could only be the fulfillment of the Hebrew Scriptures if he combined prophecy and wisdom.

Conversely, the Buddha was not just a contemplative sage. Like the Greek Socrates, his wisdom had a sharp prophetic edge, using reason and argument to defeat those who were too satisfied with their own opinions. He challenged his society's obsession with caste, rejecting the need for a priestly caste in particular. Later tradition, with its tendency to analyse and philosophize, blunted this edge somewhat. But in texts like the fire sermon (cited at the opening of Chapter 3), underneath the philosophical categories there rings an urgent challenge to change.

The Serene Enlightened One Versus the Man of Sorrows?

As noted by Pieris, people tend to see Jesus as sorrowing and the Buddha as smiling and serene. We tend to picture Jesus as the 'man of sorrows' and perhaps anger. And Leong remarks that

During one of my Zen classes, I asked my students to close their eyes and visualize Buddha. After that, I also asked them to visualize Jesus Christ. Then I asked them what their pictures of Buddha and Christ were like. Not surprisingly, most of them described Buddha as a smiling figure and Christ as a sober figure. (p.14)

But is this sobriety something longstanding traditions of iconography and sermonizing have imposed? Though the tragic element in Jesus is as old as the first gospel, that of Mark, it is never a monotone, but something more like that of Shakespeare's *King Lear*, bearing a rich vein of humor.

We have only to ponder the absurdity of the birth of the King of Kings in a stable, and kings looking for a palace and finding Christ newborn in a hovel. As well as showing compassion and weeping with the sorrowful, Jesus shared good wine and jokes at his many unruly parties. His parables are full of laughable and disconcerting absurdities, like the vineyard owner who pays his workers equal wages whatever hours they work (Matt. 20.1-16), the farmer who insists on sowing seed on rocks and paths as well as ploughed soil (Matt. 13.1-9) and the servant who earns his master's respect by dodgy dealing (Luke 16.1-9). In the healing miracles we witness the spectacle of demons sent off into a herd of pigs, which promptly plunge headlong into the sea (Mark 5.1-20)! even the solemn passion narrative begins with the mighty Messiah riding, not a horse, but a donkey, escorted by riotous children. And after the resurrection, comedy resumes with two disciples lamenting their lost master while all the while he is walking alongside them (Luke 24.13-25)! All such stories bring us down to earth, carrying us away from the solemn pomposity to which Church authorities would like to lead us, to see the merry absurdity of ordinary life.

Among our scholars, the 'radical' wisdom-focused ones would probably affirm this jovial side of Jesus, while the more Jesus is seen as the angry prophet who got crucified, the more somber our image of him will become. And the more remote will

Jesus become from the radiant serenity of the Buddha.

From the Womb to the Tomb?

In the Nicene Creed, recited every Sunday, Christians affirm that Jesus Christ "was incarnate by the Holy Spirit and the Virgin Mary, and was made man. And for our sake he was crucified". Jesus moves straight from the womb to the tomb! Seen in this perspective, the shadow of the cross is cast back over the whole of Jesus' life. Jesus becomes the man of sorrows because his whole life is seen in the context of a sacrificial, redemptive purpose. That perspective includes important things Christians would not wish to ignore, but there are other things about Jesus – joy, openness, humor, a capacity to enjoy good things and both good *and* bad people, and even a certain detachment – which such a perspective marginalizes or obliterates.

So we should not let the shadow of the cross, important as it is, overshadow the face of Jesus so completely that we cannot see the radiant face of the transfigured and the risen one. Maybe the serene Buddha can help us to contemplate this face of Jesus. Maybe too the sorrowing Jesus can help us see the depth of the Buddha's compassion, and the way in which he wrestled with demons in the dark before his enlightenment. In this way each figure may serve to bring to light – as noted at the end of the previous chapter – the 'shadow side' of the other which later tradition ignored or repressed.

The familiar polarizations, it seems to me, probably owe more to the different ways in which liberation has been conceived in the two religions than to the different personalities of the founders. The Buddha is revered as showing a way out of suffering, while Jesus is seen to have embraced it and worked through it. Gautama Buddha is serene because suffering is the problem he has overcome. He is wise and meditative because insight is how that problem is overcome in Buddhist tradition. Jesus Christ is a prophet because sin is the problem he challenges us to change. And he is the man of sorrows because he sets us free, in Christian tradition, by bearing the burden of our sins. No doubt this reflects some difference in the original teachings, but it clearly also has to do with the different ways in which the two traditions have understood the liberation the teachers brought, as explored in the previous and following chapters.

Uniting the Images Around the Original Liberation

On my web page www.holydust.org/christandbuddhapics.htm you will see three images of Jesus and the Buddha (in once case, an angry Tibetan meditation-Buddha rather than Gautama Buddha). We see how each figure can be serene, wrathful or blissful. But it seems to me that if we recall the paired sayings with which this chapter began, we can see that the liberation they express has all three aspects. Liberation means serenity because it springs from a non-discriminating openness. It includes wrath and sorrow because we can only find it by challenging very hard the values by which we are accustomed to living our lives, and this often provokes (more clearly in the case of Jesus) a vicious defensive reaction in us. And liberation involves mirth because it regards all beings with tenderness, conviviality and wit.

A possible exercise would be to meditate on one pair of faces – the serene Jesus and Buddha in the middle – and once the image is stabilized in your mind, hear the teachers saying their paired sayings. Then move to the wrathful pair at the bottom and do the same, and again, the same with the jovial pair at the top. This exercise may impart an intuitive sense of the liberation both teachers bring. It may also help you see what I mean by the 'Christic' shadow in the Buddha and the 'Buddhic' shadow in Christ.

But now we need to move from imagining liberation to analyzing in more detail what in the light of the two faiths we are liberated from, what liberation consists in, who we are liberated by (ourselves or the 'mediator'), and how in practice we may be liberated. These are the tasks of Chapters 3, 4, 5 and 6 respectively.

Summary

1. There are remarkable parallels between the teachings of the Buddha and Jesus.
2. Seeking the 'original' Jesus and Buddha inevitably distorts more than it clarifies. For our purposes it is better to compare the traditions of sayings ascribed to them.
3. The teachings of Jesus and the Buddha show a remarkable ethical convergence which is different from any universal 'common sense' morality.
4. In many ways Jesus challenges our habitual ways of seeing like a Zen master.
5. This justifies using the same term, 'liberation', to describe the transformation both teachers advocate.
6. Though often Jesus and the Buddha are opposed to each other as prophet to sage, Jesus is very much a wisdom teacher, and the Buddha presented a prophetic challenge to his society.
7. Jesus is often presented as a 'man of sorrows', contrasting with the serenity of the Buddha. But this derives partly from the Christian theology of the cross.
8. We can discern a 'Buddhic shadow' in Jesus Christ, joyous and serene, and a 'Christic shadow' in the Buddha, overwhelmed by human suffering and wrestling with temptation.
9. Reflecting on the two, and their shadows, together can enhance our grasp of the liberation they taught.

Chapter 3

Everything on Fire: Suffering, Sin and Their Causes

The kingdom of God has come near; repent (metanoeite, turn your minds around) and believe in the good news.
Mark 1.1

All things, O monks, are on fire.
And with what are these on fire?
With the fire of passion, with the fire of hatred, with the fire of infatuation; with birth, old age, death, sorrow, lamentation, misery, grief and despair are they on fire.
The ear is on fire; sounds are on fire... the nose is on fire, odors are on fire ...the tongue is on fire, tastes are on fire
...mind-consciousness is on fire...
And with what are these on fire?
With the fire of passion...
(Buddha: The Fire Sermon, in Humphreys, 1960, p.45)

These are the first words ascribed to Jesus in Mark's Gospel (generally acknowledged to be the first Gospel written) and almost the first ascribed to the Buddha, the opening of his famous 'fire sermon' delivered at Bodh Gaya a few miles south of Varanasi in India.

They are stirring words, full of urgency; terse in one case, in the other case expansive and overlain with philosophical analysis that cannot conceal the 'fiery' rhetoric at the core. They are words inviting us to transformation. Because they are faiths inviting us to change our lives, Christianity and Buddhism contain both good and bad news. Both faiths are focused on how

77

wonderfully different life might be; but both include or begin with a description of how bad life as we live it actually is. Later chapters will look at the good news of how our lives can be changed. But this chapter will focus on the bad news, looking at what Buddhism and Christianity say is wrong with the world.

We shall see a deep difference, but also that by using both visions of what is wrong, in conjunction with some modern insights, we will be able to create a deep perspective on the nature of 'evil', a perspective that is realistic but which will not paralyze us with fear. For by looking at the darkness realistically and unflinchingly, we will begin to see how change can occur, in us, in our communities and our world.

The Moth in the Web: Buddhism on Suffering and its Origin

Essentially for Buddhism the bad news is the *dukkha*, the suffering and discontent which, as relentlessly stated in the fire sermon, pervades all experience, all feeling and all thought. The Buddha's own journey towards enlightenment began when he, as a cosseted young prince, first encountered the suffering involved in sickness, old age and death. As summarized in the Introduction, the first of the Four Noble Truths declares that all existence is subject to suffering. The second states the cause of suffering, the *trisna* (Sanskrit) or *tanha* (Pali), the clinging and grasping that makes us want to get things and hold onto them. This book will use the most common translation of this word, 'desire', but the Buddha's teaching suggests the experience of an insatiable thirst that tries to slake itself on seawater. *Tanha* is a kind of fidgeting that cannot keep still, or an attempt to clutch and hold onto water. These connotations are important to keep in mind, for as we shall see there are kinds of desire that can be seen as more positive.

Because all things are impermanent and without enduring soul, this grasping always leads to the pains of frustration, loss, and fear of loss. Furthermore it generates bad karma, keeping us trapped in Samsara, the wheel of birth, death and rebirth. We are like moths caught in a spider's web; the more we struggle against the impermanence of things, the more entrapped in the world of suffering and decay we become. Life becomes infected with the three 'poisons' of greed (or rage), hatred and delusion. Later chapters will explore the third and fourth Noble Truths; this chapter is about what is wrong, which is the subject of the first two truths.

The Buddhist negative is black and bleak indeed. The chains of karma that bind us to the world of suffering are said to go back infinitely in time. Buddhists in worship confess, not the sins of the past day or past week, but bad karma 'accumulated from beginningless time' (see Chapter 6). And in Theravada Buddhism at least, there is no one to liberate you from the wheel of suffering but yourself alone, and the struggle will normally take millions of years, countess rebirths, many of which will be in terrible hells or realms of hunger-tormented ghosts, or in the dim and desire-wracked consciousness of animals.

Where does it come from, this grasping desire that causes these unimaginably long chains of suffering? Buddhism speaks of the twelve *nidanas* or spokes of the wheel of causation, whereby rebirth, desire and consciousness themselves are traced back ultimately to *avidya*, ignorance – ignorance of the unreality of the self, and of the impermanence and ultimate unreality of everything. It is because we believe things are real, and that we have real egos, that a desire for the ego to possess things can arise. But conversely, it is because we grasp and want to hold onto things that we generate the illusion that they and we are real and solid and enduring. So the twelve-spoked wheel keeps turning.

Circles can begin anywhere, but in Buddhism the beginning is our ignorance of the true nature of reality, or rather, unreality. The ignorance from which grasping and suffering arise is that of thinking things exist when really they do not. More precisely we could say it is the ignorance that isolates things in space and prolongs them in time. We think of all things – and ourselves – as isolated and separate, because only so can *I* hold on to *them*. But there is no me here to grasp, and no separate, independent object to grasp, outside of the act of grasping itself. But at the same time as isolating and separating things, my ignorance also prolongs the continuity of my own existence, and that of the object, through time, because again if I am to hold onto things, I and they need to endure. I am continually disappointed, not because things are really other than I want them to be, but because my self and my possessions only exist 'in my wanting them to be'. They have no real substance at all.

In later chapters we shall see how this understanding worked itself out in the doctrines of no self and in the Mahayana understanding of the emptiness of all things. The vast and baffling structures of Mahayana Buddhist metaphysics are all in a sense an outworking of the core Buddhist analysis of the human condition, which is shared by Theravada alike and may derive from the often anti-metaphysical teaching of the Buddha himself. The metaphysics is perhaps best understood as the answer to a simple question: what is the 'world' like without desire? Except of course that the very concept of a world is built of desire, and we have to think otherwise than of a *world*; indeed to arrive at Nirvana, in its unutterably other glory, *we* have not to *think* at all.

The Fruit, the Murder and the Tower: Sin and its Origins in Christianity

Faced with the negative, with evil or bad happenings, Christianity on the whole asks the opposite question from Buddhism. Buddhism asks, "Why do such things *happen* to us – why is there so much suffering?" Buddhist faith and practice represents an attempt to answer that question by showing us a way of avoiding suffering and finding peace and freedom. Christianity (and here on the whole it stands with the other monotheistic faiths, Judaism and Islam) asks, "Why do people *do* such things – why is there so much wickedness and sin?" Even the so-called 'problem of evil', which looks at first sight like a question about suffering, is actually a problem for Christians because of their belief in a Creator God, which immediately turns the question of suffering into the questions, "Why does God allow such things? How can we absolve God of the charge of sin?" Or if the suffering is clearly caused by a person, it turns into the questions, "What should be done with this person? Should he be punished or forgiven?"

One way of putting the difference is to say that Buddhism sees evil as a happening, while Christianity sees it as a deed. Buddhism asks "How can we cope?" while Christianity asks "Who is to blame?" Buddhism looks at pain with a view to the victim, and asks, "How can she overcome it?" While Christianity looks at it with a view to the perpetrator, and asks, "Why did he do it? Is he to blame?" From these questions arise the great concern the monotheistic faiths have shown for the institutions of law, justice and judgment, while Buddhism has been more concerned to provide people with practices that liberate them from inner hurt and pain.

Monotheism allows only one God, who is good; there is no room for a rival, evil God. So for the monotheistic faiths the first question of all is why, in a world that is entirely God's doing, the doing of bad things – sin – should arise at all. The Hebrew Bible opens with three stories that serve as an answer to this question. Most Christians have dispensed with two of the stories and will tell you about the 'fall' from the naturally sinless state of God's creation in terms of just the first of the stories. But the three stories were surely brought together into the first eleven chapters of the Bible for a reason: namely that they complement and enrich each other as accounts of what sin is, and by implication, of the wonderful 'original' creation of God that might be ours if 'sin' were overcome.

The first story is the most familiar one (Gen. 2.4–3.24). God makes man and woman and puts them in a garden where they can enjoy an immeasurable richness of sensual delights. Only one fruit is forbidden. And of course, tempted by a snake, they eat the fruit, and an angry God expels them from the garden into the world we know, full of pain and suffering. This is the story that St. Augustine (354-450) elaborated into the account of sin that is almost universal in the Western Church (though different accounts exist in the Orthodox Church, not to mention Judaism). According to this account, sin is a contagion passed on, not like karma through cause and effect, but almost genetically, spreading from the first couple to the entire human race. Augustine saw this sin as causing all our suffering, not just because the karmic nature of sin is to make people suffer, including the perpetrator, but because God himself has to punish sin, that is, make people suffer for the wrong they do. In the traditions that derive from Augustine, this extrinsic understanding of sin as deserving punishment comes to overshadow the intrinsic account of sin as entailing its own punishment.

On this account sin comes to be defined as an act of disobedience to divine command. And it is motivated by what Augustine called concupiscence, which translated the Greek *epithumia*, desire. Concupiscence – a word which sounds to the uninitiated like a delicious fruit, perhaps an exotic variety of pear, or perhaps the fruit in the original garden! – denotes the craving of Adam and Eve to grasp and possess the one thing that was not theirs. It sounds a little like *tanha*.

Despite several references to it in the New Testament (Heb. 11.4, 1 John 3.12, Jude 1.11), the second story (Gen. 4.1-16) has had less of a press in the Christian tradition. It is about two brothers, Cain and Abel. Abel the shepherd sacrifices one of his sheep to God, who graciously accepts it. Cain, an agriculturist, offers some of his wheat, and it is rejected. Cain is jealous, and murders his brother. God is angry with Cain and makes him a homeless wanderer, but significantly protects him from those who would avenge Abel's blood. In this story, sin originates not from desire and disobedience, but from frustrated obedience leading to rivalry and jealousy. Cain desires to avenge what he experiences as a wrong, namely the unfair treatment he receives from God *vis-à-vis* his brother. It is as if God sees how the desire for vengeance could make murder lead to more murder, and chooses to limit the chain reaction by forgoing his own right to avenge.

At the same time, as with the Eden story, there is a hint of divine responsibility. Just as God put the forbidden fruit in the garden, so it is God who provokes rivalry by receiving one brother's offering but not the other. The Bible here seems to affirm both our human responsibility for how we deal with the temptations and injustices of the world God has made, and God's own responsibility for those temptations and injustices.

In the third story (Gen. 11.1-9) people start to envy God. They decide to build a tower so they can ascend it to be on a level with God. This makes God angry and he destroys the tower and confuses the people's tongues. With their different languages (and religions and cultures?) people will not be able to co-operate in this way again, and probably will not want to. Here the root of sin is pride, wanting more status, and imagining that with a bit more effort we can be equal to God.

It is noteworthy that in the Gospels (e.g. Matt. 4.1-11) there is a possible echo of the stories in the three temptations of Jesus. Unlike Adam and Eve, Jesus resists the desire to satisfy his appetite with food not given; unlike Cain, he feels no rivalry or envy that might lead him to want to rule the world; unlike the makers of the Tower of Babel, he is not attracted by the notion of climbing to a high place and demonstrating divine powers.

Desire and disobedience, which are the focus of the first story, do not loom so large in the other two. Though Augustine and his teaching of 'original sin' have dominated Western Christianity, another tradition has survived for which the root of sin is not desire but pride: the way we place ourselves, instead of God, at the center of our world.

And even for Augustine, desire in itself is not evil; it is disordered, disobedient or obsessive desire, desire out of control, that is evil. The Christian tradition differs from the Buddhist in according a positive place to authentic, undistorted desire. Such desire is generally called by a different name; not *epithumia*, but *eros*, the passionate love which the soul can feel for God. And the commonest word for 'sin' in the New Testament is *hamartia*, which describes an arrow 'missing the target'. In one important tradition, sin involves, in the better cases, being deflected from our true goals and target, and falling short to hit secondary goals. In worse cases, the arrow is not aimed at the target at all, but dangerously, elsewhere. What does this mean?

The desire (*eros*) of the soul for God and of God for the soul is at the heart of orthodox Christian spirituality and ethics. St. Thomas Aquinas (1224-74) arranged the seven deadly sins of the monastic tradition in order according to the degree to which this core desire becomes corrupted. In his *Divine Comedy*, Dante gave his scheme a wonderful illustration in the imagined structure of Mount Purgatory. The least bad sins – lust, greed and avarice – consist in desire becoming excessive and focusing on means rather than ends. A healthy life is a good goal to have, and we need to eat and earn money to keep ourselves and our dependents healthy and alive, but greed fastens upon this means and makes it an end in itself. The result is very often far from healthy. Likewise lust desires for its own sake the bodily pleasures that should be the means, not the end, to union with another in love. And avarice makes money or possessions ends in themselves, to be accumulated, rather than as means that (in moderation) can help us lead happy and generous lives. Disordered desire is 'endless' in two senses: without a clear idea of its natural end or goal; and therefore lacking a point when satisfaction can be identified, so going on endlessly and without limit.

Next in the seriousness of sins comes sloth or despondency, which arises not from an excess but from a deficiency of *eros*. We fail to desire good things as much as we should; they fail to move us, so we fail to act. The Buddhist overcoming of desire can seem to Christians like sloth, and it is often criticized for insufficient thirst for justice; we shall see how such criticisms can be answered.

Finally, the worst sins of all are those that desire not good, but harm of some kind or another. Anger desires to harm another in order to defend what the agent believes to be good, or avenge what the agent perceives to be harm. Envy hates the good another enjoys and seeks to deprive him of it. Pride, worst of all, effectively denies the independent good of other beings altogether, seeing the self (in place of God) as the sole end all others should serve.

Comparisons

The Buddhist and Christian understandings of evil and harm seem very different, but also to converge significantly at some crucial points. This chapter will explore the differences, and then the convergences; the next will look at a point of view that challenges both understandings equally.

Doughnut or Hole?

The difference between the two faiths is not well captured in the widely held stereotype that Buddhism is pessimistic, world-renouncing and individualistic, while Christianity is optimistic, world-engaged, and corporately Church based. There are elements of truth in this depiction, but it is highly biased, and more untrue than true. And equally, to see Buddhism as a faith of tough realism and Christianity as committing us to a blind and naive faith is surely mistaken, for as Paul Williams points out, optimism and hope are not necessarily less realistic than deep pessimism and despair (2002, p.19ff).

But Williams goes on to cite an anonymous ditty:

Twixt the optimist and pessimist the difference is droll –
The optimist sees the doughnut, the pessimist the hole.

He suggests that Christianity is a religion of the doughnut, while Buddhism is a religion of the hole. But both Buddhism and Christianity have extremely hole-based varieties. There can be few world views more gloomy than the Calvinist account, according to which the vast majority of humankind is predestined by God, whatever they do, to the eternal fires of hell. At the same time most Buddhists I personally know radiate happiness, not world-weariness. And this is perhaps because our suffering, however huge, has a cause in us – our grasping and holding onto things. That is something we have power to overcome, and this can bring great bliss known not only to Buddhists:

The deepest truth I have discovered is that if one accepts... loss, if one gives up clinging to what is irretrievably gone, then the nothing which is left is not barren but enormously fruitful. Everything that one has lost comes flooding back again out of the darkness, and one's relationship to it is new, free and unclinging. (Robert Bellah, 1970, p. xx-xxi)

This chapter is looking at the huge holes in life that Christianity and Buddhism, more than any other faiths perhaps, have depicted; but both faiths describe huge holes because they offer us huge doughnuts.

Suffering or Sin?
Nevertheless the 'hole in life' is described very differently. This

86

difference is best captured, I think, by the point noted, that Christianity presents us with a world of actions generated by intentions, by the will, whereas Buddhism describes a succession of experiences tied together by karma, cause and effect. For Christianity the primary ethical model is that of the archer with the bow, and the main question is what he is aiming at and whether or not he succeeds in hitting his target. The Western world, based largely on Christianity, is a world of plans and targets and achievements and failures. For Buddhism the core model is that of the stone thrown into the pond. The crucial moral question is not what the stone was aimed at, but the ripples of karmic cause and effect that spread across the pond far beyond what the stone can know, and ultimately ripple back to the stone itself. Though concerned about intention, Buddhism offers us an ethic of consequences spreading way beyond what we consciously intend. Many would argue that this is precisely the kind of ethic we need in order to deal with the complex chains of ecological cause and effect that bind our planet together. (Meanwhile Judaism and Islam offer a different ethic again, concerned with God-given laws and procedures, and with whether an action conforms to or obeys these laws or not.)

If we take, as a down-to-earth example, someone who masturbates imagining a beautiful married man or woman he or she knows and is attracted to, the question for a Christian would be what the person's intentions were. The conclusion would probably be that the person was imagining an act of adultery and would commit such an act if he or she had the chance. So morally – if not legally – the person is guilty of adultery. This is exactly what Jesus seems to be described as teaching (Matt. 5.27). A Muslim or Jew would be more interested in whether the commandment against adultery was objectively being infringed. Islam, I am told, humanely encourages masturbation if it is a way of avoiding adultery – dissipating the feelings that might otherwise lead to the seduction or harassment of the person desired. Finally, Buddhism would be more concerned with the karma involved. Masturbation might be a way of avoiding the infliction of bad karma, through a sexual encounter, on the person desired. The perspective of the potential victim comes more clearly into focus than it does in the Christian case – the woman who is lusted after in Matthew 5.27 would probably prefer that to actually being sexually coerced! But the person masturbating would have also to consider the karmic effect of his imaginings on his own future state.

Which perspective is to be preferred? Nietzsche saw the Buddhist focus on suffering as showing its greater honesty and straightforwardness. "Buddhism as a hundred times colder, more veracious, more objective [than Christianity]. It no longer needs to make its suffering decent to itself by interpreting it as sin – it merely says what it feels – 'I suffer'" (1968, p.132). Nietzsche argues that we can make suffering bearable in two ways, by regarding it as a punishment for sin, claiming the nobility of penance, or by eliciting a righteous anger at the sins of those who inflicted it on us, claiming the nobility of victim status. Just to say, without adornment, "I am in pain", without the satisfactions of self-abasement or resentment, requires an unusual kind of moral courage. But that is what Buddhism *at its best* enables, and what I hear, for example, from many Tibetan Buddhists as they describe the great suffering that has been inflicted on their people, especially in the last half century.

'At its best.' Of course, quite often karma seems to be described as a kind of punishment, so that, if someone is suffering, it is acceptable because the person must deserve it because of deeds committed in this or a previous life. But karma is not a law of divine punishment, merely a description of consequence. There is no sense in which I can be to blame for what 'I' did in a past life I cannot now remember, any more than I can be to blame for what happened in my earliest, now forgotten infancy. But I suffer the consequences of both, and at some level I need to come to terms with that.

It is not always realized what an utterly different under-standing of morality this implies, from either the Judaic-Islamic or the Christian understandings. Rightly understood, Buddhism implies a universe without blame; for when I suffer from the bad actions of another person, I know that he is doing what he does because of the bad karma that is lodged in him. If I am aware of this I may be able to deal with his bad karma inflicted on me in a way that he cannot deal with it in himself. That, curiously, brings us to a notion familiar in Christianity: that one person's sin can be redeemed by another person's consequent suffering, if the latter chooses to bear it. Chapter 5 will argue that this gives us the best possible insight into the suffering of Jesus.

But there is a sense in which a world without blame is a world beyond morality as we in the West have come to understand it. In the monotheistic faiths, the last word is the word of Judgment, our accountability before the judgment throne of God or Christ. But

> in Buddhism... what is essential for salvation is not to overcome evil with good and to participate in the supreme Good, but to be emancipated from the existential antinomy of good and evil. In the existential awakening to Emptiness, one can be master of, rather than enslaved by, good and evil. (Abe, 1985, p.132)

This brings us to the next point, about whether our problem is primarily an ill will for which we will be called to account, or a slavery that is the consequence of our lack of awakening. Are we at root wicked demons, or foolish sleepwalkers?

Ignorant Fancy or the Deflection of Desire?
We saw how in Buddhism the root of suffering is ignorance: our believing too much in the independent existence of ourselves

and other beings. In Christianity on the other hand, our problem is the opposite: that we do not believe enough in the reality of the other, so that our will gets too easily deflected from our real ends. We begin to treat things that should simply be means as ends in themselves, and beings who should be ends in themselves as mere means to serve our ends. If we really believe in the target, we will not let the arrow fall short. "Buddhism sees the ego as 'false', while Christianity presents the ego as 'sinful'" (Kiyoshi Tsuchiya in Schmidt-Leukel, 2005, p.82). Or as Leo Lefebure puts it, "while the Buddhist tradition finds the origin of suffering in the cravings that come from ignorance, for Augustine the root of all sin is turning away from God" (1993, p.129).

But Lefebure goes on to qualify this.

> This turning-away is itself a form of ignorance of who we really are and gives rise to cravings very similar to those found in Buddhist descriptions... Where Augustine presents the main categories of sin as pride, curiosity, and concupiscence, the Buddhist tradition has described the three poisons of human life as ignorance, anger and greed. (p.129)

Both traditions speak of evil in terms of a turning to self – Christian 'pride' – accompanied by an obsessive and disordered clinging to the other – *tanha*, concupiscence. In both cases the overcoming of these tendencies leads to openness to new energies, unobstructed by the self; to a new wisdom in oneself and a new love of others. But Buddhism relates this to ceasing to believe in a separate self and objects, and ceasing to desire; while Christianity relates it to a new relationship to God and the created world, in which a different kind of desire flows.

Redeemed from Fire by Fire?

And there we uncover a difference that goes to the root of Buddhist and Christian spirituality. At the heart of the former is meditation, which seeks to loosen the tight tangle of the desire that presupposes ego and object. It seeks to still the struggling moth, so that it can untangle the web of karma and slip free. But at the heart of the latter is the healing of desire, so that it can attain its true object, God. It seeks a kind of desire in which the self is burnt and purged of all lesser desires, ideals and idols, enlightened with the vision of its true goal, and poured out in the love of God that is *eros* in its fullest sense.

Traditionally the Christian mystics describe these three stages as purgation, illumination, and union with God, to which some mystics (for example, Richard of St. Victor) add a fourth, the return to created beings filled with the self-emptying love of God for them. If the Buddha's fire sermon identifies the universal fire of desire burning in all our faculties, and teaches us how us to put it out, in Christianity we are, in the terms of T.S. Eliot's *Little Gidding*, "redeemed from fire by fire" – saved from the desire with which our egos burn by the desire that burns our egos away.

This Christian perspective supposes that over against the grasping kind of desire, in which we are continually trying to fill ourselves, and battling against our fundamental emptiness, there is a kind of desire that empties the self and so finds the fullness of the self-emptying God (of whom more in Chapter 8). There is an impoverishing craving for self-enclosed completeness, which could be called plerotic, 'filling' or 'self-fulfilling' desire. But there is also an enriching desire that empties us of self to live in God, which I will call kenotic desire.

When we fall in love (or when we are absorbed in a creative 'labor of love' like writing a book or a piece of music), our love of the beloved person (or subject) tends to empty us of self-awareness: we lose ourselves in the other. No longer self-sufficient, we find we become needy and dependent on the other for our existence. It is the beloved's returning love, or the existence of the work we are creating, that sustains us and makes life worth living. But this creates a radical openness and vulnerability to the other. If the other does not respond (or if the work of prose or art does not work out or gain an audience) we feel our universe is collapsing around us. The ego senses itself in mortal danger, and it reasserts itself in obsessive possessiveness of the other (or in a demand that others recognize our masterpiece). So *eros* is always tending to slide into *epithumia*, an obsessive, possessive desire that makes the beloved person or work a kind of safely-walled extension of the ego.

This sliding movement can be detected in many different realms. It is seen when lovers move from selfless devotion to the mad jealousy that would sometimes even rather kill the beloved than see her 'belonging' to someone else. It is seen when prayer and worship – a radical longing openness to God – degenerates into the obsessive ritual whereby God becomes our support structure, and serves us in a kind of egoism that is routed via the selfless love of God. We offer ourselves to God in selfless devotion, but on the understanding that he has a special and providential love for us uniquely. The same movement is seen in the descent from the admiration of bodily beauty – which includes sexual adoration but much more – to the pornography that enables what we adore to be our objectified possession. It is seen too when patriotic devotion to a country becomes uncondi- tional service of the leader, and we identify ourselves wholly with his triumph over his enemies, whom we regard as our own.

Plerotic and kenotic desire coexist in us. This becomes clearest at times of prayer, when on the one hand we feel encompassed by a presence full of beauty, drawing us out of ourselves in a kind of slow and sober ecstasy of self-forgetfulness, while at the same time obsessive thoughts flit around us, clamoring for attention and arousing the kind of desire that comforts and reassures us that there is still an ego there.

Clearly self-emptying desire is risky, because we are always tempted to fill the unbearable emptiness and turn to plerotic desire. Christian mysticism suggests that union with God in love and desire is to be attempted only by those who can endure a 'dark night of the soul' without flinching spiritually. Buddhist caution, which recommends a dissolving of *all* desire, is understandable.

Should we tell the moth to struggle harder, because only the tight chords of true desire will break the false desires that imprison it? Or should we urge it to be still, because only so will the chords of those desires begin to loosen, until finally they fall away? I wonder if the differences between Buddhism and Christianity do not amount to their different answer to this question. Maybe Christians believe in a self and a God and a real cosmos because they believe that we cease desiring in the plerotic sense through finding that there is a truer and deeper desire. That deeper desire implies there must be a desirer and a desired (God and self being both), and a cosmos that is held together by desire: a universe sustained by nothing but love. Buddhists do not believe in these things because they believe true insight will only come when all desire falls away.

But the best thing for the moth might be both to stop struggling – most of the time – but at the *right* time, when the web has worked loose enough, to flap her wings with all her might.

Summary

1. Both Buddhism and Christianity are religions of transformation. They both start with an account of what is amiss and needs changing

2. In Buddhism the emphasis is on the web of suffering in which we are caught like moths by our desire, which springs from the illusion of permanent things and self.

3. In Christianity the emphasis is on the way human beings cause suffering by their sin. The three stories in Genesis trace this sinfulness to our grasping, envy and pride.

4. Both faiths describe a big negative 'hole' because they are offering a huge 'doughnut' of liberation.

5. In Christianity the 'hole' is seen from the side of those who cause it, the perpetrators who need to be held to account. In Buddhism it is seen from the point of view of those who experience it, which is all of us.
6. But in both accounts, both sin and suffering originate in self-seeking desire.
7. However, whereas Buddhism seeks to quiet all desire, Christianity affirms an authentic love that can empty us of self. Self-centered desire is a deflection or distortion of this love. It needs not to be quieted, but redirected to its true goal in God.

Chapter 4

Webs of Desire: The Politics of the Self

The first law is no desire. Your heart seeks one thing after another,
creating a multitude of problems. You must not allow them to flare
up. Desires are like the roots of plants. Since they are buried deep
below the earth you can't see them and don't know they are damaged
until the buds of the plant begin to wither and die.... This cuts us off
from the roots of Peace and Joy. That is why you must practice the
law of no desire.

(Lost Sutras, p.81)

The most striking characteristic of the modern world view, which
distinguishes it from Buddhism and Christianity alike, is the way
its understanding of reality and ethics centers upon the free,
autonomous ego. The French thinker Descartes (1596-1650)
famously declared "I think, therefore I am", thereby ascribing his
existence neither to divine creativity nor to evolutionary process,
but to his own thought. The human mind was for Descartes a
free 'thinking thing', haunting a mechanistic physical body, or as
Gilbert Ryle famously put it, a 'ghost in the machine'. With the
German philosopher Immanuel Kant (1724-1827), the autonomy
of this thinking thing – its ability to make its own free decisions
independently of religious and other traditions – became
essential. If we are motivated by our own good as described by
tradition, we are not unselfishly obeying the moral law. But
according to the late nineteenth and early twentieth century
existentialists, the autonomous ego even had to make up the
moral law for itself. And these days, whether you are neo-
Thatcherite or an eco-feminist, and whether your concern is
material prosperity or spiritual growth, 'personal fulfillment' is

95

assumed to be what your efforts should be all about.

Yet in all sorts of ways this centrality of the human self has long been wearing thin. It is questioned from numerous points of view that are by no means otherwise in accord. Psychology with Sigmund Freud opened a huge area of the unconscious mind that make the autonomous conscious ego look like the small visible tip of an immense, anarchic, iceberg. Karl Marx and his followers contended that the supposed autonomy of the few is based on the economic slavery of the masses. And in our own time genetics asks whether we really are much more biologically determined than we would like to think; while the ecological movement asks whether the earth has not had enough of the human ego and its self-seeking, and invites us to define ourselves anew in terms of what unites us with the rest of life, rather than what supposedly distinguishes us. Finally, as we shall see, a new theory of desire teaches that, far from choosing what we want, there is a sense in which our wants choose us. A new world is opening up, which many describe as 'postmodern': a world that exists 'after' the collapse of the autonomous ego.

This chapter explores what the implications of this change are for a Buddhist Christianity. Though neither faith has championed the ego, both have cause to be rather ambivalent about the prospect of its demise. Buddhism, though it declares the ego an illusion, has made much – especially in its Western forms – of the importance of self-help and personal responsibility. Christianity is the opposite on both counts: much more skeptical about our freedom to liberate ourselves, but insisting on the eternal reality of the soul.

The chapter begins by looking at an important critique of both faiths, which says that neither has attended to the political aspect of liberation, and the ways in which some people, to be free, may need to assert their egos not less but more. Then it plunges into an exploration of desire in four dimensions, from which it emerges that the self is shaped and formed by the desires it thinks it freely has. That leads into a consideration of the Buddhist doctrine of no-self in comparison with the Christian self, and some thoughts on why the 'autonomous self' is so often so deeply unhappy. Finally a model will be offered that combines Buddhist and Christian insights, and suggests how we the unfree might summersault into true freedom.

This is perhaps the most complex chapter of the book, but also the most important to the argument, in that it goes to the heart of the difficulty we all find in even really wanting true freedom. It forms the bridge between the consideration of sin, suffering and desire in the previous chapter, and the need for a subtle balance between own- and other-power explored in the next. As we carefully journey across this bridge, I hope that the value of a Buddhist Christianity will begin to emerge.

Uncoiling the Snake of Political Vision

Buddhism and Christianity – the previous chapter argued – present us with different perspectives on what is wrong: that of the victim who experiences wrong, versus that of the sinner who causes it. But in modern times a third, political perspective has arisen that calls for a plague on both Buddhist and Christian houses. In this perspective, both faiths are seen to be looking at wrong from the perspective of individuals. One looks at the moth and asks how it can be freed from the web; the other looks at the spider and asks how it can be freed from its compulsion to spin webs and catch moths. But what we should be looking at is webs. If webs were disallowed from the universe, moths would not be caught, and spiders would have to find less oppressive ways of making a living. (Probably the analogy falls down a little at this point; this is unlikely to happen in the case of spiders, but it might in the case of capitalists and others!)

So – it is argued – we need to look not at individuals but at the structures and social systems in which the desire to exploit is taken for granted and even encouraged. Until we do that, individual spiders and individual moths can never both be happy; they are locked in rivalry because we allow webs. Capitalists and workers, men and women, masters and slaves, people of different cultures and races, will be locked into conflict and wrong until we 'change the system'.

The political perspective highlights ways in which both Buddhist and Christian understandings of virtue and vice have been developed primarily from the point of view of those advantaged by the political system. It is surely right to urge the master not to vent his anger on the slave, the man to be humble and gentle with 'his' woman, the wealthy capitalist not to be self-satisfied and proud. But to break the system, does the slave not need *more* anger, the wife *less* self-abasement, the worker *more* pride in his work and worth? There is a perspective of the victim which both Buddhism and Christianity have often underplayed.

In response to this question a shift has occurred, at least in parts of Christianity. Jesus the humble and kindly gentleman, condescending from the glory of his family home with the Father and the Spirit, has been replaced – in some quarters – by Jesus the angry peasant, identified with women and outcasts. (I do not know of any equivalent shift in the case of the royal Prince Gautama, though parts of Buddhism have also come to embrace the political struggle.)

To break the system that enslaves, we need to get beyond the encouragement of individual virtues and vices – just creating a slave-based society where the masters are kindly, marriages where the male breadwinner is generous with *his* earnings, and so forth. We need more than changes of heart. We need changes of laws and institutions, to change society.

Righteous Anger?

This point is explored in an enlightening dialogue between two feminists, one Christian and the other Buddhist (Gross and Ruether, 2001). The Christian, Mary Radford Ruether, remarks that during the struggle of black people for civil rights, many white Christians urged that what was needed was not legalistic improvement but a change of heart, so that whites came to 'love' blacks. "The blacks retorted angrily with something to the effect that 'we don't care if you love us or not. What we want is to make sure that you will be prevented by law from discriminating against us.'" (p.124) Ruether goes on to remark that though the whites who now have to line up along with blacks at the lunch counter do not 'love' the blacks any more than they 'love' the whites in the line, they accept their right to be there. In our terms, something in the objective web of oppression has been changed.

So we need to be aware of a dimension of liberation that goes beyond the largely personal agendas of traditional Christianity and the no-self traditions of Buddhism alike. The angry response of the blacks is understandable and probably at certain points liberating and creative. On the other hand, in the longer haul, can anger liberate? Is anger, which is something felt by individuals toward other individuals, a relevant emotion in relation to impersonal systems? Will it not always personalize the political agenda and make personal enemies? Will anger not miss the real webs of oppression that turn people into oppressor and oppressed? Will it not – as has so often happened in violent revolutions – simply make the spider and the moth change roles?

Zen teacher Gabrielle Roth expresses well the ambiguity of anger: creative in the moment, destructive if held on to for too long.

Anger... is a 'no' to wrong, a violation. It draws lines and throws up barricades. Proper anger cuts like a knife through water. It is quick, clear, needs no explanation. It's the bared teeth of a bitch protecting her litter, the arched back of a cat threatened by a coyote. There is nothing cleaner, more effective than appropriate anger...

Internalized, bottled-up anger is pandemic in our society and its consequences are catastrophic domestic violence, violent crime, all kinds of inappropriate aggression, war at all levels, despairing destructiveness. (1998, p.62-4)

Think of the difference between Robert Mugabe and Nelson Mandela. Both, as young men in the struggle against racist governments and structures, were full of appropriate anger. To my mind the face of the young Mandela looks the more angry and determined at this point. Both condoned the use of violence against violent regimes – or what their enemies would term terrorism. But on liberation, Mandela was determined that the whites as well as blacks needed to be liberated in the new society. He developed structures in which old angers could be expressed and old cruelties confessed without recrimination and with the possibility of forgiveness. His face now is radiant with a universal and innocent compassion that persuades the old enemies and brings the old powers tumbling to the dust. Meanwhile Mugabe went on hating. He found new enemies to hate. Some comrades remain loyal to him as the liberator of old, but Mugabe has few friends, and persuades nobody who is not already persuaded of the rightness of his cause.

In political struggle, how do we become more like Mandela than Mugabe? Rita Gross's Buddhist response to Ruether (pp.107-120) gives a key part of the answer. She relates a little of her own story: a childhood in which she was oppressed and limited as a woman by a narrow Christianity, the liberating feminism that taught her to be angry, and finally her move towards Buddhism and meditation. She says that if she had been told how her meditation would dissolve her anger she would have avoided it. Having become steeped in meditation she remains critical of Buddhist friends who tell her that her feminism is attaching her too strongly to the political world. But she has found through it a new perspective in which ego-based perspectives are dissolved.

Clinging to or aggression against others, in defense of the ego, are the primary emotions (*kleshas*) of the untrained mind. But it is not the thoughts and emotions themselves that are the problem; it is the extremely close identification of ourselves with those thoughts and emotions, the uncontrolled way in which they dictate what our lives and our actions will be. (p.110)

What meditation does is create a space between us and our thoughts and emotions.

Thoughts and emotions occur and then there is a gap, some space in which one can bid the old familiar pattern hello and goodbye without buying into it. There is good reason why one of the traditional analogies for the process of waking up is 'like a snake uncoiling'. (p.111)

Through meditation, the snake of understanding is given space to uncoil, free from her still existing personal anger. Gross finds she can see the structural element of oppression more clearly and less personally. This enables her to speak of it in a way that is no longer angry and alienating, but quietly strong, humorous and convincing.

The Parliament of the Soul

One way of understanding what meditation can do here is to see it as helping to create a kind of just inner politics, which mirrors the outward just politics we are striving to establish. Without the space meditation can give, we tend to react to thoughts and feelings in one of two ways. We can identify with them and allow them to rule us; or we can push them away and repress them.

In the former case our life consists of a succession of *coups d'etat* by different thoughts and feelings. When we first try to meditate, we realize how far we are ruled by first this thought, then that feeling, and how difficult it is to throw off this chaotic inner tyranny. In the latter case we disown feelings we do not want to acknowledge as part of us. The problem is, to use a Buddhist analogy, you are only burying bad karma like a seed in the ground; when the time is ripe it will sprout and grow rampantly. In Jesus' terms you are like the man who casts out a demon and sweeps his house clean; later on seven worse demons come along and enjoy the nicely swept house (Matt. 12.43-5)! It may be that you hated a severe father but repressed the hatred; then you encountered a cruel teacher and repressed your hatred; then a ruthless bishop or abbot, and repressed your hatred for him; finally a gentle person utters a mildly authoritarian remark, and suddenly, without apparent reason, all the hatred you have built up is unleashed on him!

Meditation and similar techniques open up another place to take your thoughts and feelings. You neither let them rule, nor push them away, but allocate them a place in the parliament of your soul from which they can be called to speak when you need to hear them, or have their say when they need to.

In former times I was a stalwart defender of the institutional Church. But gradually many things the bishops did began to enrage me. The Anglican bishops seemed to be tearing the Church apart over issues like homosexuality. The Orthodox bishops seemed to be doing the same over issues of jurisdiction, while the Roman Catholic hierarchy was becoming ever more reactive and remote from the people. At first my fury did considerable damage. It led me to dream up all sorts of inane responses. I would leave the Church, I would expose the bishops in my writings, I would even... become a Buddhist (for all the worst reasons)! But if I had done those things, neither the Church, nor I, nor the cause of Buddhism, would have benefited at all. Alternatively I could have repressed my anger, but that too would only have brought further harm. In the end what I have done is to allow a very angry, anti-bishop, anti-establishment person a place in my soul. I call him the 'Anglican Dissident'. I often go to listen to him, but I listen to the older voice of the 'Defender of the Faith' too.

Oddly enough the Anglican dissident is the most Anglican part of me now. The Defender of the Faith always thought that (Eastern) Orthodoxy is where the true faith is to be found, Anglicanism being fuzzy, compromised and heretical. It often seems to be the case that angry people retain or acquire the features of those they despise: as the biologist and atheist campaigner Richard Dawkins might be likened to a heresy-hunting Grand Inquisitor, and the ex-Catholic feminist Mary Daly a redoubtable nun! That is yet another weakness of anger that is allowed to reign; it never really moves out of the framework it opposes, or lays to rest the ghosts that haunt it. History is littered with republics that repeat the oppressions of the regimes that were overturned by angry revolutionaries. In my case, thankfully, there are other voices and frameworks that have grown stronger since, like the Buddhist, who listens in bemused silence as the Anglican Dissident and the Defender of the Faith have it out with each other! It would be hard to go back to the loyal servitude of the Church that was once mine, but I am not compelled to be the Church's enemy either. A third space has opened up in which I find myself being – I hope – a good and reliable but critical friend.

Now having a rich and varied 'inner politics' can make us far more effective when it comes to playing our part in the outward political scene. If we have dialogued inwardly with an oppressor, we are more likely to persuade an outward one than if we have been captivated by rage against him. We will have heard all his arguments before, internally, and will be familiar with the case that may bring about a change of heart in him. However – and this is the crucial point – without some disciplined practice like meditation to open up a space within us, and allow us as it were to be plural, the inner dialogue or 'multi-logue' is hard to achieve. But as the section below on the chariot will explore, the Buddhist doctrine of *anatta*, no-soul, is based on the notion that we are plural, made of many elements. And in meditation we learn to watch those many seething elements as they rise and fall within the field of consciousness, often presenting themselves in neat logical form, but actually coming and going without any essential logic at all.

Four Aspects of Desire

Political and sociological analysis suggests four aspects of desire which traditional understandings have sometimes overlooked. I will explore these aspects, and then show the profound implications they have for the formation of the self (or not!), and therefore for the whole question of how liberation comes to us.

1) Desire Needs Lack

Economically, value – the measure of how much things are desired – is related to scarcity. By the law of supply and demand, items that are scarce in supply will increase in value. That is why gold is valuable, oil increasingly valuable, water is cheap (though may not always remain so – it is already, in America, being bought from farmers by water hungry cities) and air is entirely without value, being (so far) abundant and free. The first Genesis story expresses this clearly: in a world of abundance Adam and Eve have to take the one thing that was 'scarce', forbidden and not given. Which of us would not have done the same?

An anecdote related by the Slovenian Marxist writer Slavoj Žižek (2009, p.75) tells of a witch who visits a peasant and offers him two alternatives: either she will give him one cow and his neighbor two, or she will take one cow from him and two from his neighbor. Without hesitation the peasant chooses the latter. What he wants is what our egos always crave – not simply to have more things in absolute terms, but to have more of them relative to others, to have what others lack. That is why those in relative poverty in affluent societies seem often more alienated and unhappy than those who are poorer in absolute terms in societies where everyone suffers the same lack.

Of course not all value originates in this way. There is the kind of value we place on something because it serves our ends. A comfortable house serves our need to have a place we can live and relax in. But a large, impressive and costly house can often be less pleasant to live in than a smaller, cozier one. Gardens and rooms become hard work to maintain. It is here that the desire to have more and better and bigger than others has overtaken consideration of what is useful to achieve our ends. The means have become an end in themselves – our desire has become, in Aquinas' terms, disordered and sinful. But we are often unclear about which ends matter to us. That may be partly what makes us so obsessively accurate about measuring how much of the 'means' we have.

For our society is certainly obsessed with measuring things. Without a quantity, an assignable degree of abundance or scarcity, things in our world cannot be valued. So in hospitals, for instance, pastoral and spiritual care has to have definable targets and measurable degrees of attainment, otherwise in the eyes of the managers, it simply does not exist! The same is true of education; losing sight of the traditional goal of a broad and balanced education of the whole person, we evaluate schools on exam grades, and university departments on the quantity (not always quality) of material published.

This is why God, who is freely available to everyone who desires him, is of no value at all in our society – unless the priests can make God scarce and in short supply, so they can begin to make business out of God, as they have always needed to do. Jesus' Good News (cited at the head of the chapter) was that the Kingdom of God is (in the English translation) 'at hand', readily available to everyone who wants it. People therefore needed to 'repent', that is, change their whole mind and aim, which was based on the idea that God was in short supply, being available only at Jerusalem and through careful and complex observances. That was bad news for the priests and their business.

Now, though the collapse of global communism has made Marxism less fashionable than it was, the heart of Marx's theory remains very relevant to the question of desire and delusion. The difference between real value or usefulness to serve our ends, and market value, is what Marx termed 'surplus value'. The worker makes a real difference to the usefulness of what he works on, when he turns, say, bits of wood into a chair, or bits of silicon and so forth into a computer. But the worker can only sell the labor he uses at the market value. And competing with other workers, he ends up offering the lowest price he can afford to live on. This will generally be much less than the real value of what he has done to the material he has worked on. The difference – 'surplus value' – is what the capitalist appropriates as profit.

It is this profit that enables the capitalist to invest in new materials, creating new markets for labor. So profit is what circulates as the main energy driving the market economy, enabling it often to expand and progress so dramatically. But this means that capitalism is driven by delusion, by precisely the mismatch between real or natural value and a socially constructed illusion called market value. The young Marx actually saw the capitalist world as committed to a 'fetishism of commodities' in the same way that religion is committed to what he regarded as idols and fantasies.

To find an analogy, we must find recourse to the mist enveloped realms of the religious world. In that world the productions of the human brain appear as independent beings endowed with life, and entering into relations both with one another and with the human race. So it is in the world of commodities and the products of men's hands. (1954, Vol. 1,1,1,4, p.76)

If this is true, the capitalist market raises issues about reality as well as justice, and any spirituality that wants to base itself on reality has to grapple with the foundations of capitalism.

What circulates in the market is mainly money, which is an imaginary thing in which the use value is reduced to, and consists solely in, its exchange value, that is, in the competitive desire it represents. Apart from what it can be exchanged for, the use value of a five pound note is extraordinary small: I might use it as (very inferior) toilet or tissue paper, but that is all. But money enables a new kind of interchange, a curious interweaving of our desires and delusions, replacing the natural interchange between human beings with a kind of 'interlacking'. For money is a kind of lack I can hold in my hands, waiting to be exchanged for the desired object that will fill it.

Possessive desire springs, as the Buddhists say, from illusion. But this is not first and foremost the illusion of the individual soul. Rather it emerges from the way desire self-propagates in society through the competition that is quantified in the corporate illusion that is money. Where lack is lacking it gets created 'out of nothing', in order to serve our need to exist over against others. In that sense – as Buddhists would be the first to recognize – our sense of individual existence depends not on a feeling of self-fulfillment but, on the contrary, on our lack, on what is not, rather than on anything that really is.

2) Desires are Imitative

As well as wanting what others do not have, we want what they want. According to one bold but challenging and in many ways convincing theory, all desire, far from springing direct from ourselves, arises from the imitation of others. This is the theory of mimetic desire, devised by the French cultural theorist Réné Girard. The English Roman Catholic theologian, James Alison, has promoted this theory as a helpful way to interpret the Western Christian notion of original sin.

As described by Alison (1998, p.27ff), the theory states

1. **Desire** – or at least the characteristically human forms of desire – originates in imitation, *mimesis*. The baby begins life with an instinctive tendency to imitate others – especially, at first, its mother. This is how we learn language and all sorts of skills, but we imitate not only what the other is and does but what they have and what they desire to have. Learning a language involves, after all, not just imitating the sound but grasping what the person intends or wants in uttering that sound.

2. **Mimetic Rivalry.** But because we desire what others desire, we are immediately thrown into competition with others for the same thing. Children want not just shoes but precisely the same brand of trainers as their friends have. So they get jealous, they may fight for the same things, or argue with their parents to give them precisely the desired object they want. (Or course the economic structures noted above exacerbate this tendency; things get valued because others value them and compete for them, making them expensive.) So antagonism comes into the world.

3. Society could not survive if this antagonism were not resolved. The solution that all surviving cultures have arrived at – according to Girard – is to find a **victim or scapegoat,** an individual or a minority group to blame for society's unrest. By means of the sacrifice of the scapegoat, aggression against one another is diverted into aggression against a common enemy. This replaces division with solidarity. The Gospels show this happening: Jewish Herod and Roman Pilate become friends (Luke 23.12) as the Jewish priesthood and Roman rulers find a common enemy in Jesus. The scapegoat becomes a highly ambiguous figure, despised because he is the object of everyone's hatred, but often also godlike because of the

peace and reconciliation his death brings. (This of course is also true in the case of Jesus.)

4. Because of the guilt this primordial murder incurs, however, these violent origins of society have to be forgotten or denied, and the society's myths or ideologies tell of the prevalence of peace. If violence is necessary, it is always claimed to be in order to safeguard peace and preserve the nation. (The words ascribed to High Priest Caiaphas expresses the kind of logic usually cited: "it is better to have one person die for the people than to have the whole nation destroyed." (John 11.50))

Girard believes his theory explains the prevalence of the notion of sacrifice in all societies, from the more 'primitive' in which humans or animals are actually killed, to modern societies which reject such rituals but nevertheless tend to need to scapegoat minorities and find common enemies to fight. There is indeed something very puzzling about the moral universe of human beings, which Girard's theory helps us understand. On a 'micro' scale – families, neighbors and so forth – people seem on the whole kind and courteous to each other. But on the 'macro' political and economic scale, there is vast injustice within and between nations, and regular cycles of war and genocide. Though we like to think our Western, 'civilized' society has left behind the barbarism of our ancestors and of 'third world' atrocities, or at least the mass violence and terror of 20th Century Europe, events in Afghanistan and Iraq have shown that we have not lost our compulsion to wage war. We wonder how cultured people with good family values and often strong Christian faith in, say, Nazi Germany could in some cases knowingly approve, and in others actively organize, the concentration camps. Were they, underneath the cultured veneer, beasts?

No, the fact is that culture and family values and piety on the micro scale not only coexist with violence on the macro; Girard has shown, frighteningly, a sense in which they rest on it. The peace of our communities actually rests, according to mimetic theory, on violence against the other, and where no 'other' exist, one has to be invented 'over there' in the form of a common enemy to preserve the peace 'right here'. (This is perhaps why family values and piety were not absolute to either the Buddha or Jesus; the former left his own family in the search for enlightenment, while the latter stated that his true family was formed of all who did God's will (Mark 3.35).)

Now in terms of the three Biblical stories, it would seem that the Garden of Eden tells of mimetic desire – Eve imitates the intent of the serpent, and Adam literally imitates Eve, finding himself wanting the fruit because she does, and perhaps because God seems to be guarding it with a special possessiveness. The story of Cain and Abel tells us of rivalry and the violence it can beget, and the Tower of Babel tells, perhaps, of the co-operation that can arise between peoples united in a supposed peace, and also a common imitation of the gods; what is 'forgotten' is that the ziggurats of Babylon – of which the tower of Babel seems to be one – were like the Aztec equivalent, places of sacrifice.

Now according to Alison, the process just outlined takes place at the origin of the self. It is not, he urges, as if we first have a sure sense of our existence, and then notice that we are desiring things and falling into rivalry. A sense of self arises from the experience of mimetic interaction with others, leading us to exclude others from our sense of identity. Prior to the process, the baby is what the writer Arthur Koestler called a *holon*, a "purely psychological being, the structure of which is permanently becoming in the midst of continuous exchanges with other structures" (Alison, 1998, p.31). For "the 'me' of each one of us [is] an unstable structure, one that is changeable, malleable, and other-dependent... The rival is always anterior to me'" (p.30). It is the third person – the rival, whose desire for the other I make my own, and then become the rival of that other – that turns pure *eros* into Greek *thumos*, or Buddhist *tanha*: desire fraught with envy, grasping, possessiveness, obsession, pain.

But we deny this. Our sense of self also includes the forgetting of this very dependence, for our rivalry thrusts us into an assertion of independence and self-reliance, as we claim the desires that run through us as our own self-originated, self-chosen desires. In that sense the self is founded upon the 'murder' – the elimination from memory, the silencing of the voices – of all the others who constitute me. The self is just what is left when all that is 'other' is excluded and negated. "This is our condition. This is what we start with, living on the brink between a wisdom which enables us to recognize where we have come from, and a self-deception, an exacerbated unknowing, which binds us further into violence towards ourselves and others, a violence in which we are all ineluctably constituted" (p.33).

Now Buddhist liturgy speaks of "bad karma accumulated from beginningless time". Interpreted literally this would require time and causality to be without beginning. Though Buddhists have traditionally understood them to be so, modern cosmology tends to suggest otherwise (see Chapter 7), so it might be better to understand this language metaphorically. I wonder if it does not express the same strange truth that Christians name as 'original sin', namely this inability to do the right thing, or even to want to do it. As St. Paul wrote, "I do not do the good I want, but the evil I do not want is what I do" (Rom. 7.19). This strange inability seems to arise from no fault of our own, and yet it makes us feel blameworthy because there is no clear reason why we might not do the right thing. There is a way in which we are pitted against others and even against our own fulfillment (since this lies in our interrelationship with others) for reasons that originated before we came into being. Bad karma causes – and so predates – the beginning of our separate consciousness and hence the time in which we carry out our own good and bad actions. For us, bad karma has always been around.

The Buddhist confronts the immensity of his own evil as an eternity of bad karma inherited from his past, while the Christian confronts it as his offence against an eternal God before whose judgment throne he is to stand in the future. But both are grappling with what makes evil both something infinitely bigger than us, something in which we are imprisoned against our will, yet also something that is our own personal responsibility, for which we are called to account.

It is crucial to this understanding of desire that it is not a natural or inevitable part of us. There is nothing in principle to stop us being free from it and realizing what Buddhists would call our essential Buddha-nature, and Christians the Christ or image of God within us. We crave, not because it is natural to crave, but because we are born into a world of rivals. Sin in Orthodox and Catholic (but not Protestant) Christian thought is our condition, not our nature. Our true nature is the interdependent *holon*. We do not *have to* be exclusive selves; we just always are, for reasons that are historical rather than natural, having to do with the way humans have formed society together from time immemorial. The fact that we do not have to live in this way, though we all in fact *do*, is crucial, for it means that it is possible to live without this illusion. An ego-free way of life is possible for the interbeings that we are.

3) Desires are Not Natural

This crucial point probably seems counter-intuitive. Surely we have wants that derive from our natural instincts? This, I think, is obvious. Mimetic desire has very enthusiastic advocates that would see it as the source of all our wants. But we clearly do have drives that derive from our animal makeup. These are perhaps best distinguished from desire as 'drives'. It is mimesis, however, that turns satiable drives based on needs into insatiable wants. The mimetic turns the genetic into the memetic (the memes or ideas that copy themselves from one mind to another – see Chapter 7).

Thus animals show aggression where needed for survival, but humans turn aggression into limitless war and genocide. Animals possess sexual drives in order to propagate, but humans lust after each other outside the times when a female is fertile. Animals kill to eat, but even the much maligned fox only kills a hutch-full of chickens so that (ifpossible) it can take them away and store them to provide for leaner times. Only humans eradicate entire species to satisfy exotic tastes, or just for the 'fun' of it.

Drives are rooted in our bodily reactions – hunger, for example is felt in the belly, and sexual arousal in the erogenous zones – and it would be absurd to suggest they arose through some form of imitation. Neither Buddhism nor Christianity in their authentic forms encourage the kind of asceticism that seeks to overcome natural bodily needs. However, what we learn by imitation are the social forms in which these drives are felt to be appropriately satisfied. The desire for caviar or fine wine is not a natural drive; it is socially learned. Romance, courtship, flirtation, seduction, pornography, masochism, sadism and child abuse do not arise from natural drives, but from our social formation or malformation. They are leaned by, as well as encouraging, some kind of imitation. It is here that the question of moral value arises, and the transformation of the person becomes an issue.

We like to think our 'base drives' come from our animal nature. But our excesses are a social distortion, entirely unnatural, and lacking natural boundaries. As noted, so as not to destroy itself in rampant rivalry, society has to impose artificial boundaries and controls through punishments and scape-goating, and the internalized scapegoating called shame and guilt. A split is created between our 'lofty' spiritual nature, of which we are proud, and our animal and bodily drives and lusts, which we repress in our shame.

So Morris Berman (1990) argues that in hunter-gatherer cultures, animals are sacred members of a world that is at once nature and society. Animals are primary objects of human mimesis. Then in agricultural societies animals are divided between the wild and the tamed, the hostile and the useful. Finally in modern society for the first time animals are largely absent from daily life in our towns and cities. They become focuses of our dreams – a pure and adored 'nature' menaced by the corruption of society – and our nightmares – terrible images of our own ferocity and rapacity, in a nightmare that culminates in "nature red in tooth and claw" and the "selfish gene" (see Chapter 7). In the process our 'animal nature' has become the 'carnal' and 'bestial', the despised scapegoat for our cravings, when the irony is that it is our human tendency to mirror and rival one another that has amplified natural drives into competitive and destructive cravings.

We thereby become what novelist John Fowles called 'nemos' – no-bodies. Having disowned our bodily feelings we feel hollow inside and need all the more to find identity through imitating what others desire. As will become clear when we explore the Enneagram, "all our acts are partly devised to fill or mark the emptiness we feel at the core" (1968, p.51). Berman argues that this split between our spiritual image and our bodily drive accounts for much in the history of the West, while the Buddhist writer David Loy (2002) accounts for this history in terms of a struggle with different manifestations of 'lack'.

4) Gender Difference?

I have found that while men often quickly recognize mimetic theory as applying to them, with women it can be a little different. Certainly, the genetic basis that mimesis amplifies and distorts is known to be different in males and females, and not just in the case of the human species. It is frequently noted that in a huge number of mammals and birds – mainly those animals where the offspring need protection and learning in order to survive – the male most often acts competitively, fighting off other males in order to sire the maximum number of offspring from different females. Females, on the other hand, are more typically social and nurturing. And this is easily explained in terms of genetics: the male is programmed to propagate as many of his genes as he can, while the female can only propagate one clutch of offspring at a time, so naturally desires to look after and protect them so that their chances of survival are maximized.

This means that in human society it is easier for women to be 'good' in terms of a peaceable and caring nature and sexual commitment to one partner. Of course in patriarchal societies two things happen: a morality is devised in order to bring the competitive aggression and sexual promiscuity of the male under control, so that it does not destroy society. And paradoxically, just as we saw how the animal becomes the scapegoat for the human, so the woman becomes the scapegoat for the man. She is blamed for seducing the males and encouraging rivalry.

Many feminists would resist the emphasis on genetic origins, for it can be used to make male superiority look natural. (Though in terms of Christian and Buddhist virtues, it actually suggests the male is by nature inferior!) All the same, many feminists (e.g. Catherine Keller in Cobb and Ives, 1990, p.102-115) have argued that the moral universe that (in Buddhism and Christianity alike) condemns desire, egotism and pride is the construction of men. Women, it is convincingly argued, frequently experience themselves not as desiring but as the objects and victims of desire. Their problem is not that they desire too much but that they conform too much to the desires and expectations of others. To be liberated, therefore, women may need not to sacrifice their desires but to learn to own and assert them. They may need to become more self-possessed and less selflessly orientated to others' needs. I know this rings true for many women. So Keller asks "will the Christian-Buddhist dialogue offer the worst of both worlds to women? How can the two patriarchies, with their common problem of the inflationary male ego and their common solution of selflessness, fail to redouble the oppressive irrelevance of the 'world religions' for the liberation of women?" (p.106)

However, even if this means the personal journey of women may need to be different from men, in the social and political arena the problem remains the same: ego-centeredness and desire. Overcoming the ego and its desires involves overcoming those of others and the hold they have on us, as well as overcoming our own egos and their desires. And a subtler point: the hold other egos have on us is as strong as our own egos' need of their desire and esteem. A person is entrapped in the desires of others only insofar as she or he desires their desire. Egoism and pride are not sins we possess in isolation, but factors that chain us to one another in the desire to have one's ego recognized.

The importance of the feminist critique is that it warns us of a kind of damage that can be done by patriarchal, individualist conceptions of sin, and reveals the need for a wider struggle against a world based on the ego and its dreams. As this book will repeatedly emphasize, such a struggle needs to be social and political as well as personal. Liberation concerns the social and material delusions of the world 'out there' – a world that is crafted by desire and crafts our desires in turn – as much as the desire felt 'in here', in us.

The Chariot and the Buddhist Denial of the Self.

The teaching of *anatta* or no-self, is one of the most distinctive and – to many – disturbing features of Buddhism, distinguishing it not only from nearly all other religions, but from all but the most reductionistic humanist views. Often – especially in the Theravada tradition – the teaching is presented very negatively; the self is an illusion, like a candle flame. The flame looks real, but it has no enduring substance, only an ever-changing flow of gaseous substances. In the same way we seem to remain the same, but after seven years, none of the atoms that make up our bodies now will still be there. And in the end the flame will 'blow out' - extinction is the literal translation of 'Nirvana'. Christians often contrast with this their more positive belief in an eternal soul that will find its ultimate realization in a union with God.

In Buddhism the soul is analyzed into five 'bundles' or *skhanda*: form, perception, consciousness, knowledge and action. None of these consists of a permanent entity we could call the self or soul, nor is there some other permanent entity we can discern apart from these elements. The famous dialogue between Nagasena and King Milinda uses the chariot as an analogy (Conze, 1969, p.148). The king arrives to see the sage on a chariot. but when asked to describe what this chariot is he admits it is not the pole, the axle, the wheels, the framework, the flag staff, the reins or the goad stick, or any other part. Nor is it something else outside all these things. So the king is forced to admit that he came on no chariot at all. And it is the same with us: the elements that make us up change all the time and we know of nothing outside these elements that stays the same.

Now it could be protested with some justification that the analogy is misleading. The human being is, like other living beings, capable of assembling itself – or rather, growing – and moving itself about intelligently, in a way in which no chariot is. Unlike the chariot, it can reproduce little copies of itself that in turn grow up to full-sized versions. It clearly has a more substantial kind of unity than a chariot. We do not need to resort to an eternal soul here, but clearly the whole human being is greater than the mere sum of its parts, in a way that justifies the term just introduced, *holon*.

In *Holy Ground* (1990) I used the term *diousia* to describe a kind of being that arises through relationship and exchange. The term suggests a *dialogue* but with *ousia* – our whole being – rather than merely *logos*, words. Thich Nhat Hanh, expresses the same idea with his term 'interbeing', which is really a compression of the Buddhist idea of 'dependent co-arising' – the idea that nothing has substantial reality in and for itself, but gains whatever being it has from its relationship with other things. For example, a heart is no heart at all without the other organs of the body. The other organs depend on it to pump blood to them, but it depends on them to control and nourish it. The body – the interdependent whole or *holon* – cannot be reduced to parts, because if we take it apart the parts are not even parts! What was the brain is only a slimy mass; what was the heart a piece of meat. But when the parts of the body do interrelate within the whole, this is not because some extra spiritual organ, the self or soul, is added, but because of the *diousia* or interbeing of the whole.

Not only are we – our bodies – themselves interbeings of various elements. We are also interbeings in relation to others in society. There is no father without a son, no husband without a wife, no priest without worshippers, and so on; social reality is itself all interbeing with no isolated self-sufficient beings within it. I shall use the term 'interbeing' from now on to express all these ideas, mainly because it is readily intelligible, and also because it has a venerable pedigree in the work of Thich Nhat Hanh.

Nagasena's chariot analogy, then, rightly denies the need for any special self or soul to form our unity, but fails to grasp the interbeing of our parts. A chariot wheel is still a wheel; its 'wheelness' does not depend on its belonging to a chariot. That is why a chariot is not an interbeing, but a machine. But in practice Buddhism affirms this. The doctrine of *anatta* does not mean that we are soulless machines or zombies. What Buddhism rejects is the idea of a soul as an eternal entity separate from and dualistically opposed to the material world.

Although a great deal of Christian tradition affirms precisely that kind of dualism, that understanding is widely believed these days to owe more to the Platonic tradition of Greek thought than to Judaism or early Christianity. For the latter, the whole human being is both physical and spiritual, and inherently related to God and other beings. There is no immutable soul, but without the immanent breath or spirit of God we would perish, and will do so but for God's power to raise the whole human person from the dead. The earliest theologians like Irenaeus of Lyons (c.130-200) preserved this understanding, and only later did Christianity commit itself to the eternal soul imprisoned in a body, which many Christians now take for granted. De Silva (1979) argues this ancient Christian understanding of whole-persons-in-relationship – affirmed in much recent theology – is quite compatible with the Buddhist teaching of *anatta*, which denies the self-sufficient, eternal soul but affirms our 'interbeing' with all other beings.

The Butterfly Dream and 'Interbeing'

Can we imagine what it might be like to live as an interbeing woven out of interrelationships rather than an independent self? The Zen Buddhist Kiyoshi Tsuchiya (in Schmidt-Leukel, 2005, p.53ff) provides a powerful image of the contrast between the 'cosmological ego' of Taoist and other Chinese thought – including Zen Buddhism, which was heavily influenced by Taoism – and the 'relational ego' of Judeo-Christian and much Western understanding. The cosmological ego is a process of life that is at one with the universe, an interbeing. Tsuchiya offers as an image for this self the butterfly of the Taoist sage Chuang-tzu.

> Once Chuang-tzu dreamt he was a butterfly. A butterfly flitting and fluttering around, happy with himself and doing as he pleased. He didn't know he was Chuang-tzu. Suddenly he woke up and there he was, solid and unmistakable Chuang-tzu. But he did not know if he was Chuang-tzu who had dreamt he was a butterfly, or a butterfly who had dreamt he was Chuang-tzu. (Chuang-tzu, 1964, p.45)

119

The image depicts a beautiful harmony between oneself and the universe, such that it becomes impossible to know who is subject and who is object – who is dreaming who.

Now modern science teaches us that real butterflies are utterly unlike the beautiful brightly colored fluttering thing we see. Rather they consist of bundles of millions of unimaginable particle-waves bounding through what is largely emptiness. And one modern understanding is that we are dreaming – producing images in the mind – all the time, but in our waking life these dreams are constrained by the input and output of the nerve-impulses that control our bodies. In sleep both the sensory input and the motor output are closed off, and the mind goes on producing its images freely. So when we 'see' a butterfly, we are in fact dreaming a butterfly dream occasioned by certain sensations.

And this dream image of the butterfly – which is the butterfly I 'see' – derives in turn partly from my desire and the way it structures the world, in part from our language and culture about butterflies. Both desire and culture – a culture itself formed, we have seen, by desire – conspire to present an objective world over against a subjective soul. Desire needs to have real objects to possess and a free ego to desire and choose. But Buddhism teaches us to relax our competitive desires, and allow self and object to interpenetrate as the parts of the cosmic process both really are, beyond all rivalry. Thich Nhat Hanh expresses beautifully how this can happen:

We are like an ocean wave that believes it is fragile and ugly and that the other waves are more beautiful, more powerful. The wave has an inferiority complex. But when this wave gets in touch with its true nature, water, it sees that water goes beyond all concepts of beautiful, ugly, high, low, here, and there. Whether it's a large wave or a small wave, half a wave or a third of a wave, it's still made out of water. Water is beyond all these qualifications – it is without birth and without death. (2007, p.102)

Kafka's Beetle and the Relational Self

Tsuchiya opposes to the butterfly the 'Western' notion of the relational self, the self that is constituted by its relationships to and responsibility toward God and other people. He criticizes the definition of the self by the Danish philosopher Søren Kierkegaard (1980, p.13) as "a relation that relates itself to its own self", arguing that this leads to a self steeped in anxiety because it has no grounding except in relationships with others and ultimately, to itself. Moreover, it has no relationship to the cosmos, being alienated from the natural world in a way that has contributed to our contemporary ecological crisis. (Kierkegaard would have been the first to agree that the self is permeated by anxiety and dread, but believed this could be overcome when the self accepted the paradox of Christ as God incarnate, and became "grounded transparently in God" through Christ.)

Tsuchiya believes that the relational self ends up alienated from its natural roots and imprisoned in its desire to please and be acceptable – like the wave with its 'inferiority complex'. He sees the relational self parodied in Franz Kafka's terrifying tale (1961) of a man who woke up to find he was a beetle, encased in a shell like a prison and unable to move. Pathetically the beetle still seeks acceptance from his family, even as it slowly rejects him. The beetle is Kafka's image for the most nightmarish form of Western monotheism, for which God and our neighbor are primarily guilt inducing and persecuting, forcing us to protect ourselves with heavy soul-armor.

There is a well-known Zen *koan* which asks "What is the sound of one hand clapping?" The relational self seems to me rather like that one hand. On its own it can only hit empty air. It has to find a way of making a noise. There are many ways in which we try to make a noise: through possessions, through being loved and admired by another or the wider public, through wielding power and control over others, or through surrendering our autonomy to a powerful leader... All of these seem to give the relational self an other against which it can sound itself. The cosmological self – on this analogy – would be like a hand that likes just to be open and feel the wind.

The contrast between the beautiful butterfly and the terrifying beetle is not altogether fair. The Christian God, though often conceived of as wrathful, is in Christ primarily loving, forgiving and reconciling. Indeed, the butterfly is an old Christian symbol for the resurrection. The butterfly bursts from its chrysalis-armor as Christ bursts from the tomb. The legalistic system that demanded repression and sacrifice gives way to a new order in which the soul loses its old self-protective isolation. It seems to me that the resurrection stories in the Gospels have a dreamlike quality; it is not clear if the risen Jesus is the disciples' wonderful dream, or if he has brought them into his dream of what we might be once liberated from the ego.

Nine Roots of Wrong: Nine Petals of the Lotus

The Enneagram is a diagram of obscure origins, not belonging to any specific religious faith (though claims have been made for the Sufis and the Christians). It is now quite well known as a model for the psyche, and I will not explore it in detail here; my interest at this point is twofold. One is the way it seems to be able to synthesize Buddhist and Christian understandings of sin and desire. The other is that it is based on the kind of vision we have been exploring in this chapter.

The basic notion behind the model is the idea that even our best ideals are rooted in a compulsive need to bolster our egos. But the Enneagram also suggests that if we can go against the grain of this compulsion, a new and liberating desire can grow from it. In our terms, plerotic desire can be transformed into kenotic desire. The very channels our habitual sins have carved out can become the channels of the divine. In ways we shall explore in the next chapter, the lotus of liberation grows out of the mud in our murkiest depths.

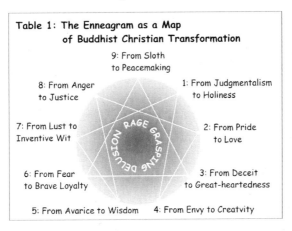

Table 1: The Enneagram as a Map
of Buddhist Christian Transformation

9: From Sloth
to Peacemaking

8: From Anger
to Justice

1: From Judgmentalism
to Holiness

7: From Lust to
Inventive Wit

2: From Pride
to Love

6: From Fear
to Brave Loyalty

3: From Deceit
to Great-heartedness

5: From Avarice to Wisdom   4: From Envy to Creatvity

As in **Figure 1**, the nine 'points' of the Enneagram are ranged around three 'centers': heart or feeling, guts or will, and head or mind. Each of us lives primarily from one or other of these primary centers and identifies our 'self' with it. It is possible to relate this to the genesis of the false self according to Alison. Heart-centered people are those who yearn to establish identity through the rapport of relationship and mutual imitation; gut-centered are those who do so through rivalry and the imagined (or real) elimination of others; and head-centered are those who do so through a denial of both relationship and rivalry, striving to become independent and self-sufficient, sacrificing the need for others. (However, at the middle point of each center – those numbered 3, 6 and 9 – the core yearning proves too great to acknowledge at all, and is suppressed.)

The heart-centered people are the 2s, 3s and 4s, whose lives are based on the seeking of relationship and, if unredeemed, can manifest various forms of the Buddhist 'poison' of possessive grasping.

2: Seeking to be on the giving side of the early mother-child relationship: living through generosity. The vice here is a need to be needed, a kind of pride that can be quite swamping of the other's independence. But when this obsessive need is overcome, kenotic love can easily pour out in selfless service of others.

3: Suppressing personal relationship in the interests of success in society, 3s develop the vice of deceit, hiding their true nature under the public persona of the successful businessperson or politician. If 3s can become more open and honest, their sense of strategy can achieve much of benefit to humanity. They can become magnanimous – 'great hearted'.

4: Seeking to be on the receiving 'child' end of the early rapport, needing to be special and beloved in the eyes of others. The vice of envy easily arises. But redeemed, 4s can allow a generous creativity to flow through their own 'performances' and creative work.

Among the gut-centered people are the 8s, 9s and 1s, whose lives are based on self-assertion and exhibit some form of the poison of hatred or rage.

8: Seeking self-identity through rivalry and power over others, with the characteristic vice of hatred. Redeemed, their angry sense of justice can lead 8s to overthrow power on behalf of the victims of society.

9: Seeking identity through suppressing the aggression to which they are tempted and always looking to see 'which way the wind is blowing'. The characteristic vice of 9s is sloth or laziness, an easygoing attitude that always chooses the path of least resistance, often deriving from a denial of anger. Redeemed 9s can be gentle peacemakers, using their flexibility and diplomacy to bring together rival factions.

1: Seeking self-identity through perfection and fulfilling legalistic demands. The characteristic vice is a judgmentalism which frequently leads to anger with 'rivals' on the path of perfection or those who do not do things the 'right' way. Redeemed 1s can be called to genuine holiness of life.

Finally the head-centered people are the 5s, 6s and 7s, whose lives are based on withdrawal from the real world – the poison of delusion.

5: Seeking identity through the cognitive and acquisitive side of the mind, building a sense of self through what one has and what one knows, rather than relationship. The characteristic vice is avarice or stinginess. Redeemed 5s can become philosophers, lovers of wisdom, turning from their isolation to share their insights.

6: Seeking identity through suppressing the independence of thought of which they are innately capable, avoiding anything menacing, and leading a 'safe' and conformist life. The characteristic vice is one not on the Buddhist or Christian lists, but all important: fear, not the rational fear of real dangers but a generalized fear of the unknown and 'what might go wrong'. Redeemed 6s can be profoundly loyal, transforming fear into courageous service of good causes.

7: Seeking identity through the decision-making side of the mind, in endless fantasies and projects that rarely come to fulfillment. The characteristic vices are greed and lust, escaping from the burden of the ego through indulging the body. Redeemed 7s can be witty and sparkling, enriching people's lives with their irrepressible inventiveness.

Those who have used the Enneagram will appreciate the subtlety with which it dismantles our pretences and leads us in new and

125

creative pathways. In connection with the feminist criticism noted above, it has the advantage of being, I think, fairly balanced between typically 'male' and 'female' sins, if we wish to use those categories; the 'maternal' 2 is seen as being as potentially dangerous as the stridently 'masculine' 8. And it seems to me that it is a tool well adapted to a Buddhist Christian vision, providing a way of relating their accounts of sin to the mimetic theory of how the self arises. It takes forward the Buddhist notion (but familiar to Christian mystics) that the self is formed of delusive desire, but also suggests a Christian notion (but suggested in some strands of Buddhism) that desire can be released from its bondage to the needs of the ego to become a living focus of interbeing within the life of the world.

Whether this might be, and how, is the subject of the next chapter.

Death's Honey

This chapter has drawn together several different accounts in order to deepen our understanding of desire in the negative sense of possessive grasping. We have seen that this kind of desire is built into the economic structure of society, based as it is on scarcity, and into the way we gain a sense of self by imitating the desires of others. Ultimately following our desires does not make us free because we do not choose our desires. They choose us and make us the separate, rival selves we find ourselves to be, in the process creating a split between our infinite 'spiritual' cravings and our natural desires, between our souls and our bodies, between male and female, and between the human and the animal, in which the latter becomes the scapegoat for our inevitable failure in the arena of the former. But just as the last chapter showed how desire needs to be distinguished from *eros*, a kind of love that can empty us of self, so this chapter has made it clear that desire needs to be distinguished from our natural drives. In the next chapter we shall see that what arises spontaneously and instinctively (*jinen* in Japanese) can become a crucial basis of moral life.

I will end this chapter with a poem of mine that connects with many things this chapter has discussed through a telling of the story of the raising of Lazarus (John 11.1-44). The poem describes 'a lost shadow in the caverns', a response to our original calling that lies buried behind the 'posturing we have become'. This lost shadow is our original 'interbeing', a 'you and I' mother-and child mutuality of which I was part. This interbeing was sacrificed to form the isolated, monad-like 'me'. But Christ calls from the shadows to which I had consigned it a 'honey' that I have distilled like a bee, a richness that is an 'eternal life' that can only become freed through the death of the self. The next chapter will have more to say about this liberation.

Waking monads, we climb up
        out of dark that subsists, subtle
as the world's origin's keening echo: for the call
to be reverberates on behind the posturing
we have become, a lost
        shadow in the caverns: the you
and I they killed to make
us me.
        Then he, the brother
-keeper, Almighty and bright
        -sinewed, unsheathed Light's
ultimate arrow towards us, calls
        one last grieving time
our leprous name, and the winding sheets
        fall, unselving from our secret cells
what the spirit's bee has there distilled:
death's honey: eternal life.

Summary

1. Both Christian and Buddhist accounts have been challenged for ignoring the fact that many aspects of suffering and delusion require a political solution.

2. Nevertheless political action can be motivated by unresolved anger. Meditation can enable us to create a space for diverse voices within us that aids our ability to engage with outside forces and voices.

3. Desire relies on economic scarcity and the illusory realm of the 'commodity'. So liberation cannot avoid political and economic struggle.

4. Desire is social in that it originates in 'mimetic rivalry'. Ultimately we do not have desires, they have us.

5. Desire needs to be distinguished from natural drives that originate in our animal nature.

6. The male emphasis of both Buddhism and Christianity have ignored important differences between male and female. Desire is the 'problem' for both genders, but in different ways.

7. Buddhism does not deny the organic unity a person is, but the notion of the self as separate and eternal.

8. Though desire leads us to imagine ourselves as separate, rival beings, the separate self will always be unhappy and engage in destructive ways of relating to others because it both needs others and needs its 'independence'.

9. The Enneagram embraces Christian and Buddhist, and 'male' and 'female' ways of seeing the false moves we all make to secure our self-identity, and also how these moves can be challenged and redeemed.

Chapter 5

Faith for Fools: Liberation and Atonement

Doing things for mundane reasons is not part of your true being. You
have to cast aside vain endeavors and avoid shallow experiences.
Otherwise you are deceiving yourself. It's like being aboard a ship on
the ocean. The sea water rolls and swells with the wind, creating
waves that force the ship this way and that way. There is no peace on
board, everyone is worrying they will sink. We live our lives veering
this way and that: we do things for the sake of progress and material
gain, neglecting what is truly important and losing sight of the Way.
That is why you must distance yourself from the material world and
practice the law of no action.
(Lost Sutras, p.82)

Buddhism and Christianity are often contrasted as a religion of
reason on the one hand and blind faith on the other, or hard
work on the one hand and reliance on God's grace on the other.

Negative stereotypes of both religions follow from this
contrast. The stereotypical Buddhist is a lone meditator,
following a path that is in principle equally available to all, but
which is so spiritually demanding that only a spiritual elite – the
Sangha – attain it. One reason Paul Williams (cited in Chapter 3)
converted from Buddhism back to his earlier Christianity was
because he saw the latter as a religion for sinners, a religion that
mediates God's grace to ordinary, muddled people like him
(2002, p.99ff).

But the stereotypical Christian is no better. A weak-minded
sinner, he is content to have grace and truth mediated to him by
an institutional Church that has led him, and gullible souls like
him, to believe it has a monopoly of the grace needed for

salvation. A happy relationship exists. The Church lets him off the need to be good and to think for himself, while he delegates to the Church all the power it wants. Both are agreed that we have neither the wit nor the will to work out our own salvation. To be kind, the Church has to be powerful, and if need be compel people to hold the true faith which they need in order to be saved. Many have moved in faith in the opposite direction from Williams, because they want a religion that will treat them as adults.

These stereotypes are strong and damaging to both faiths. This chapter will therefore examine the issue that lies behind them: whether we are saved by our own effort or by an under-served gift received by faith. It will emerge that both faiths are more complex on this issue than the stereotypes suggest, and that the Christian understanding that we are saved not by ourselves but by the work of Christ can benefit from some Buddhist insights.

Self-power and Other-power in Buddhism

The balance between 'self-power' and 'other power' – whether we achieve enlightenment or salvation solely by own effort, solely through trust in the power of other(s), or through a balance of the two – is one of the chief issues on which Christians and Buddhists are divided not only from each other, but among themselves. So we will look first at the Theravada, then the Mahayana, and then the special case of Shin Buddhism, before turning to Christian approaches to the issue.

Theravada – the Long Haul

In the Theravada tradition enlightenment is presented as a long slow haul lasting millions of years of reincarnations. In this process only one's own effort can lead to reward. So the repeated refrain of the Rhinoceros Sutra advises solitude 'like a rhinoceros' in order to concentrate one's effort.

He who is kind toward much-beloved friends loses his own good from his mind becoming partial; observing such danger in friendship, let one walk alone like a rhinoceros. (in Stryk, 1968, p.220)

And elsewhere we are taught: "live as islands unto yourselves, being your own refuge with no one else as your refuge" (from the *Digha Nikaya*, in Walshe, 1995, p.245).

The austere ideal is the Arhat or Noble One who has become enlightened, being free of all attachments to the world of Samsara, and having lost the desire for sex, food or human company. The Theravada tradition also teaches the possibility of the Pratyekabuddha who, never having had the benefit of knowing Buddhism or any other teaching, works out his own enlightenment all by himself, simply by reflecting on the nature of reality. Since Buddhism does not rely on revelation or leaps of faith, but the appeal to reason, there is no reason in principle why a person might not work out her own path to liberation.

On the other hand, Buddhism avoids heroic efforts of asceticism. The Buddha himself learned to see his early asceticism as a mistake, "trying to gain enlightenment by force of will, by sheer force of ego-directed effort" (Sangharakshita, 1994, p.45). And though of course it requires much self-discipline, meditation is generally taught as a state we do not achieve by effort but rather fall into, as into sleep, as mental and physical activity subside.

Even in the Theravada there are practices that suggest the transfer of merit. In funeral rites, for example, the bereaved ask that their own good karma may be used to enable the departed to achieve a better rebirth. And Nirvana is not reckoned to be a state we can 'achieve' for ourselves.

It is incorrect to think that Nirvana is the natural result of the extinction of craving. *Nirvana is not the result of anything.* If it were a result, it would be an effect produced by a cause. It would be *samkhata*, 'produced' and 'conditioned'. Nirvana is neither cause nor effect... It is not produced like a mystic, spiritual, mental state such as *dhyana* or *samadhi*. TRUTH IS. NIRVANA IS. The only thing you can do is to see it, to realize it. There is a path leading to the realization of Nirvana. But Nirvana is not the result of this path. You can go to the mountain along a path, but the mountain is not the result. (Rahula, 1978, p.40.)

So Nirvana is not a state we create for ourselves, but something we discover. Zen Buddhists in particular have pointed out that, being the extinction of all desire, it can only be found after we cease to desire it and strive for it. We can walk the path to it but we cannot make it happen – it is there, given, the ultimate gift of reality itself, found at last after eons of illusion. To that limited extent, even in the Theravada there is something like what Christians call grace.

Reflected Moonlight – the Mahayana Tradition

Mahayana Buddhism allows a far greater variety of ways in which merit or good karma can be transferred from one sentient being to another, so that we can receive merit which we have not earned for ourselves, but simply received in trust. In the Shin form of Buddhism this receptive trust becomes the sole means to enlightenment, but before looking at Shin let us look at the main elements of the wider Mahayana tradition that make for a greater emphasis on 'other power'.

a) The Bodhisattva ideal, though not entirely absent from the Theravada tradition, becomes much more central in the Mahayana. Here the solitary figure of the *Arhat* gives way to the ideal of the one who, deserving enlightenment, chooses instead to transfer his good karma to save all sentient beings, vowing not to enter rest until they are all saved. This ideal transforms Buddhism in two ways. The ideal for the practicing Buddhist – who at a certain stage is invited to make the Bodhisattva vow for himself – becomes more generous and other-orientated, somewhat closer to the Christian ideal. But the Bodhisattva is also one from whom one might receive grace in the form of transferred merit. The Bodhisattvas become ideal, almost divine figures to whom one can pray for release from bad karma. Worship, trust, devotion and prayer come back into the mainstream of Buddhist life. The notion that one might oneself become a Bodhisattva, and the idea that Bodhisattvas are realizations of the Buddha Nature that each of us possesses, make these figures very different in essence from the divinities of polytheistic faiths.

b) In some forms of Buddhism, including the Vajrayana and Zen, there is great stress on trust in one's guru or teacher. The disciple offers him great devotion, almost worship, trusting him as a personification of the *Dharmakaya* or Buddha himself.

c) In Vajrayana Buddhism especially there is great emphasis on the importance of balancing one's own rational faculties with *day-pa*, confidence or trust (cf Dalai Lama, 1996, p.112). Ritual devotions and visualizations help the disciple, and "there is no bad karma, no monolithic negativity that cannot be overcome. But – and this is the key – there must be real belief that the power of this practice can eradicate and purify all negativities. If there is the slightest doubt, then the whole process weakens" (Too, 2003, p.75.)

d) *Bodhicitta* is a Mahayana term meaning 'enlightenment consciousness' or 'awakening mind'. It denotes the awareness that leads one, on encountering the vast open emptiness of reality, to become a Bodhisattva and seek to save all beings. It is as if the openness of existence itself, once realized, creates a total openness to all beings. Wisdom creates a compassion that fills all beings indiscriminately, like moonlight reflected everywhere:

> The crystal dews on the quivering leaves reflect her like so many pearls hung on the branches. Every little water pool, probably formed temporarily by heavy showers in the daytime, reflects her like so many stars descended on earth. Perhaps some of the pools are muddy and others even filthy, but the moonlight does not refuse to reflect her immaculate image in them. The image is just as perfect there as in a clear, undisturbed, transparent lake. (Suzuki, 1963, p.102-3)

Christians reading this might immediately think of the grace of divine love that falls like the sun and the rain "on the righteous and on the unrighteous" (Matt.5.45).

e) But Mahayana waxes even more radical. Not only is wisdom bestowed without regard to merit; some traditions suggest that lack of merit may actually enable growth in enlightenment. The image of the Lotus – the beautiful flower that has its roots in mud and slime – is at the heart of Buddhism; and a Mahayana text proclaims

> Yas kleshas, so bodhi, yas samsaras tat nirvanam.
>
> (What is sinful passion, that is wisdom; what is Samsara, that is Nirvana.) (cited Suzuki 1963 p.352.)

The second part of this statement expresses a fundamental divergence from the Theravada, for which Nirvana is a remote future state; in the Mahayana perspective, Nirvana can be experienced while in Samsara, the world of birth, decay and death. But the first part suggests the perspective of the Enneagram, where our worst vices hold the seeds of our potential virtues. By no means does all of Buddhism hold such a perspective; but the Vajrayana encourages the use of bodily practices and sexual energies which traditional Buddhism regarded as impure. And in a very different way, Shin Buddhism embraces the same paradoxical process. Buddhism becomes a faith for fools.

A Faith for Fools – Shin Buddhism

Ask not, "How could Amida receive me into his Pure Land, seeing that I am so vile and sinful?" For there is none of us but possesses a complete set of germs of worldly passions, sinful lusts and evil deeds. But the compassionate power of Amida is so infinitely great that he can and will translate us into his Pure Land if only we are willing to entrust ourselves wholly unto him. Neither should you say on the other hand, "I am good-hearted enough to be sure to be reborn into the Pure Land." For that Pure Land can never be reached so long as we rely on our own power of merits. (Shinran, cited in Nakai, 1946, p.112)

Perhaps because it does not offer the stark alternative to Christianity many Westerners are looking for, Pure Land Buddhism – which originated in 1st or 2nd century India – is often sidelined in Western accounts of Buddhism. But it is has the largest following of Buddhists in Japan (more than Zen, which is so much better known in the West), has influenced many other forms of Mahayana Buddhism, and has spread worldwide. It is based on the simple idea that Amida Buddha – the Buddha of Light – has promised rebirth in the Pure Land far in the West to all who lead a good life. The Pure Land is a land of delight where true teaching is easily available and easily followed, enabling people to enter Nirvana.

In 10th century Japan the radical Shin version of Pure Land Buddhism was founded by Honen (1133-1212) and radicalized by Shinran (1173-1263). Honen despaired of achieving the standards that the Buddhist texts required.

I realize that I have not observed a single precept or succeeded in the practice of meditation... The mind of the common man... is like the monkey which flits from branch to branch, confused, vacillating and unable to concentrate... Without the sword of undefiled wisdom, how will we extricate ourselves from the fetters of unwholesome karma and evil passions? Unable to sever ourselves from the fetters, how will we deliver ourselves from the bondage of transmigration through birth and death in the delusive worlds..? This is indeed lamentable and disheartening.

(Honen, cited in Brazier, 2007, p.37-8)

Honen's breakthrough came when he realized that enlightenment depended not on our perfection but on the perfect generosity of the spiritual realm: All we have to do is ask. Whoever recites Amida's name – *Namo Amida Bu*, 'Hail Amida Buddha!' – in heartfelt faith that this promise will come true, will be reborn in the Pure Land. And according to Shinran, even the recitation would be a work we needed to achieve by our own power. But salvation comes solely by 'other power' from Amida himself. So the recitation of the name became a response of gratitude to liberation already granted.

A sutra from the Pali Canon compares us to an ant hill that contains, buried, a melee of strange objects such as forks and toads, axes and pieces of raw meat, symbolizing our unruly passions. But at the heart of the ant hill is the coiled serpent, the naga, symbolizing our spiritual potential. "Our spiritual nature is buried in our wayward nature" (Brazier, p.53). It is dangerous to try digging out all the bad objects since we might throw out the serpent too. As with the wheat and the tares in Jesus' parable (Matt 13.24-30) it is better to accept the mix of good and bad we inevitably are. In this light, Shin Buddhism regards human beings as unavoidably "foolish beings of wayward passion" or in short, fools, *bombu*. We bring to Amida the whole heap, both our *bombu* nature and our spiritual core, and let him do with us what he needs to. For "despite our bottomless capacity to create trouble, we are still inhabitants of a benevolent universe" (p.197).

The founder of Protestantism, Martin Luther of course would have counseled exactly the same; we are always sinners, always redeemed, justified by faith, and sinning boldly that we may boldly rejoice in our salvation. It even helps to be sinful. In Amida's unhindered light

> The ice of our blind passions necessarily melts
> Immediately becoming water of enlightenment
> Obstructions of karmic evil turn into virtues...
> The more the ice, the more the water;
> The more the obstructions, the more the virtues. (Shinran, 1997, Vol. 1, p.371)

The faith required is not something we have to strain to do, otherwise it would be just another self-induced effort. Rather it involves *jinen* – the spontaneous naturalness that occurs when we let go of conscious effort, trust the power of Amida and his vow. It is like learning to swim: you have to let go of any conscious struggle to keep yourself afloat and allow the natural power of the water to buoy you up. (As a child I never could let go in this way; but one day I fell into a pool that was deeper than I had thought, and found myself pushed back to the surface by the water. After that I trusted the water and I could swim!)

Self- and Other-Power the Same?

Despite its resemblance to Christian 'grace', however, the 'other power' of Amida is not a power that comes to us from beyond.

> Amida is not a transcendent Other standing opposed to, and independent of, sentient beings. Amida is inherent in all

sentient beings... Amida is therefore at once innate and transcendent... To be awakened to the depth of the Original Vow then means to attain the enlightened wisdom to know who one really is. (Soga Ryojin, in Franck, 1982, p.223)

And writing about the practice of meditation in all schools of Buddhism, Alan Wallace writes,

The benefits of this practice are not created by myself as the thinker, but instead occur spontaneously as the mind gradually settles in its own calm, luminous ground state. If I regard that space of inner purity to be outside myself, or to belong to God, then the benefits of this practice can be attributed to grace. But if I regard that space as a deeper dimension of my own being, then I don't need to look outside myself for liberation. So who draws the boundaries between what is inside and outside the self? (2009, p.59)

'Other power' is therefore not ultimately to be contrasted with 'self-power'; the contrast is rather between effort and letting go. When we let go, the One who is both other than us and our own true identity can get to work.

Faith and Works in Christianity

Christianity, unlike much of Buddhism, has always seen salvation as something we cannot achieve for ourselves, something that is primarily God's initiative and accomplishment in sending his Son to die for us and his Spirit to live in us. But controversy has raged over whether, once set free by this work of God, we can co-operate with God's grace in a synergy or working together between our wills and the uncreated energy of God's Spirit in us (the Eastern Orthodox view); whether God creates in us virtues that, though they are his work, are genuinely our virtues, which merit salvation (broadly, the Catholic view); or whether nothing we can do can deserve salvation, and all we can do is trust the power of God (the Protestant understanding of salvation by grace and faith alone).

This last view is close in many ways to the Shin form of Buddhism. The life of Honen, mentioned above, has often been compared with that of Martin Luther (cf Lefebure, 1993, p.109ff). Both seem to have been moral perfectionists with an earnest desire to fulfill the requirements of their respective scriptures; though both, too, had an endearing earthiness, a sense of humor and a freedom from any ability to pretend to more virtue than they had. You could say they had the misfortune (or ultimately, the fortune) to be earnest and moralistic without being at all hypocritical. Both came to despair of ever achieving what seemed to be required of them. Both were dramatically converted, via the insight that their salvation did not depend on them but... and here of course is the difference. Luther expressed what he believed saved him through the categories of medieval Christianity, in which the cross of Christ loomed large, including the theory of atonement. Honen believed it was Amida and his vow that saved him.

Do We Need Faith?

Out of the discussion so far, it seems to me that there emerge three questions relating to the issue of whether we can liberate ourselves, or need faith in powers beyond us.

Question 1: Can We Overcome Self by Ourselves?

It has often been noted that there is something seemingly contradictory about a faith that believes there are no resources outside the self to help us liberate ourselves, but also believes there is no self. If liberation is to be possible at all, one or both statements need to be qualified.

The notion that there are no resources outside the self has already been qualified by the ways we have noted in which 'other power' actually functions even in Theravada Buddhism. And the notion that there is no self cannot mean that there is no responsible agent. At an ultimate level, the Buddhist would say, there is no real separation between self and other; we are all both effects and causes in a karmic process that propagates like ripples in a pond. The pond is the reality; the ripple looks as if it is some thing that moves across the water, but there are no continuous water molecules in a wave, only a chain of cause and effect whereby one piece of water makes another move according to a pattern. In the same way a bundle of thoughts, feelings and actions called 'Ross' propagates itself through cause and effect from one moment to the next – and even, according to Buddhism, from its death to its next rebirth. But though it is only like a propagating wave, this self can still come to realize its wavelike nature, and it could be that each self-wave can only come to this realization by its own work. Other waves may only confirm its illusion that they and it are permanent realities. It has to realize its own insubstantiality for itself.

I would not want to suggest it is absolutely impossible to achieve liberation by one's own efforts, since that is what we do seem to see in the case of the Buddha. His enlightenment reveals the fact that delusion and ego-centered desire are not our necessary state. But if there is 'other power' available, it may make the path much easier to find and follow. Some Buddhists acknowledge this.

> As a Buddhist I feel that Buddhist self-effort is not an easy way. Often self-effort leads to the opposite of the Truth. Though the Truth is formulated as the empty nature of self, self-effort or practice in Buddhism hardens the shell of self far away from the truth of emptiness. Arrogance or an inconsiderate attitude are often derived from the wrong view that is created from practice or self-effort. (Bokin Kim, in Gross and Muck, 2003, p.570)

In other words, self-effort is a risky and difficult way to overcome the self; it is likely in many of us to have the opposite effect.

On the other hand 'other power' can reinforce the ego too, by creating objects of faith to which the ego is over-attached. It is perhaps easier to dissolve the illusion of the self when it is not attached to and invested in the kind of illusory, self-serving understanding of God we find in fanatics of all persuasions. Nobody is more insuperably egocentric than the suicide bomb 'martyr' who sacrifices himself and many others for his God.

Become What You Were Before You Were

The previous chapter suggested that the core of our willing and choosing is not free. It represents our core delusion. This means there is a profound sense in which we do not want to be liberated. What we want is the fulfillment of the obsession around which our ego is built, as the Enneagram summarizes so well. To begin the process of liberation by ourselves involves a peculiar kind of inward gymnastics, an uncontrived summersault in which 'we' turn over against and leap up free from our 'selves', levitating ourselves by our own bootstraps. Tibetan Buddhism calls this the "turning about in the deepest seat of consciousness".

For most of us this is quite impossible, and liberation probably begins through the intervention of 'other power'. This can happen (and did happen to me) through a catastrophe in which the house that the ego has carefully built for itself is blown aside like a pack of cards. Yet looking back, it can become possible to see how the ego itself began to engineer its own liberating catastrophe. It becomes harder, in fact, to see what has happened by 'self power' and what by 'other power'. For what is liberating is not in the self and not in the other, but in that which overcomes the dualism between the two. It is that which, in Christian terms, is God, and in Buddhist terms, is Buddha-

Nature.

Liberation begins in a recovery of the innocence that was before the 'I', opposed to the other, came into being. A Sufi saying urges, "Become that which you were before you were..." (cited by Simon Parke, Church Times 14 Sept 2007, p.14). We have to find the original being that was there before the 'I' with all its hurts and demands came on the scene. Then we can begin to will and desire from the soft center of that being, rather than from the tough core of ego-compulsion. We can begin to receive "hearts of flesh" in place of our "hearts of stone" (Jer. 31.31-34). But this is no regression to early childhood. The Sufi saying goes on, "...but with the memory and understanding of what you have become." All the rich experience we have gleaned in life is not discarded, but experienced from this new center, from which it can become wisdom.

And this will include the experience of political struggle.

Question 2: Is Liberation Personal or Political?

Chapter 4 suggested that egocentric desire is inherent in our belonging to society. If this is the case, to overcome our delusion of self we have to overcome the illusion of the other too. The struggle against desire (in the sense of jealous grasping, rather than instinctive drive) has to be social and political as well as personal. If society is, so to speak, the ocean on which the wind of desire moves, breaking the surface into countless individual-seeming waves, then for a self to overcome desire is like a wave trying to stop the wind.

Peter Rollins (2006) tells a serious joke about a paranoid who believes he is corn and that the chickens are out to eat him. It's not enough, says Rollins, to convince the paranoid that he is not corn; the chickens have to be convinced too. In the same way it is not enough to convince an individual self that her desire for the latest fashion or the most expensive delicacies are wrong; the fashion and food magazines have to be convinced also. As noted in

Chapter 4, desire for such things is not a quirk of the individual ego. It is a social delusion evoked by the structure of our consumer society, including its advertisements and the whole apparatus designed to encourage and necessitate desire. The struggle to overcome desire has to tackle the ideological apparatus of society, and it has to tackle it as a society, or at least a community, if it is to stand any chance of success.

At times when we do enter a period of solitude and silence – in a retreat, for example – we may come up against this social dimension in two ways. Firstly, in the silent depths we may encounter the deep-rooted voices of the others who have made us what we are: the stern voice of the perfectionist father sounding as conscience and guilt, perhaps, or the longing for recognition by mother. The Enneagram – remember – told us not so much who we are as what other voice we have most made our own, and allowed to dominate the community within us. And secondly, when we return to society, all the tensions of the communities we inhabit – at work, in the home, or wherever – can easily rush out at us again and sweep aside whatever precious changes to our life we have resolved to make. It can be as if the time of solitude never was, as we find ourselves falling into the old obsessions and passions of fear, envy, anger or whatever, slotting back into our normal place in others' regard.

For our desire is inherently a social phenomenon, inherently in competition, and as such, inherently unhappy. To overcome this root unhappiness – the *dukkha* the Buddha identified – we need to overcome envy, overcome our alienation of the other, and create a community where people are not rivals. The Bodhisattva, perhaps, desires to save all beings partly because only by saving them can she ultimately be saved herself.

Hence both faiths have constructed communities of trans- formed desire: the *Sangha*, the Church and communion of saints. As societies these will tend to repeat the same sins and delusions as society at large; ambition, pride, avarice, envy and hatred are by no means absent, I believe, from such communities. But their aim is surely to build a society in which the self and desire are overcome in the other as well as in the self, in which new relationships are established which are not rival or ego-bound, and a new mode of 'interbeing' ripples outward to transform society at large.

Question 3: Has Liberation been Achieved for Us?

These considerations call into question any understanding of liberation based on solitary self-effort alone, and that includes many Buddhist accounts. I now turn to look at questions about the Christian understanding of salvation as an achievement of Christ alone on his cross.

Here two questions need to be distinguished: (a) whether enlightenment or liberation is something realized within ourselves, or something bestowed upon us gratuitously as a result of sacred events that have happened outside our control; and (b) whether the realization comes by our own effort or by faith in someone or something beyond us. Question (a) is about where liberation originates or comes from, so to speak, and question (b) about how it is realized in us.

Buddhists are unanimous in giving the former answer to (a). Enlightenment cannot be conferred by special historical events, because that places too much religious power in the institutions that confer it, or are 'in the know' about the events in question. Salvation has to happen in us and for us if it is to happen at all. But as we have seen, they differ greatly regarding (b), whether this happening arises, as it were, through our making it happen, or through our letting it happen.

Christians, likewise, are unanimous – and different from Buddhists – regarding (a); for all of them salvation is first and foremost something that has happened to the world in history through the death and resurrection of Christ. Like Buddhists they answer (b) differently, Protestants emphasizing faith alone, and

Catholics and Orthodox balancing faith with good works. Protestants believe that we are saved by faith that the events have saved us personally, Catholics and Orthodox that we are saved partly via the good works we do and the sacraments in which we share in the saving events.

That makes for a big difference between Protestant Christians and Pure Land Buddhists. They agree about the role of faith, but put their faith in radically different places. D.T. Suzuki (1974) expresses the difference in a very strong way.

In Christianity God's will or love of humanity, I may say, is expressed in the crucifixion of his only Son, that is, a concrete event in the history of karma-bound beings; whereas in Shin Buddhism Amida's will takes the form of intense determination and its solemn declaration. The latter may seem insipid, inane, and evaporating compared to the Christian realism. But in point of fact the Shin... has been the most irresistibly inspiring power in the history of Far Eastern Buddhism, and this power has been exercised without ever shedding blood, without committing cruelties, without persecuting heresies. (cited in Buri p.118-9)

In other words, Christians put their trust in a (partly) known historical person and an historical event (the crucifixion), while Buddhists trust a being (Amida Buddha, not the historical Buddha) outside history. They trust Amida without knowing him or having any kind of personal relationship with him (Brazier, p.119). In some ways the Christian trust is less 'blind', and its personal emphasis has impressed some Buddhists. For example Kenneth Tanaka (in Gross and Muck, 2003, p.101ff) writes movingly of the way a child's simple relationship with God in prayer can form the basis of a growing spirituality, while Buddhist meditation can be a remote and demanding practice removed from the practicing lives of non-monastic Buddhists.

At the same time, being more personal, the Christian approach can be more risky. As noted, it can generate a kind of egoism routed via God. The Christian renounces self-centeredness and trusts in God, but on the understanding that God loves him and in his providence makes the world revolve around him. I know of Christians who claim that God has answered their prayers by giving them nice cars and even ensuring they have a parking space! The Christian's personal assurance has often been exclusive in a way that the more remote Buddhist versions are not. Though salvation in Christ is offered freely to anyone who wants it and believes it is freely given to them, those who reject this free offer reject salvation itself, and the Church – for most of its history – has regarded them as bound for hell.

But now it is time to look at the very specific and historical way in which Christians have understood salvation to be offered, namely the atonement wrought by Christ on his cross. After discussing and rejecting one prominent way of understanding this, I shall offer a Buddhist way of understanding it, which Christians, if not Buddhists, may feel is an improvement!

The Suffering Servant and the Infinitely Offended God

If the idea of a unique incarnation of the one God in Jesus Christ causes deep problems for Buddhists and for most non-Christians, the doctrine of the atonement causes more. For D. T. Suzuki, depictions of the cross remind him of 'the gap that lies deep between Christianity and Buddhism'. (1957, p.128) He goes on to argue that 'as there is from the first no ego-substance, there is no need of crucifixion' – we do not need our egos to be nailed to the cross with Christ, because our egos do not exist in the first place. As John Maransky puts it, "Christ's passion and death has been understood as an atonement for the sins of persons, which take the burden of sin from the self. But the Buddha's activity is understood to trigger a recognition in persons that there is no such self to grasp or defend, hence no real basis of sin," (in Schmidt-Leukel, 2005, p.177-8). So Buddhism focuses on the self's own realization, albeit the realization of its non-existence, while Christianity focuses on the salvation achieved by another outside the self, albeit the salvation of the self.

Now the atonement has never been officially defined as a doctrine of the mainstream Christian churches. It does not appear in the traditional creeds, though it is a required belief in many Protestant denominations. In the Bible itself and the early Church fathers it is approached through a variety of different models. But there is one model that has become predominant in the West and especially among Protestants, and this model is often called *the* doctrine of the atonement.

As a broad idea the atonement depicts Jesus Christ as the 'suffering servant' or 'lamb of God' who bears in himself the consequences of the sins of humankind, and offers us in return the purity and bliss that comes from God. In words ascribed to St. Paul, "[God] made him to be sin who knew no sin, so that in him we might become the righteousness of God," (2. Cor. 5 21). As such the idea is profoundly important in all Christian traditions, and indeed to me personally, for two reasons.

One is the moving way it depicts God as able, in the person of his Son, to take into himself all our wounds and sins, and transform our bad into his good. The other is the way this liberates me from the incredible burden of having (taking up a familiar image in Buddhism) to construct my own raft of salvation from whatever driftwood I can find while at sea. Instead, a raft has been given in the atoning work of Christ; I can climb aboard, and my own efforts, far from being rendered worthless, can now actually achieve something in terms of paddling the boat, which they could not while I was foundering in the sea. Of course, many Protestant versions of Christianity offer the spiritual equivalent of a power-boat, in which I need make no effort at all. But I will argue that the liberation effected by Christ sets us free; the power of the cross and resurrection is an enabling power. It eliminates the sin that binds us, but imparts a responsibility to use our freedom well.

When people use the term 'atonement', however, they often have in mind the specific theory of 'penal substitution'. Though many parts of this theory precede him, it was St. Anselm of Canterbury (1033-1109) who put the pieces together in a systematic, worked-out way, using the theory of justice that was prevalent in his medieval times. According to that theory, the punishment a crime deserves depends not only on the gravity of the crime but also on the status of the victim. So to rape or murder a slave or peasant might be overlooked, while merely insulting a noble or a king might deserve the death penalty.

Now because God is infinite in 'status', sins against him, however slight, deserve an infinite punishment. All sins are in the end sins against God. So God's justice demands that we all be punished eternally in hell. But God loves us and does not want to see his precious handiwork burn in hell; so he has a dilemma. He solves this by punishing his own Son instead of us. Because the Son is infinite and divine, his punishment satisfies the demand for an infinite punishment, and God in his love can now acquit us – or at least those who believe his Son has done this for us – from the fires of hell which we all deserve.

We do not these days believe sins are serious in proportion to the status of the one sinned against. At least, that is thankfully not how our legal system is meant to work. (Though some may wonder if in some ways it still does!) But many seem to have preserved this notion in the case of God. They feel their tiny sins deserve a terrible punishment because somehow they hurt or offend God. Anselm's doctrine really does depend on that notion, which most of us – Christian, Buddhist and others alike – would see as a pathological and destructive guilt that is belittling to God, making him terribly easy to hurt and offend.

Moreover, translated into modern politics, to think of God as both infinitely exacting in his legal demands for righteousness and (thanks to Christ) infinitely merciful and forgiving of our transgressions is to think of him as the ultimate totalitarian leader. As Slavoj Žižek comments, "one of the strategies of totalitarian regimes is to have legal regulations... so severe that, if taken literally, everyone is guilty. But then their full enforcement is withdrawn. In this way, the regime can appear merciful: 'You see, if we wanted we could have you all arrested and condemned, but do not be afraid, we are lenient..'" (2009, p.135). Perhaps just this explains why so many Russians apparently wept at the death of Stalin as if for a loving father. Rather than hating him for the millions he killed or sent to the gulag, they loved him for not doing the same to them, though they deserved it too. In the theology of Paul, the law serves exactly the purpose of ensuring that "all have sinned and fall short of the glory of God" (Rom. 3.23), so throwing us into dependence on his mercy, shown (exclusively) in the cross of Christ.

Buddhists, of course, reject not only the petty tyrant God behind Anselm's version of the atonement, but the very idea of a God who administers pain as a punishment, and the very idea that salvation can be won by one being and conferred on others 'from outside'. Instead, punishment is seen as a process intrinsic to the universe, working through the law of karma, whereby the harm someone does will inevitably come back to cause them suffering. Most profoundly of all, in Buddhism 'salvation' is not a matter of being good and escaping punishment, but enlightenment.

That is why the Zen scholar D.T. Suzuki argues that the physicality of Christian salvation – the brutal suffering on the cross, the drinking of Christ's blood in communion, and even the resurrection – smells too much of the body by comparison with the more spiritual 'resurrection' of Buddhism.

What is needed in Buddhism is enlightenment, neither

crucifixion nor resurrection. A resurrection is dramatic and human enough, but there is still the odor of the body in it. In enlightenment there are heavenliness and a genuine sense of transcendence. Things of earth go through renovation and a refreshing transformation. A new sun rises above the horizon and the whole universe is revealed. (1957, p.132-3)

Jesus as a Radical Bodhisattva?

But we have seen that there are many exceptions to the rule that nobody can benefit from another's karma, notably the notion of the Bodhisattva. The Bodhisattva is both an ordinary human contributing to the salvation of the universe, and a savior figure bringing grace as it were from beyond. So could Jesus – who for Christians is both human and divine – be regarded in Buddhist terms as a radical form of Bodhisattva, who not only transfers his merit to us, but absorbs in his own sufferings the effects of our bad karma? After all, the Bodhisattva's transfer of merit involves remaining in the world of suffering for the sake of other beings.

This idea is not new. The Dalai Lama himself has suggested that Buddhists might regard Jesus as a Bodhisattva. And Rita Gross, a convert from a strict form of Christianity to Buddhism, writes, "Jesus seems more like a Bodhisattva than like a Buddha to me. This is because of his willingness to suffer on behalf of others and the extent to which... he puts the well-being of others before his own comfort," (Gross and Muck, 1999, p.46-7). Of course both Christians and Buddhists might not like this comparison. For orthodox Christians, Jesus' death and resurrection has saved the entire universe from the effect of sin, but for Buddhists the notion of a Bodhisattva who had already by his sufferings resolved the bad karmic effects of the entire universe would wreak moral havoc. Freed from the consequences of bad actions, we could live in total irresponsibility. While the notion of a salvation that works without the unhappy notion of an angry and offended God would be welcome to Buddhists, the burden of seeking enlightenment would be lifted from the shoulders of the individual to an unacceptable degree.

However, we have just called into question the sturdy individualism behind this criticism, and argued that liberation is inevitably a corporate struggle. And once Christ is seen as a Bodhisattva, taking to himself bad karma for which he is not individually responsible, the struggle with evil becomes corporate. It is a struggle carried by the community of those committed to sharing his death in order to share also his life with the whole world (2 Cor. 4.11).

That much, I think, a Mahayana Buddhist might not quarrel with. It might remain a matter for personal decision whether to join this (Christian) community of corporate struggle, or to pursue the struggle for liberation in a more traditionally Buddhist way. The offensive aspects of Anselm's atonement theory – the angry God who demands 'satisfaction' for insults against him, and the suggestion of some Christians (but not Anselm, so far as I know) that liberation is 'conferred' exclusively on the few who accept this theory – are overcome if we see Jesus as operating through the immanent workings of karma.

Meanwhile the aspects of the broader idea of the atonement which attract so many Christians – the deeply loving act of the 'lamb' who embodies God but endures our pain and death, and the sense of liberation that comes through being given a raft to paddle together, which we could never have built for ourselves – are retained in this understanding, without the implication that everyone has to buy into this belief in order to be saved. This understanding of the work of Christ preserves what Christians feel to be true in their own case, without forcing them to make claims about how salvation works for other people, claims which could never be known to be true.

Of course no one would claim Jesus saw himself as a Bodhisattva. That Buddhist concept was certainly not available to him. But for the same reason he could not have seen himself in

Greek terms, as one of the Trinity, consubstantial with the Father, or in medieval feudal terms as repaying humanity's debt to its offended Lord. The concepts that were available to Jesus, and which he or (more likely) the early Church used to interpret his passion – the Suffering Servant, the Passover Lamb, the Scapegoat sacrifice and the ransom paid to release captives – are as well captured by the Bodhisattva idea as by Anselm's theory.

What Sins are We Saved From?

On this understanding, exactly what sin does Jesus save us from? Is it all sin, all bad karma? And can we be delivered from all this sin only by Jesus' atonement? Might there be others who also redeem evil by their innocent suffering? Is Jesus a representative of all who do so, or is he the only one who has done so? In the latter case, we are forced to see Jesus, after all, as the unique savior of everyone, and Buddhists will understandably be offended by that.

It is obvious that Jesus does not save us from all the effects of our individual, voluntary wrongdoings. After his death and resurrection, people go on sinning, and suffering the just and unjust effects of their own and others' sins. To deny this would undermine the basis of responsibility in a way that would be unacceptable not only to Buddhists. But Chapter 4 made it clear that there is a kind of sin, or rather, an entanglement in sin, which individuals can do nothing about for themselves. This is the 'original sin' or 'bad karma from beginningless time' that is at the root of our separate selves.

I suggest it is this radical tangle that Jesus has cut – like the Gordian knot – by his dying and rising, setting our hands free to work. To return to our analogy, his atonement offers us a raft in which our own work for salvation can begin to be possible. But it does not just wash away sin and leave a clean self, as if this sin were something extrinsic to us, clinging like dirt. The sin that Jesus has saved us from, I suggest, is the sin at the root of the self, and the knot he has cut through is the self itself.

In the Gospel accounts, Jesus is described as declaring that "the Son of Man [or 'the Human Being'] must suffer many things and be rejected by the elders and the chief priests and the scribes, and be killed, and after three days rise again," (Mark 8.30-32). But why must he? Later tradition (already established by the time of John's Gospel) sees Jesus as making for his cross in full awareness that he is the Son of God, accomplishing the purpose of which he was sent, the sacrifice that would redeem the world. But in the three earlier Gospels the crucifixion seems to happen much more by the chance interaction of forces. The necessity involved is the necessity for (Roman) state power to establish itself against threats, combined with the necessity for (Jewish) religious authorities to eliminate the heretical other, plus whatever obscure psychological necessity was operating in the mind of Judas. The necessity is described not as a neat unrolling of divine destiny, or the procession of a fore-ordained tragic hero, but more as what Buddhists would describe as the inexorable and messy necessity of society's bad karma working itself out.

To understand the crucifixion with clear and fresh eyes, we need to embrace this element of atrocity. It is just one more example in history of people being degraded, tortured, broken and finally killed because of the necessity for scapegoats, of others we can eliminate as others to define and solidify who 'we' are. This need for scapegoats is human, not divine. The Gospels make no attempt to deny this element, even describing Jesus as praying for escape and seeming to be ignored and abandoned by God. Nor do they glorify the suffering as something a heroic Jesus triumphs over. Jesus is plunged by history into an abyss of terror; in the words of the Apostles' Creed he "descends into hell". But gradually that hell of nothingness becomes the great openness of God.

Chapter 3 touched on the way sometimes people cannot deal

with their own bad karma, but that karma may be resolved by others who receive the bad effects of it and suffer it in themselves, bringing it from numb darkness to a place of pain but light. In the same way, but to a vastly greater degree, I suggest, Jesus has taken the negativity of the world into the nothingness of God. The absence that is dereliction has become the space that is freedom. The painful nothingness of Good Friday has become the quiet Sabbath emptiness of Holy Saturday and then, on Easter Day, the open freedom of a new kind of interbeing.

Resurrection and Nirvana

In the Easter stories we hear of the disciples' relationships with Jesus, not merely restored to what they were before, but inhabiting a new freedom: erotic desire without grasping, envy and possessiveness for Mary Magdalene (John 20.14-18); friendship without an enemy, and companionship and table fellowship without the shadow of grief and loss for the disciples on the road to Emmaus (Luke 24.13-35); a faith based not on accounting and paying for sin but in forgiving and freeing people from it, given with the breath of Jesus' Spirit in the locked room (John 20.19-23); collaboration without the threat of scarcity, and leadership without hierarchy and rivalry, in the lakeside appearance, with the sudden abundance of fish and the charge to Peter by the lakeside (John 21.1-14). It is this new beginning that makes Christians feel that the death of Christ was not only a random atrocity (though it was that) but a taking of the deepest karmic tangle of sin into a new open space where it begins to be resolved.

If that is so, Jesus the radical Bodhisattva has done something unique and necessary for the salvation of the whole universe. However, he is not unique in doing something unique, and it may be that other Bodhisattvas and the Buddha – and perhaps even unsung children and solitary old folk we do not even know about – have also carried out unique acts indispensable for the liberation of the universe. Perhaps all of us are called to do something unique and indispensable, each of us being a Christ or a Buddha in our unique way? If liberation is a corporate and not a purely private affair, then this kind of thing is to be expected.

Mixing the metaphors once again, we do not need to know exactly – and none of us knows completely – how the web of salvation has been spun, we just need to participate in that web with all the energy, wisdom and compassion we can muster. For though the root of sin has been unraveled by Christ, sin and bad karma still go on; indeed they do not seem to have abated at all. But from Jesus Christ we can learn how to find the Christ in ourselves, as a space where we can receive the violence and pain others cannot cope with, and through suffering it 'mindfully' (as the Buddhists say) bring it into the redemptive process that flows from the death and resurrection of Christ.

Were it not for the experience of Christ risen, which is at the heart of Christian faith, it seems to me that there is nothing in the crucifixion itself that would compel us to see it as any more than an atrocity. There is nothing redemptive in the cross without the resurrection. But there is something about the resurrection that forces me to think of it as Nirvana happening in history; just as conversely, perhaps, Nirvana can be thought of as a resurrection happening in the depths of the seeker. An unconditioned freshness beyond pain and blame is common to both resurrection and Nirvana, and is what makes it so easy for Suzuki (above) to use resurrection imagery to convey the latter.

And I suggest, very tentatively, as something for Buddhists and Christians to ponder, that we might see the Buddha as the one who showed that Nirvana is possible; that there is no natural necessity for us to remain chained in bad karma and possessive desire. And Jesus is the Bodhisattva who acts in history to break the ancient, historical hold that bad karma and desire actually have on us, making Nirvana not only possible, but actually already here among us operating in our history, in the way Christians call the resurrection, the life of the kingdom to come present even now.

Summary

1. Buddhism is not a religion of strenuous self-effort alone; in all its forms, some kind of 'other power' is involved.
2. This emphasis is strongest in the Shin form, which enables Buddhism to relate to ordinary people.
3. Christianity likewise varies in the balance required between our own effort and faith in God's grace.
4. If the self is rooted in desire it is extremely difficult to achieve liberation solely by our own efforts.
5. Liberation requires corporate, political and historical as well as personal effort.
6. Christians believe – and Buddhists do not – that liberation has been accomplished for the world by Christ.
7. Anselm's widely followed account of how this happens presupposes an unacceptable view of God.
8. The Bodhisattva ideal can help us understand how the death and resurrection of Christ have overcome the tangled roots of desire, setting us free to strive for our liberation.
9. The resurrection is Nirvana unleashed in history. Nirvana is the resurrection realized within us.

Chapter 6

Butter Sculptures: The Arts
of Transformation

*Don't be concerned with facts, forget about right and wrong, sinking
or rising, winning or losing. Be like a mirror. It reflects one and all;
blue, yellow and all other colors; long, short, any size. It reflects
everything as it is, without judging. Those who have awakened to the
Way, who have attained the mind of Peace and Joy, who can see all
karmic conditions and who share their enlightenment with others,
reflect the world like a mirror, leaving no trace of themselves. This is
the law of no truth.*
(Lost Sutras p.83)

The previous chapter argued that liberation requires trust in
'other power'. But it equally requires skills we can learn. Even
the trust may be something I have to work at, like learning to
swim, or paddle. Kenneth Leong (encountered in Chapter 2)
relates what a friend said about his father, who was a Protestant
minister:

> "To him, all good things – trout as well as eternal salvation-
> come by grace, and grace comes by art and art does not come
> easy." This is one of the most beautiful Zen statements I have
> come across. All good things are the result of *grace, art*, and
> *work*. (Leong, 1995 p.136)

To extend the analogy, we note that trout only come to the bait by
grace; we cannot force them to bite, only wait in hope. But we can
learn the art of fly-fishing.

Both Christianity and Buddhism have a rich variety of 'arts' to make it more likely that 'other power' will be drawn to us and made our own. It is to these arts – practices and skilful means of meditation and worship whereby faith may be both evoked and expressed – that we now turn.

Should Practices be Merged?

This book has arrived at a much stronger sense of the way Christianity and Buddhism can help one another than I had when I first began to write. It seems to me now that there are ills in traditional Buddhism – notably its sturdy self-reliance and its tendency to withdraw from 'the world' – which are at odds with other parts of Buddhism, and which only a strong sense of other power and corporate engagement with evil can cure. We find such a sense well (though by no means uniquely) exemplified in Christianity. Meanwhile there are ills in traditional Christianity – the jealous exclusivism and even violence implicit in the kind of monotheism it inherited – which are at odds with the peacefulness and openness of its founder and his early followers, but which Buddhist concepts may help Christians overcome. In both cases each faith is helping the other to be true to itself, but only by issuing a strong challenge that can be quite threatening to traditional understandings.

But though the concepts and understandings are profoundly related to the spiritual journey we make, it is possible for them simply to remain concepts. We might effect a wonderful intellectual integration of the two faiths, giving us a vision of the ego as something to be overcome and Christ as the Bodhisattva who releases us from the ego's very root. Yet our actual egos might remain as walled in, and our cravings as strong and jealous, as ever. So the question just raised becomes urgent: what practices and 'skilful means' are available in the two traditions that might root these ideas into my life's journey? What arts might I learn that would realize in me and my community the kind of ego-free, non-violent 'interbeing' that has come to seem so valuable?

That, of course, is quite a Buddhist question. Christians, when they learn from the teaching of Christ or the Bible that some action or way of life is right, tend to ask, "What can we do to put this ideal into practice?" Buddhists typically ask, as it were, "What practices will put this this ideal into us." Both are concerned for practice, but in a different way. The risk for Buddhists is that they will go on forever doing practices that instill loving-kindness, without ever putting that into practice in the wider world. The danger for Christians (and perhaps, Western activists generally) is that they leap into action on the assumption that everybody already wants in their heart of hearts to do what the teaching requires. Then a lot of guilt and contradiction arise when people realize they do not really want what everyone expects them to want, or what they themselves feel they 'ought' to want, and their heart is not in the action.

This chapter will mainly be about practices as answers to the second question. A lot has been said about Buddhist and Christian ethics, or practice as considered in the first question. But a question remains as to what kind of practice will root the kind of Buddhist Christian vision this book has been developing. Will it be an amalgam of the two traditions, with bits of Christian prayer and worship blended with Buddhist meditation and mandalas?

I have not actually developed such an amalgam myself. My main practice is a fairly normal Christian pattern – I sing Morning and Evening Prayer daily with my wife at home, and attend the Eucharist on Sundays and Festivals, and on at least one weekday. I am involved with my local Anglican Church community, though I am not a central 'pillar' of it. I attend an Eastern Orthodox liturgy about once a month. My Buddhism is only apparent in periods of meditation morning and evening. This is normally *vipassana* (see below), but sometimes my own amalgam of Ignatian and Tibetan visualization based on the Gospels.

159

Why have I not opted for a stronger Buddhist mix? Because, I think, it is important to me to belong to a tradition; to be doing what I do as part of a community that stretches over the globe and over the centuries. Of course I have adapted that tradition to my own personality and circumstances. But I have resisted a 'spiritual supermarket' approach, taking from the Buddhist and Christian shelves packets that suit me. For one thing, that would take little packets out of the context in which they have their fullest meaning. For another, it would insert them into a new context – me. My own ego would become the final arbiter, and there would be a great danger that I would select the packages that bolster rather than threaten my own ego. And more subtly, my whole spirituality would become a consumer spirituality; it would fall prey to the very delusions which the spiritual 'arts' of the two traditions are designed to release me from.

What follows, then, is not some heady new Buddho-Christian-mix, but a look at the main elements of the religious practices of the two faiths, with a view to where each might impact on and enrich the other without doing violence to the integrity of either tradition. To achieve this it seemed best to sort the different practices according to the 'part' of us they involve, so that practices from each faith that engage the same part could be considered together. So they are arranged as practices of the mind, seeing, hearing and voice, the heart and devotion, and the body. Vajrayana Buddhists will recognize that the order descends the 'chakras' or spiritual centers in the body, though incompletely (seven chakras are traditionally identified), while Enneagram practitioners will recognize that the first two categories relate to the 'mind' center, the next two to the 'heart' and the final category to the 'guts' or 'will'. Inevitably this approach simplifies, not least because all faith practices engage the whole person at all levels. But there always seems to be a first 'port of call' for any spiritual practice, and this seemed as good a way of organizing the subject as any.

1) Practices of the Mind

I look first at practices that engage the mind in the first instance and in the broad sense, meaning practices that focus on consciousness and even the unconscious mind. Alan Wallace notes (2009, p.15ff) the degree to which the West has tended to focus in great detail on outward events – even in religion, much more in science – but has very few techniques for exploring the inner world; so much so that science often dismisses the very reality of consciousness. The East, on the other hand, has developed incredibly subtle techniques and categories for exploring and directing the mind, which to untrained Westerners can seem baffling. It is here that we have probably most to learn in terms of Buddhist Christian practice.

Meditation

Many think of 'meditation' either as the main or only spiritual practice of Buddhism and other oriental faiths, but completely lacking in Christianity; or as a kind of psychological relaxation technique which can be divorced from any faith context and profitably used by anyone. Neither understanding is quite right, on three counts.

Firstly, meditation is a long-standing part of the Christian tradition, dating back to the desert monks and nuns, though for them it meant something rather different from Buddhist meditation. Secondly, meditation in Buddhism exists alongside the many other practices described later in this chapter. It comes as a surprise to many Westerners to learn that many Buddhists actually pray and practice rites more than they meditate, if they meditate at all (Faure, p.66ff). There are sects, like the Shin, that reject meditation altogether. It has been argued (Lopez, 1995) that it was in response to colonialism and Christian mission that Buddhists came to emphasize meditation as their own spiritual practice, distinct from the faith commitments of Christianity. Buddhists also made meditation central to its own mission to the

West, where the practice had largely disappeared and left a gap. It is in this context that a form of meditation divorced from faith began to spread in the West, notably with the popularization of 'transcendental meditation' and the like from the 1960s onward. There is no doubt that the techniques used in meditation – sitting still, cross-legged, focusing on the breathing and/or on specific objects like a candle, bringing all thoughts 'back to the breath', and so forth – can have a therapeutic effect of relaxing the body and calming the mind, independently of any religious belief.

Thirdly, in Buddhist terms this kind of meditation is 'tranquility meditation' (*samatha*). Though widely used, Buddhists do not regard it as distinctively Buddhist, but as part of a much broader heritage that pervades Hinduism also and has been traced back to the ancient Indus Valley civilization that peaked 3000-2500BCE. It is not on its own a means of achieving enlightenment but an accompaniment of the more specifically Buddhist 'insight meditation' (*vipassana*). Insight meditation focuses on specific themes like wisdom, compassion, impermanence and death, as well as developing a deep and liberating mindfulness (see next) as to what is going on in the mind and body.

Christianity has its own variants of both tranquility and insight meditation. The desert monks developed many techniques for stilling the distracting thoughts and obsessions which they called *logismoi*, a kind of incessant inner chatter. These included the use of repeated prayers synchronized with the breath, as in the Jesus Prayer, discussed later. What is described in Christian tradition as 'meditation' involves the repetition or chewing over in the mind of some Biblical phrase, until it, as it were, becomes part of the believer. This has a tranquility-inducing effect, giving the mind something to do so that it will not distract the deeper work of prayer. But the phrase itself may lead to insight, and so form the bridge from the reading of scripture, to prayer, in which the practitioner speaks to

God, and so in turn to contemplation, in which she passes into a loving attention to and rapport with God that goes beyond all words. The traditional mystic way involved the 'purging' of obsessive thoughts and cravings, leading to insight or illumination, leading in turn to loving union.

Now there was a great wind, so strong that it was splitting mountains and breaking rocks in pieces before the Lord, but the Lord was not in the wind; and after the wind an earthquake, but the Lord was not in the earthquake; and after the earthquake a fire, but the Lord was not in the fire; and after the fire a sound of sheer silence. (1. Kings 19.11-12)

In many ways Christian meditation is like this experience of the prophet Elijah on the mountain. Like a mountain ourselves as we meditate, we need to keep still, and not let the wind of our thoughts or the earthquake of our emotions or the fire of our desires persuade us that God is anywhere other than in the "sound of sheer silence".

So can Christians learn from and incorporate the Buddhist practices? Well, many Christians already do practice what they regard as Buddhist meditation, though as Rita Gross (Gross and Muck, 2003, p.152) points out, this is usually *samatha*. The lack of specifically Buddhist content enables *samatha* either to replace or to complement the techniques just discussed as cases of tranquility meditation, enabling us to interact as whole persons – body, breath, mind and spirit – with God and her Word and Wisdom, rather than merely engaging intellectually or emotionally. And it can dissolve the opaqueness of the self and open up a space in which God may speak to the soul.

When Vajrayana Buddhists speak of our thoughts being experienced in meditation as so many clouds that scud across, and temporarily obscure, the blue sky of our inherent Buddha-Mind, Christians can relate that image, perhaps, to the pure eternal light of the inner Christ – or even, changing from a visual to an auditory metaphor, to the "sound of sheer silence". But there is a difference. In Christianity, we noted, desire is overcome not by tranquility but by the broader and deeper desire for God. So Christian meditation leads not to emptiness, but to dialogue with God and ultimately to silent love of God and being loved by God, an ultimate 'interbeing' that consumes the self.

Though Christians, when they adopt what they regard as Buddhist mediation, mostly employ *samatha* as a quieting down that prepares the way for contemplative prayer, a few writers (Meadow, 2007 and Cowan, 2004) have encouraged the use of *vipassana* to purify and open us to Christ. A Buddhist Christianity might benefit greatly from insight mediation that focused our whole being on Christian concepts like the Trinity or events in the life of Christ. I am currently working on this.

Mindfulness

Right 'mindfulness' or attentiveness is enjoined along with right concentration (*samadhi*), as the final two parts of Buddhist Eightfold Path. It involves an attentive awareness of the body, sensations, mind and internal phenomena like thoughts and feelings, such that we are not automatically directed by them. Rather, being fully aware of them just as they are, we are able to be in more control of them. For example, instead of being led by anger to violent words or actions, one simply rests with the awareness of the anger. A space then opens up, in which one is free to act mindfully in the presence of the anger as seems best.

Mindfulness is often explained as living totally in the present, but this can be misleading, as it could mean suppressing memories and living passively without any intentions. In fact, mindfulness includes awareness of past memories and future intentions. However, it is awareness of those things as they exist now, in the present. Instead of being driven by past experience (or suppressed memories) to dream up and dwell on intentions, mindfulness enables us to be aware of the memories that are shaping us, and the intentions that are beginning to form in us, right now. That gives us space to decide how we really want to respond in the present.

The Christian desert tradition included, as well as meditation, much teaching about mindfulness or what was called 'watchfulness'. In the words of one interpreter, we are encouraged to "observe the fear or the anger or the envy – whatever the thought-feeling – and not the story we spin about the fear, the anger, the envy," (Laird, 2006, p.84). When we feel envy, do not get caught up in our familiar yarns about how inferior the person we envy really is, or alternatively, how bad we are to feel envious. Just watch the envy, as something happening in us now, and let it pass in its good time.

Often we multitask, doing many things at once, while thinking about other things – memories from the past, intentions for the future. Mindfulness is about bringing our whole mind back to the here and now, and what we are doing in the present, noting all the sensations involved as I peel the potatoes or walk along the street, dispassionately and objectively, noting but not being carried away by any pleasure or pain. Mindfulness can be practiced anywhere at any time, and I know of no reason why it could not enrich a Christian's life, enhancing her sense of belonging to and enjoying being in this material universe, and celebrating what the French spiritual writer de Caussade (1675-1751) called the "sacrament of the present moment".

Mindfulness can be extended into a deepened awareness of love, which again Christians can only welcome:

Let your love flow outward through the universe, to its height, its depth, its broad extent, a limitless love, without hatred or enmity. Then as you stand or walk, sit or lie down, as long as you are awake, strive for this with a one-pointed mind; your life will bring heaven to earth. (*Sutta Nipata:*

Buddha's Discourse on Good Will.)

The 'one-pointed mind' is an aspect of the *samadhi* or concentration that is the eighth part of the Eightfold Path. It denotes an awareness that is not distracted but totally focused. In a similar vein, the unknown Christian writer of The Cloud of Unknowing speaks of prayers like sharp pointed arrows piercing into the depths of God, while in the Sermon on the Mount we hear: "if your eye is single, then your whole body will be full of light," (Matt. 6.22). The word for 'single' is sometimes translated 'healthy' which is more logical but less accurate; *haplous* means single, simple, transparent, uncomplicated. To do something mindfully is to do it with an uncomplicated eye and both hands; not with one hand on the steering wheel and one on the mobile phone, while your eyes range all over the place looking at the shops!

Reading and Preaching

The reading and preaching of Scripture is at the heart of the Jewish and Christian traditions. The belief that in the Word of Scripture God reveals Godself made these the central practice in the daily synagogue services, which came to form the backbone of the first part of the Christian Eucharist, the 'Ministry of the Word'. Meanwhile the monastic office consists almost entirely of the recitation of psalms, biblical canticles and scriptural texts, which also became the basis of the scriptural meditation just mentioned. Lectionaries have developed for the reading of scripture at morning and evening prayer and at the Eucharist, in which virtually the whole Bible is read day by day through the year. This immersion in the whole of scripture knows no parallel in Buddhism, where the looser definition and far greater variety of scripture would make it much harder to achieve. However, chanting the sutras, silent reflection on them, and expounding them to laypeople, are important practices in Buddhist monasteries and temples.

One great objective for Christians who desire to tap the depths of Buddhist wisdom on a regular basis might be to design a supplement to the lectionary whereby Buddhist texts could be read in harmony with the Christian ones at appropriate seasons of the year. The Buddha's birth could be read about, for example, at Christmas, his temptations during Lent when we read of those of Jesus, his achievement of Enlightenment at Easter and his PariNirvana or passing out of the world of Samsara at the Ascension. The interilluminations – both the likenesses and the differences – would be a rich source for reflection. Meanwhile of course there is no reason why Buddhists might not read and expound Christian texts – as indeed Buddhists like the Dalai Lama, Thich Nhat Hanh and Kenneth Leong do so well, often bringing to light meanings more easily perceived from their Buddhist perspectives.

Koans

Hyakujo wished to send a monk to open a new monastery. He told his pupils that whoever answered a question most ably would be appointed. Placing a water vase on the ground, he asked: "Who can say what this is without calling its name?"

The chief monk said: "No one can call it a wooden shoe." Isan, the cooking monk, tipped over the vase with his foot and went out.

Hyakujo smiled and said: "The chief monk loses." And Isan became the master of the new monastery. (*Gateless Gate* 40, in Reps p.124)

This is a typical *koan*, a teaching form unique to Zen Buddhism. While most teaching is designed to make points that pupils understand, the point of a *koan* is not to make a point, not to be understood. The *koan* offers paradox that cannot be resolved by the normal intellect. "The whole intent [is] to help the pupil break the shell of his limited mind and attain a second eternal birth, ...enlightenment. Each [*koan*] is a barrier. Those who have the spirit of Zen pass through it," (Reps, 1971, p.93). The *koan* is reflected on in *zazen*, sitting meditation.

> In our *zazen*, it is precisely at the point where our small, foolish self remains unsatisfied, or completely bewildered, that immeasurable natural life [*jinen*] beyond the thought of the self functions. It is precisely at the point where we become completely lost that life operates and the power of the Buddha is realized. (Uchiyama, 1993, p.61)

The writer on spirituality Michael Sells argues (1994) that a lot of spiritual writing employs a "language of unsaying", in which propositions cancel one another out and create an "anarchic moment". As in a joke, language subverts the very expectations it generates, creating an anarchic "punch line". The mind is confused, but reality is felt like a "punch" in the guts. It is the same with *koans*. They raise questions like, "What is the sound of one hand clapping?" We think it is going to be easy to answer because the sound of two hands clapping is so well known. Of course, the very notion of clapping involves two hands, so the attempt to answer is defeated from the outset by the language of the question. The imagination, drawn to so concrete an image as a hand-clap, finds itself closing on nothing. Perhaps (as suggested in Chapter 4) we feel we are like one hand clapping. The inconceivable emptiness of things (*Sunyata* – see especially Chapter 8) is encountered: amazing, alarming, hilarious.

Parts of the Bible – such as the wisdom sayings of books like Proverbs, Ecclesiastes and the Psalms – lend themselves to being read in a *koan*-like way. The Hebrew in which most of the Old Testament is written is an open-ended language in which a word can mean a number of different things, leaving all sorts of open possibilities that invite imagination. (Be careful what translation you use, though, because some modern ones close these options down in the interest of a clear and simple message.)

Many of Jesus' parables are designed to confound us in the same way, but the veil of familiarity often blunts this confusing edge because we have heard so many sermons telling us exactly what they mean. For this reason it may be helpful sometimes to turn to the unfamiliar versions of the parables found in the apocryphal Gospels like that of Thomas:

> When you bring forth him whom you have within you he will save you. If you do not have him within you, he will kill you. (Thomas 70 C, in Morrice p.107)
>
> Know what is in front of you and what is hidden from you will be uncovered to you. For there is nothing hidden which will not be revealed. (Thomas 5 B, in Morrice p.108)
>
> His disciples said to him: "When will the kingdom come?" Jesus said: "It will not come by expectation. They will not say: 'See, here,' or 'See, there.' But the kingdom of the Father is spread upon the earth and people do not see it. What you expect has come but you know it not."
> (Thomas 113 A, in Morrice p. 106)

It is worth reading passages like these after meditation has established an open frame of mind that can 'ponder in the heart' without rushing to glean a quick moral lesson. Then perhaps you can turn back to the familiar versions and ponder them in a koan-like way too.

2) Practices of Seeing
This section considers practices that involve visual objects or imaginative visualization.

Visual Objects
Christian and Buddhist art are very varied as traditions, as well

as very different from each other. There is nothing in Christian art like the meditative maps called mandala, but then the mandala is a mystery to Buddhists outside the Vajrayana Tantric traditions in which it makes sense. And there is nothing in Buddhist art like the Orthodox icon, but then, the icon relies on the notion that Christ and the saints are present in the act of worship, and disclosed to the believer through the icon. Outside that framework – which not all Christians share – the icon does not make sense. Meanwhile many Protestant traditions in Christianity and the Shin tradition in Buddhism reject the use of any art that depicts objects, preferring in places of worship to depict nothing at all, but often displaying words – the nembutsu invocation of Pure Land Buddhism, or key texts like the Ten Commandments in the case of Protestantism.

In mainstream Buddhism images play a larger role than is often realized, as a trio of essays in *History of Religion* (Vol, 34 no. 3, February 1995) makes clear. Bruce Owen tells how the Buddhist deities are invested in their divine power by human ritual among the Nuer of Nepal; Matthew Kapstein describes how Tibetan art involves a kind of "weaving of the world" through the art; and Donald Swearer describes how Thai Buddhist statues are consecrated in all-night candlelit vigils of meditation. Human activity in some sense creates the power of these images. This should not surprise us, since according to Mahayana Buddhism at least we all share Buddha Nature, and there is no divinity that is not in some way projected from within us. In the next section we shall see how important it is also to take back and dissolve the projected image into oneself, and to realize one's fundamental identity in it.

The process of 'writing' and consecrating icons is equally important in Eastern Orthodox Christianity, and again it is ultimately the context of worship that consecrates the icon . But in other ways the perspective is very different. There is something of the icon in a lot of depictions of Christ, and this something contrasts with what we find in images of the Buddha. My web page www.holydust.org/christandbuddhapics.htm shows Albrecht Dürer's mirthful face of the risen Christ, the dead Christ from the Pieta of Villeneuve-les-Avignon – whose tranquil closed eyes still somehow address us – and Piero de la Francesca's Risen Christ, returning like a traumatized warrior from his battle with death. All of these depict Christ face on to the onlooker, in closed self-contained curves and straight lines, as if communicating a gaze from the beyond that holds things together, and fixes on and holds the onlooker in a relationship that includes love, or awe, or both. These features are typical of icons.

In Buddhist art – whether it is a laughing Japanese Buddha or a serene Thai Buddha or a wrathful Tibetan Bodhisattva (all depicted on the same web page) – the lines flow out energetically beyond the figure, and the gaze (except in the Tibetan case) fixes on somewhere else, on a state of realization yet to be attained by the onlooker. Christianity fixes transcendence in God, believer and their relationship within a self-contained universe; Buddhism finds transcendence in the state – Nirvana – which the Buddha has found and the onlooker seeks, within a cosmos that is radically impermanent, always on the move.

When – as at the prayer place of some of my friends – a smooth three-dimensional grey Buddha is placed alongside a two dimensional icon with its bright colors and angled curves, I experience a kind of discord. Is this just a matter of aesthetics, or is there a kind of clash of world views involved? And if the latter, by what right do I juxtapose Christ and the Buddha and their world views in this book? Perhaps I can do so in this book because I try to develop from the two world views a mental 'space', in which both can find their place. It is a bit like the way the different visions we receive in each of our two eyes can fuse to create a three-dimensional space; or to change to an auditory metaphor, like the way two distinct melodies can blend in a new harmony. But maybe my friends have done the equivalent of this blending in the physical and imaginative space of their rooms. If so, why do I find it difficult to do that? I do not know.

Imagination

The real clash between the Buddhist and Christian images has to do I think with our inward powers of visualization – our imagination – and in particular, how we imagine past time relating to the present day. Icons always depict an event from the Bible believed to have taken place, or else a saint believed to have existed in history. Icons find their proper place in the Christian Eucharist, where the past life, death and resurrection of Christ are made present to his people now. In the icon, imagination serves to make the past present. The icon is rooted in the Judeo-Christian conviction that past and future are as real as the present, and give it meaning.

It is the same with other Christian uses of the imagination in prayer. For example, the popular Spiritual Exercises of Ignatius of Loyola invite us to imagine scenes from the Bible, not only visualizing the scene also imagining what we might have heard and smelt and felt and thought. But the purpose is to bring us into a dialogue with the Jesus who was present in the historical scene we are imagining, but is also present in the one doing the imagining. Imagination forms the bridge between the incarnate Christ of history and the inner Christ who speaks to us and in us now.

With Buddhism it is different. On the whole, imagination is discouraged. Along with thought and feeling it represents a distraction from the tranquil mindfulness that is sought. And imagination can stimulate unwanted desires and cravings. But in the Vajrayana Buddhism of Tibet, there is a rich place for the imagination, and even for the delight and desire it evokes. The imagination is invited to focus on vivid figures such as the yidams and the five Dhyani (meditation) Buddhas, figures which in Tibetan art are characterized by their different colors and genders, by the objects they hold, or sit on, or which hover above their heads, and the compass direction from which they appear. Some have many arms, some are serene, and detached, some smiling and compassionate, others again wrathful. Devotees imagine these beings as they recite the detailed descriptions in their puja (worship), and they may be invoked with their specific mantra.

However, "these deities are quite different from the deities of monotheistic religions... They are not ultimately separate from the meditator, who identifies himself with the deity by visualizing himself as the deity" (Rita Gross in Gross and Muck, p.48). As his mantra is said, the 'deity' is 'dissolved' – allowed imaginatively to disperse into thin air –and then visualized as a power emanating from the meditator himself, usually from the heart center. The background belief here is in the unreality of time and of self and of all forms of separation. The imagination is used not to make history present, but on the contrary, to transcend the separation of the self and its objects. The divine is vivid and in a sense real, but only as a realization of mind, a skilful projection of what is within us.

This approach finds its most dramatic presentation in the wonderful sculptures the Tibetans make out of butter, and the intricate mandalas they make out of colored sand, for the great festivals. Intricate designs are sculpted and traced with painstaking love over many hours and days. But when the weather warms, the butter melts, and the whole wonderful edifice is dissolved. And when the wind blows, or the sweepers come after the feast, the designs are dispersed.

The emphasis on the mind and impermanence in visualization practice enables Vajrayana Buddhists to visualize what is terrifying and apparently evil in a way that would be unbearable for the more realistic Christian approach. Tibetan art depicts wrathful beings that look like they are about to tear you apart and devour you – an example is on the bottom left of the web page. But ultimately these too are dissolved and assimilated as representing the darker side of one's own mind. The imagination is used to face up to the 'demonic' in all its terror, and then to acknowledge this as part of the psyche.

Such a move is impossible for Satan and the demons in the Christian imagination, since these are seen as eternally alienated from God and consigned eternally to the depths of hell. Traditional Christianity has hated and rejected the demons, while liberal Christianity has simply denied their (psychic) reality. Jung has noted how damaging this "splitting off of the shadow" has proven, as truly demonic practices of persecution, torture and crusade, and a dark imagination of hell have emerged from the disowned shadow.

Despite the great differences regarding the reality of what is imagined, I wonder if it might be helpful for Christians to adopt some insights from Buddhist practices. The Vajrayana approach to demons seems much more healthy than the Christian. I have suggested (2008) that the eve of All Saints (Hallowe'en) might be a good occasion for visualizing our demons and then 'owning' them, just as Prospero at the end of The Tempest acknowledges the strange monster Caliban, declaring "this thing of darkness I acknowledge my own," thus setting him free.

It is possible to acknowledge the importance of history for Christians without denying the value of the dissolving and assimilation of historically manifest realities. If Christ is thought to be both historically incarnate and present in the believer, then, having imagined him in an exercise like those of Ignatius, would it not be appropriate to let Christ 'dissolve' and become one with us? Having imagined ourselves as one of the sick people in the gospels, receiving the healing touch of Christ, could we not then dissolve the imagined scene and imagine the healing Christ in the center of our hearts? We could reflect on who we might bring Christ's healing to, and what kind of healing it might be, and so forth.

Not only would such an approach guard against an idolatrous trust in our imagination of Christ; it would also enable us
to move from receiving into ourselves the blessings and the
message of Christ, to being, ourselves, the bearers of his presence
and his message in the world today. As the well-known prayer of
St. Teresa puts it:

Christ has no body now on earth but ours, no hands but
ours, no feet but ours.
May ours be the eyes through which is to look out Christ's
compassion; ours the feet with which he is to go about doing
good; ours the hands with which he is to bless people now.

This is a prayer a Tibetan Buddhist could readily use, simply
employing the name of a meditation Buddha like Chenrezig for
that of Christ. Why after all does Chenrezig have so many
hands?

3) Practices of Hearing and Voice

This section considers practices that engage primarily the mouth,
throat and voice, and the ears and hearing.

Mantras and Repeated Prayers

Mantras are series of syllables of no definite meaning. Generally
short, they can be a hundred syllables or more in length. Their
origins lie deep in ancient Hinduism, from which their use
spread into Vajrayana Buddhism and the Shingon sect of China
and Japan. Originally they may have been magic spells, but in
Buddhism they are (ideally at least) used to instill insight and
train the mind, rather than to gain power over nature and
people. They may be said repeatedly in harmony with the breath,
but also form a significant part of the puja or devotional services.
Their effectiveness lies in the sound of the syllables rather than

their meaning, though a deep and complex web of symbolism has built up around them. For example, Lama Anagarika Govinda devotes a 312 page book (1969) to explaining the meaning of the best known mantra, *Om mani padme hum*, which is widely used in Tibet.

A mantra also widely used in Tibet is '*Om ah hum*' – the three syllables here being said on the intake, peak and exhalation of the breath respectively. The following gives a flavor of the symbolism associated with any mantra.

> When pronouncing *Om* one imagines that it stands for the universal sound, the symbolic word for the infinite, the perfect, the eternal... *Om* is like the opening of our arms to embrace all that lives and exists... *Ah* is the expression of wonder and direct awareness. It is a point of stillness, of emptiness. *Ah* brings energy, openness, expansion and empowerment. *Hum* is the universality (*Om*) brought into the heart, it is the infinite in the finite, the eternal in the temporal... *Hum* brings expansiveness, infinity, essence and oneness into the human being.
>
> (www.soul-guidance.com/houseofthesun/omahhum.htm)

Christian tradition knows nothing equivalent to the mantra, but from early times the monks have used repeated prayers such as 'O God make speed to save us; O Lord make haste to help us', both in private and in corporate prayer through the day. Best known in the Eastern Orthodox tradition is the Jesus Prayer, 'Lord Jesus Christ, Son of God, have mercy on me, a sinner'. In the Prayer of the Heart this is said in conjunction with the breath and with a focus on the place of the heart in the center of the body. Its role – giving the mind a worthy focus of attention so that the heart may become still and receptive – is not unlike that of a mantra.

In modern times the Benedictine Father John Main (2006)

promoted the use of prayers like *Maranatha* ('Come, Lord') in a mantra-like way, and many Christians find this approach spiritually helpful. For myself, I often use *Om ah hum*, relating the above meanings to the Trinity as explored in Chapter 8. With *Om* and the intake of breath I focus on the coming to be of myself and all beings out of nothingness, with *Ah* and the peak of breath I offer thanks and adoration for the order and beauty of being, and with *Hum* and the breathing out I offer and empty myself into the infinity of beings. No doubt we are only at the beginning of exploring the richness that might come to Christian practice through the careful adaptation of mantras.

Music

Until modern times in the West, it has been the almost universal practice of all religions to chant rather than merely say the prayers and other vocal parts of services. As St. Augustine put it, "whoever sings prays twice" – the act of singing engages the whole body in producing the words, and seems to enable the words to go on singing in the memory. But the style of chanting varies, from the rhythmic repetitions of mainstream Buddhism, to the deep-throated earthy chant of Tibet, to the haunting melodies of Korea and Burma. In Christianity the Greek Orthodox employ solid, often passionate chants that resonate with their Jewish background, while Roman Catholicism developed the more ethereal style of Gregorian chant, and then the intricate polyphony of medieval and Renaissance times. Protestantism with its emphasis on comprehensibility, simplicity and congregational involvement restricted the use of chant, but developed a vast repertoire of metrical hymns and choruses which is now used and added to by Roman Catholics also.

In many ways in the West the music expresses the self-emptying passion and longing for God which lies at the heart of the Christian approach. The development of polyphony and harmony seems to be characteristically (though not uniquely)

Christian, and the way several melodies can combine into one harmony and yet remain distinct can be seen as expressing the characteristically Christian understanding of union with God without fusion, the threeness-yet-oneness of the Trinity, and the unity-in-diversity of the Church as the communion of saints.

In Buddhism music has moved in a very different direction. In Mahayana monastic music, the rising of the sound as a total entity, and its falling away to silence, is more significant than melody or harmony, and expresses the Emptiness and dependent co-arising explored in Chapters 7 and 8.

> Concerned less with the shapes of the melodies than with the quality of the sound... free chanting, as well as the recitation of the Buddha's name, provides a way to find... the condition of things being just as they are, all interdependently related in one constructive process.
>
> (Pi-yen Chen, 2001-2, p.45)

Christian harmony and Buddhist music both seem to express interrelatedness, but of a different kind, the one allowing for the tracing of an individual life – a melody – which creates harmonious relationships with other such traces, the other emphasizing a much more fused and spontaneous arising together of all things. In Chapter 8 I try to combine the different approaches in a way that makes religious sense. It would be interesting to see whether they could be combined in a way that made musical sense.

4) Practices of the Heart
Heart is often opposed to head as feeling to thought, emotion to intellect. I shall use it to group the practices that concern both feeling and choosing.

Confession

The examination of conscience and confession of sins is important in both Christianity and Buddhism, not as a gloomy end in itself, but in order to gain release from the hold unforgiven sin (or in Buddhist terms, bad karma) has on us. In Vajrayana Buddhism there is a very strong emphasis on the weight of past bad karma, but meditation Buddhas like Vajrasattva are there to help.

> The negative karma I have accumulated from beginningless time is as extensive as the ocean. I know each negative action leads to countless eons of suffering, yet I am constantly creating negative actions. I try... to practice positive acts, yet day and night, without respite, negativity and moral downfalls come to me like rainfall. I lack the ability to purify these faults and, with these negative imprints in my mind, I could suddenly die and find myself falling to an unfortunate rebirth. Please, Vajrasattva, with your great compassion, guide me from such misery. (Too, 2003, p.74)

There is however a difference between Christian and Buddhist approaches. Christian confession – whether sacramentally to a priestly representative of the Church or privately to God – leads to 'absolution', a release from the burden of sin in which the innocence bestowed in baptism is restored. The confession and forgiveness are related to the redemption Christ has accomplished in his dying and rising, to which baptism joins the Christian.

In Buddhism, the bad karmic effects have to be dealt by self-effort, without this externally wrought forgiveness, generally through deeds which counteract the bad karma. But in Shin Buddhism there is need for neither absolution nor self-effort. Here the discipline of examining oneself and discerning one's sins is very exacting, but confession is not followed by forgiveness. Forgiveness would suggest that we had behaved outside our nature and could return to a different way of being. It also suggests a return to the fold, a repair of the relationship. In the Pure Land view we are not forgiven because we are never judged in the first place. Universal love is unconditional. It holds us, whatever we do. Confession... does not heal a breach, for Amida has never been absent, but it may lift a veil we have created. (Brazier, p.189).

In some traditions, again, through enlightenment and the realization of Emptiness "all the evil of the past is purified. This is *mushosen*... repentance on realizing the unborn – that all is pure from the beginning" (Robert Aitken in Gross and Muck, 2003, p.79).

Though this is far from Christian practice, it seems to me to accord with a true Christian understanding. The Christian Poet William Blake (1757-1827) wrote

Every harlot was a virgin once,
Nor can'st thou ever turn Kate into a Nan.

('Kate' here stands for the original innocence, and 'Nan' for the fallen woman.) He seems to be speaking precisely of the fact that "all is pure from the beginning". Mother Julian of Norwich (1342-1417) similarly believed there was a part of the soul that never consents to sin.

Jesus, it seems to me, does not come offering a forgiveness that is conditional on repentance and confession. In many stories, like that of Zaccheus (Luke 19.1-10), forgiveness precedes repentance: Jesus says he will eat and drink with the sinner, and that 'lifts the veil' and the sinner begins to be able to make amends for sins already and unconditionally forgiven. In the parable of the Prodigal Son (Luke 15.11-32), the father is looking out for his son long before he repents and returns, and embraces him before he utters his confession. Peter himself sinned grievously in his betrayal of Jesus, but Jesus extracts no confession and pronounces no absolution; he just asks Peter if he loves him, and then entrusts him with responsibility for his flock (John 21.15-19). Whereas we so often begrudgingly forgive after an abject apology, and say that we will never 'forget' the sin or trust the person again, Jesus' forgiveness is implicit and overflowing in the trust he bestows. And it is this forgiveness that necessitates repentance so that it can make a difference to our lives.

It seems to me Buddhism and Christianity have much to learn from each other about the practice of confession. The Christian assurance of forgiveness can bring release to those strands of Buddhism – notably the Vajrayana – where immensely arduous works including thousands of prostrations are felt to be needed to gain release from bad karma. But the Christian understanding becomes unhelpful when it leads to a repeated cycle of sin, confession and absolution. Maybe confession should take place after absolution has been pronounced, or even at the end of the Eucharist, when the table fellowship with Christ has brought implicit forgiveness, and Christians are sent out to their day to day work.

Intercession

Intercession or prayer for the world and for those in need is an enormous emphasis in Christian practice, from the repeated litanies of the Orthodox Church to the Evangelical 'prayer meeting' where most of the prayer consists of very specific intercessions and petitions. Intercession means 'going between' and in it the Christian appeals to Christ the mediator who 'goes between' God the Father and humankind, asking that the benefits of his dying and rising may be channeled toward this or that specific need.

In Buddhism, by contrast, many regard prayer as absent altogether because of the lack of belief in God. But Rita Gross argues that in practice prayer is important in Buddhism in three ways (Gross and Muck, 2003, p.91ff). First there is prayer to supernatural beings who are believed to be as real as you and I. That is to say, like us they have a relative existence, but are ultimately unreal. Like the angels and saints of Catholic and Orthodox Christianity, these beings often co-opt the powers of preceding pagan spirits.

Secondly there are expressions of 'aspirations or wishes, in which no-one is addressed, but many hopes are expressed'. Typical here is the *metta* practice of Theravada Buddhism where loving kindness is wished, first for oneself, then for dear ones, then for those whom one is indifferent to, then for enemies, and for all beings. And typically a time of meditation or other religious practice will end with a prayer like this:

By the power and the truth of this practice, may all beings have happiness, and the causes of happiness. May all be free from sorrow, and the causes of sorrow... May all beings be filled with joy and peace. May all beings everywhere, the strong and the weak, the great and the small, the mean and the powerful, the short and the long, the subtle and the gross: may all beings everywhere, seen and unseen, dwelling far off or nearby, being or waiting to become: may all be filled with lasting joy.

(www.worldprayers.org/frameit.cgi?/archive/prayers/invocations)

Having realized, through meditation, the Buddha nature within her, the practitioner asks for that nature to flow in generous love towards all beings. Though specific petitions may be made, on the whole this flow is less specific than in Christian intercession, typically, as here, taking the form of the Buddha's own indiscriminate and all embracing love.

Thirdly Vajrayana Buddhism includes prayer to various

meditation Buddhas, deities and a panoply of other beings, which as noted are visualized in worship, but also dissolved. They have ultimately no separate reality apart from the one praying, any more than the one praying has a separate existence from them. Gross argues that Christians and Buddhists describe what happens in prayer in a very different metaphysics, involving a relationship with a real Other in one case, and in the other, non-dualism between the one praying and the one prayed to. But in terms of what goes on in practice there may not be such a big difference.

Each approach can learn from the other. Sometimes the Buddhist practice seems almost too global, too resistant to praying for specifics in a way that might lead eventually to specific action. As well as an upwelling of indiscriminate love, true prayer springs from empathy and compassion, feelings which are usually felt for specific people in specific situations. On the other hand Christians might learn from Buddhists to avoid the over-specific and self-indulgent shopping-list kind of prayer, and the prayer that sounds like reading the newspaper to God! God – in the Christian sense – does not need to be told what to worry about!

Finally, Kenneth Tanaka asks whether "God's monopoly of credits" (Gross and Muck, p.108) in Christian prayer is appropriate. Though in Christian terms all good things come from God, the Buddhist practice of mindfulness of all who have contributed to our well-being seems right in an age that is coming to realize our deep ecological interdependence. As well as God, should we not, in grace over meals, thank the cow, fish or broccoli, as well as the farmers, fishermen, traders and so forth, whose sacrifice enabled us to have the meal?

Worship

Now it is Christmas Eve. I am going to a celebratory party... I bathe, put on deodorants, talcum powder and after shave...

When I was involved with Buddhism we used to celebrate holy days by austerity, by extra-special seriousness. Soon, soon (we thought) the period of mourning will be over and we shall be liberated, enlightened, for ever. At the cathedral the tears we cry are tears of joy. Tomorrow we feast. And I shall drink wine.

(Williams, 2002, p.113)

Here Paul Williams contrasts Christian joy with Buddhist solemnity. The comparison is not altogether fair. Buddhists are often, in my experience, full of mirth, while Christians too have their times of intense solemnity and fasting, like Lent and Holy Week. But these fast periods are always preparations for celebrations like Christmas and Easter, in which Christians (at least the non-Puritan kinds) know how to feast and drink as Jesus is recording as having done. There is a sense in Christian worship and festivity that the Kingdom of God is given in the here and now, whereas many forms of in Buddhism, especially the Theravada, Nirvana can be very remote, with a sense of arduous struggle before we arrive.

'Worship' is the best overall term to cover all that goes on in Christian religious practice. This fact underlines perhaps the deepest difference between the two faiths. This chapter has shown that there are many practices that the one tradition can adopt or adapt from the other, and many more that contain insights that can inspire the other even if the practice itself is not adopted. But in Christianity (as in Judaism and Islam) all religious practice is directed to 'the knowledge and love of God'. It is done to express and cement a relationship with God. So it will express *eros* and *agapé*, desiring love and self-giving love. It will include elements of delight, joy and thanksgiving, and a kind of ecstasy in which the worshipper leaves self behind as she reaches out to the Other whom she knows but cannot know enough.

In Buddhism worship is not as absent as is sometimes thought in the West. 'Worship' and 'devotion' translate the term puja which is as much a regular feature of Buddhist practice as meditation, and often used to introduce it. This includes the solemn bow or prostration with hands folded before the sacred objects: the statue of the Buddha, the stupa and the Bodhi tree; the offering of light, flowers, incense, fruit, music and cleansing water; and chanting and ringing of bells. But integral as worship is in both popular and monastic Buddhism, it has a lower place than in Christianity. Liberation does not come through developing and expressing a relationship with God, so rejoicing and desire and ecstasy are not at the heart of Buddhist practice. The goal is not to reach out beyond the self but to let go of the self and achieve the ultimate tranquility of Nirvana. If there is joy in Nirvana, it is a serene, 'cool', still bliss rather than the 'warm' burning thanksgiving and rejoicing of Christianity.

Are these differences ultimate? It depends on whether the difference between having a God and having no God (or at least no personal God) is ultimate; and on whether the Christian overcoming of egocentric desire by other-centered, self-emptying desire, and the Buddhist letting go of all desire, are mutually exclusive. This is a matter Chapter 8 will explore.

5) Practices of the Body

All the practices described above involve the body in some way, because our thinking and imagining as well as our seeing and hearing and singing are all based on our bodily existence; nothing is in our minds that is not made up of images that come from our senses. So far from forgetting the body, spiritual practices like prayer and meditation involve bodily postures and actions. It is these I now describe, before turning to the special case of the Christian sacraments, where the union of the spiritual and the bodily is most strongly affirmed; and finally mentioning institutional bodies.

Bodily Acts

It is often thought that bodily posture matters in Buddhist meditation but makes no difference in Christian prayer. But this indifference is a relatively recent phenomenon. Early Christians, when they prayed, would stand, face east, and lift their hands palms upward; just as surely as Muslims, when they pray, face Mecca and prostrate. Prostrations and genuflections also have their place in the Christian act of prayer: Eastern Orthodox Christians prostrate themselves regularly during Lent, but are forbidden to do so in the Easter Season. In the Prayer of the Heart, in this tradition, a unique (and painful-sounding!) posture is recommended of sitting leaning forward with the head between the knees. The sign of the cross, the clasping of hands in prayer, and the holding together of the two little fingers and thumb in the sign of blessing, are among many gestures (Buddhists would call them mudras) widely used in Christian tradition. Even Protestant Christians who resist in principle such emphasis on posture and gesture often find themselves, when called to pray, bowing their heads and leaning forward on their seats. And in Pentecostal Christianity, hands raised in the ancient posture of adoration are a familiar sight. In the Judeo-Christian tradition, we are unities of body and soul, and we cannot pray, any more than we can clean the house or make love, without our bodies. Nor is Buddhist practice limited to meditation postures; prostrations are encouraged in many forms of Buddhism, notably the Vajrayana, which also makes use of the special dance-like hand-gestures called mudras.

According to some, the differences between the 'normal' postures in the two faiths express something of the essence of each. D.T. Suzuki contrasts the vertical position of Christ on the cross with the horizontal position of the Buddha at his death, and declares that standing is the authentic Christian position – the stance of the servant attending to his master and ready to execute his orders – while the more tranquil lotus position, rooted to the earth, expresses the essence of what Buddhism aims for. The Benedictine scholar Gabriel Bunge (1996) goes so far as to suggest that the lotus position, though adopted by some Christians, is not an authentic position for Christian prayer because it inherently expresses the Buddhist world view.

To me, such comments seem a little extreme. Christianity, after all, knows the resting Christ of the deposition from the cross, while the Buddha is often depicted standing and teaching. My own favorite position for prayer is the 'Burma' position: kneeling on a prayer stool with the weight evenly poised between the bottom and the two knees. The erect spine makes for Buddhist tranquility, but unlike the lotus position, this position allows one to express – for example in bowing forward or even prostrating – the loving devotion to which Christian meditation may lead.

The lively use of the body in dance is discouraged in mainstream Christianity and Buddhism alike, though it is found in Charismatic Christianity and the Nembutsu dancing of Pure Land Buddhism (Brazier, p.261ff). The unconventional Zen teacher Gabrielle Roth teaches people to dance to different kinds of music in a series of five rhythms she believes to be a natural outward expression of spiritual progress: flowing and graceful, punchy and staccato, chaotic and frenzied, formal and lyrical, and still. The 'still' corresponds to traditional meditation, and the 'lyrical' is to be found in the gracious, stately gestures of Orthodox and Catholic worship, but the first three rhythms are much easier for those in our culture of dance and pop to relate to. And many – she claims – find it easier to evoke and express a spirituality through bodily movement than through stillness. Each or us needs to find the natural place which we gravitate towards, and then learn how to explore the other rhythms of the soul.

Sacraments

There is nothing in Buddhism quite like the Christian mysteries (as the Orthodox call them) or sacraments, of which Baptism and the Eucharist or Holy Communion are the best known and most universally accepted. (Roman and Anglican Catholics and Orthodox also count as sacraments Confirmation, Anointing for Healing, Confession, Marriage and Ordination.) Sacraments are rooted in the incarnation of God in Christ, which is thought to enable human and material signs – like the water of baptism, and the bread and wine of communion – to be God-bearing. All of them in some way make present now the historical work of Christ, acting as a material sign and means whereby spiritual grace is given to the believer (see Thompson, 2006).

Though Buddhism is rich in symbolic acts, it does not share the understanding of history, or the idea of matter as the expression of its Creator, upon which the sacraments rely. For Mahayana Buddhism at least, matter is ultimately illusory and mind alone is real, if anything is. Sacraments, as the expression of spirit in matter, rely on a duality between spirit and matter that Buddhism does not possess – even if in the sacrament this duality is profoundly healed. The sense of participating in God through ordinary matter like bread and wine and oil and water is, for me and for many, one of the riches of Christianity we would not lightly forgo.

However, in the summers of 2007 and 2008 I was privileged to participate in a Tibetan Buddhist puja in which the Dhyani Buddha Chenrezig was imagined in great detail, only to be dissolved in the imagination as we quietly muttered Chenrezig's mantra, *om mani peme hum*. This time of dissolving felt to me uncannily like the time of receiving holy communion, despite the vast differences in the context.

It occurred to me then that the whole structure of the Christian Eucharist is not unlike a Vajrayana Buddhist puja. Both could be seen as a conversion of the ancient sacrificial practice –

the offering, dismembering and consuming of a victim – into something peaceable and spiritual. In the puja Chenrezig or another deity is corporately imagined, then dissolved, then realized in the heart center of the believer. At the Eucharist, Christians call to mind the teachings of Christ, and invoke his presence in the bread and wine, which is uplifted by the priest for all to see. So Christ is 'visualized' and 'realized' in the gathered community. But then the bread of Christ is broken, shared out and consumed. The outward sign of Christ is dissolved. And it gives way to the inner reality, Christ realized in the heart of his people, as they in turn dissolve and disperse the presence of Christ throughout the neighborhood.

After this point it becomes inappropriate to reverence the outwards signs of bread and wine. As an Anglican Catholic priest I used to be very shocked at the practice of some Protestant churches of casting the unused consecrated bread to the winds, to be eaten by the birds. But now it seems to me right that the Eucharistic presence of Christ in the bread and wine should be dissolved completely, either into those who share in communion, or into the wider cosmos.

After all, the risen Christ of the Gospels seems to dissolve himself in just this way. At the breaking of bread on the road to Emmaus (Luke 24.30-32), Jesus, once recognized by the disciples, does not linger to be adored. The moment of recognition is the very moment of disappearance. But while outwardly vanishing, he remains, as the fire burning within the disciples' hearts.

In the way in which the Evangelist lets a cult meal of the resurrected one shine through in a profane meal in the inn and lets the participants recognize him as this one in the breaking of the bread and also to disappear from their sight, we have a parallel to the quick extinguishing of the 'objective'... in favor of the non-objectifiable fire of the heart. (Buri, p.63)

Though sacraments are a wonderful Christian treasure, there is always a danger (as Protestants have seen so clearly) that they may become idols in which the presence of God is located and possessed. They should never be regarded as ends in themselves, but a variety of what Buddhists call 'skilful means'. As such, Christians have something to learn from the butter sculpture, the graciousness of allowing what is infinitely precious to us to dissolve and disappear from our sight.

The Body of the Community

As well as the individual body, a religion is embodied in a community. The Church is indeed likened by St. Paul to the body of Christ, in the interdependence of its parts (individual Christians) and in its being regarded as an embodiment of the presence of Christ on earth. Both Buddhism and Christianity sustain a rich convivial life in the communities in which they are set, and have a ministry to local institutional 'bodies'. I cannot explore all this now, merely record how much the local Christian community has always meant to me, both as a priest and as a layperson. At the same time I know that both religions have often imposed on their communities in oppressive ways.

I hope I have said enough elsewhere about the importance of engaging in a liberating way with community, politics and history. So I do not need to add anything now, except make the obvious statement that these are all part of the practice whereby the liberation the faiths promised are actually realized (or not) in life. In the end they are the most important part of this practice; which is why it is so important that the end results of the religious practices are dissolved as outward objects of veneration, to become realized in the life of the community.

Summary

1. It would not be appropriate to devise an amalgam of Christian and Buddhist religious practice. Nevertheless the

two faiths can to learn much from one another that will deepen their own faith practice.

2. Meditation is probably the most frequent oriental practice that Christians have used, though it is a shame that the Christian tradition of meditation leading to contemplation is a widely forgotten one.

3. Mindfulness can be practiced at any time, and it can root a Christian in the material world, enabling her to serve God with body as well as mind in the humblest of tasks.

4. There is rich visual imagery in both faith traditions. Christians can learn much from the practice of dissolving the imagined image rather than letting it become a permanent inner idol.

5. The reading and singing of the whole of scripture through the year is a practice that could enrich Buddhism, while Buddhist readings might well enrich the Christian lectionary.

6. Confession of sin is crucial to Christianity and many Buddhist traditions, but Christians need to ask if a sense of unconditional forgiveness should not precede every act of confession.

7. Christians can learn from Buddhism not to offer egocentric shopping lists of prayers, and that to intercede rightly, they need first to awaken ultimate love within them. But the Christian specificity of prayer serves to root it in the real world and direct it towards appropriate action.

8. Christian practice is directed towards the worship, knowledge and love of God, while Buddhist practice is aimed at a liberation which the notion of God can impede.

9. The Christian sacraments wonderfully express the active presence of the ultimate in the everyday. But to be means of grace and not ends in themselves, they need to be 'dissolved'.

All in all the exploration of religious practice opens up rich areas for possible cross-fertilization. But – especially at point 8 – it confronts a seeming impasse regarding God and the self. To see whether that impasse can be overcome, we need to look at the deep and ultimate issues which will be the subject of Chapter 8. To prepare the way for those issues, Chapter 7 will investigate how the two faiths look at the 'penultimate reality' of the universe.

Chapter 7

The Hollow Flute: Life, Time, the Universe and Everything

The antagonism of science is not to religion, but to the heathen survivals and the bad philosophy under which religion herself is often well-nigh crusted. And, for my part, I trust that this antagonism will never cease; but that, to the end of time, true science will continue to fulfill one of her most beneficent functions, that of relieving people from the burden of false science which is imposed upon them in the name of religion.
(T.H. Huxley, 1876)

One of the surprises of the early 21st century is the revival of the conflicts between 'Science' and 'Religion' (capitalized to show that they are, one way round or another, the representatives of Good and Evil) that began in the 19th century and peaked early in the 20th. Once again the self-appointed advocates of Science are on the warpath against a revived belief in a six-day non-evolutionary account of creation.

Now it seems to me that in principle there is no more conflict between science and religion than there is competition between a greengrocer's and a butcher's. Science as the experimental exploration of the possibilities of the physical world, and religion as the exploration of ultimate meanings and values, are about different, albeit overlapping things. The grocer and the butcher may overlap in their trades; both for example may sell cheese, and this will create no problems. But if a butcher starts selling cauliflowers, or the grocer venison, conflict arises. When 'false science' – for example, earth-centered astronomy or six-day creationism – is 'imposed...in the name of religion', it is like a butcher selling cauliflowers. And when science tries to dictate people's ultimate values – when it becomes what some call 'scientism' – conflict arises. Of course most scientists regard ultimate realities and meanings, and the ordering and wellbeing of society, as well beyond the scope of scientific enquiry, and shun scientism. But scientism – which relates to science rather as fundamentalism does to authentic religion – is, like all fundamentalisms, currently undergoing a revival.

The response of some theologians is to urge, in effect, that religion has nothing to do with reality as we know it. God is 'wholly other' and on the question of his existence, the scientific exploration of reality provides neither evidence nor counter-evidence. This again is odd, because it has been convincingly argued (e.g. by Jaki, 1986) that the scientific study of reality gained more headway in the West than anywhere else partly because the monotheistic faiths taught people that the universe was not a meaningless flux but precisely a creation by a Creator who reveals his rationality, his Logos, in the way the world is. This was the kind of rationality which we as rational beings might discover through scientific enquiry. It is as if the universe as a rationally designed machine, promoted by Christianity, is now turning on its own Designer, to consume everything that is not mechanistic. But what is a machine without design? Ironically the world of Buddhism, which does not hold that the universe is rationally designed, and never encouraged scientific exploration, is much less threatened by the inroads of modern science than Christianity.

I do not think that the universe 'proves' the existence of God; in many ways the world seems to me dependently co-arisen, as the Buddhists say, rather than created. But I have long believed there is a "spirituality of matter" (Thompson, 1990) and a spiritual core to the scientific study of matter; and I now believe a Buddhist Christianity shows its worth not least by the way it dovetails with such a spirituality. That is why I precede the chapter on 'ultimate reality' with a chapter on what we could call 'penultimate reality'. By this I mean going deeper than we normally do in our daily lives into how the world is, in a way that touches on, but does not settle, issues of what it ultimately means.

So this chapter is intended not to 'answer' the challenge of scientism, but to develop the encounter between Christianity and Buddhism by bringing both into a 'trialogue' with aspects of today's scientific world view. Non-polemically it will map out some paths of interaction between our two great faiths and the findings of science. We shall see that in some ways modern science offers great opportunities for a Buddhist world view, but in some less acknowledged ways the case for a Christian understanding has actually been strengthened by scientific findings. Altogether modern science represents both challenge and opportunity for both faiths, and to respond creatively, each faith may need to adopt insights from the other. In other words, a Buddhist Christianity coheres well with what science is currently saying about the cosmos; better, in some ways, than some aspects of traditional Buddhism and Christianity.

This chapter could be seen as a debate between three inner figures recognizable from my biography: the dogmatically 'scientistic' atheist of my later childhood, the Buddhist of my teens, lately revived, and the Christian who dominated for much of my adult life. It will consider five main questions about the universe which Buddhism, Christianity and science answer in different ways. But it will deal with the questions non-sequentially, because the answers are interwoven with the different departments of science in complex ways.

1. Is the universe reducible to simple entities we can understand, like atoms?
2. Is it real, and if so, in what does its reality consist – mind, matter, or both?
3. What holds it together – the law of karma, divine provi-

dence, or 'blind' causality, or indeed nothing at all?

4. Is it hostile or friendly, violent or peaceful? Does human morality run with or against the grain of the universe?

5. Does it develop and grow through time? Or is time basically cyclical or reversible?

We will look at three main areas where science has been felt to challenge religious and especially Christian standpoints. Working from the microscopic to cosmic scale, quantum physics is first considered; it raises issues 1 and 2, asking deep philosophical questions about reductionism, materialism and the nature of reality and causality which challenge traditional science as much as traditional religion. Then the book turns to biology and in particular the theory of evolution, which raises mainly issues 3 and 4, posing familiar questions about the role of divine providence, purpose, and (less commonly discussed) karma. Finally the chapter turns to cosmology: the theory of how the universe came to be, and how it is going to end, which raises questions 4 and 5, but also, via quantum cosmology, feeds back into 1. In some ways cosmology parries the thrust of the evolutionary critique. It raises again the question of the mind and purpose of God *vis-à-vis* a more Buddhist interdependent co-arising of everything, which leads into the discussion of God and Emptiness in the next Chapter.

Area 1: Quantum Physics, Mind and Matter

Since Fritjof Capra's much acclaimed and much criticized *The Tao of Physics* (1975) and David Bohm's more difficult but seminal *Wholeness and the Implicate Order* (1983) it has become commonplace in some quarters that quantum physics has sounded a death knell for the reductionistic, mechanical and deterministic world of classical physics, and opened the way to a more holistic approach that favors some religious views, especially those Eastern ones, including Buddhism and Taoism, that resist dualism, think holistically, and deny any hard and fast reality outside of mind.

This is partly true, but exaggerated. It is true that we can no longer be reductionistic, deterministic *and* objectivist about reality; we shall see that one of these features of classical physics has to surrender, but not necessarily all three. Scientists have not been dragged kicking and screaming into a holistic universe, though some have chosen to take that pathway, the door to which lies more open than before.

Unlike the evolutionary and cosmological theories discussed later, quantum physics is absolutely confirmed by all experimental evidence to date. It is the interpretation, not the theory itself, that is controversial; though quite often one possible interpretation is cited as if it were the uncontroversial theory itself.

The evidential basis for quantum physics is manifold, but best known are two effects that cannot be accounted for in terms of classical physics:

i) **Wave-Particle Duality.** When light is projected through two fine slits onto a screen, a wavelike interference pattern results. The effect is just as we would find if waves of water passed through two openings and then onto a shore. However, if the light is low the particles pass through the holes one at a time, and leave on the screen point-like marks suggesting the light consists of tiny particles. But they still show the wavelike interference. The particles, passing one at a time, cannot be interfering with each other; they must in some sense be interfering with themselves, as if each particle passed through both slits! (When I see a motorway sign saying 'use both lanes' I now get terrified that I am being asked to do as the quantum particle does, using both at once!)

ii) **Uncertainty.** The more exactly we measure the position of a particle, the less exactly we can know its momentum, and vice versa. If we measure the position precisely, the momentum can only be assigned a set of more or less probable values spread over a range, and *vice versa*.

The 18th century physicist Laplace believed in a total determinism. He told the king of France that if he knew the position and momentum of every particle now, he would be able to deduce the entire past and future of the universe. Quantum physics now tells us that we cannot know this about the particles – and not just because our measuring instruments are not up to scratch, but in principle.

On the other hand, it tells us we can know the position-and-momentum together, which is given by a wave function, and this wave function does evolve in a deterministic way. But then again, the wave function does not describe anything that can exist in our three-dimensional space and time. It consists not of quantities with straightforward values, but of operators in a multi-dimensional kind of space called 'Hilbert space'. Quantum physics is 'uncertain' in that it consists not of definable things and quantities in ordinary space, but operations in hyper-space.

You may ask, if this is quantum reality, why do we see things as existing in 3D space and causing one another in an ordered and predictable way? The interim answer is first, that upon observation the deterministic, multi-dimensional quantum description 'collapses' (unpredictably) into our 3D space; and second, on the large scale on which we exist, the unpredictable quantum effects cancel out into something more predictable, just as the random movements of atoms in a river betray *en masse* a predictable flow.

That is the interim answer. But it does not quite make sense. What on earth is the status of this strange quantum world, and what on earth do we mean by saying it 'collapses' into our familiar world when we perceive things? At least sixteen kinds of answer have been proposed, but the answers fall into three main families. Looking at these three families takes us to the heart of the shattering impact quantum physics ought to have on our thinking, one way or another.

Three Kinds of Interpretation
Essentially the options that have been considered are:

1. our everyday world is the 'real' world and the quantum world a useful mathematical 'fiction';
2. the quantum world is the 'real' world and our everyday world is a kind of fiction based on it;
3. the quantum world is real and our everyday word is a kind of sub-world within it.

The first option is the **Copenhagen interpretation** which was agreed by Niels Bohr and Werner Heisenberg in 1927 and has since become the most widely agreed interpretation among scientists. On this understanding, quantum physics does not describe an underlying reality: it is just a set of equations that prove useful for predicting events in the actual world we know. This approach applies the positivism to which many scientists subscribe, to the effect that science is about measurement, not metaphysics. The scientist's job is to get the mathematics that best correlates and predicts our measurements, not to discover reality. The motto suggests itself, "don't speculate, just calculate."

Buddhism might welcome such restraint. For there is a strong trend in Buddhism that might be given the motto, "don't speculate, just liberate!" Avoid metaphysics, and concern yourself with the practice... in the scientists' case, the practice of discovering new technologies for manipulating matter to our advantage, and in the Buddhists' case, the practice of the Eightfold Path, leading to Nirvana. Christians might respond differently, but equally positively, welcoming a scientific viewpoint that leaves to others the task of describing ultimate reality and values, rendering scientism impossible.

Other scientists however have been less happy, and have taken the second option, appealing to **hidden variables**. To the end of his life Einstein resisted the role of statistics in quantum physics, which contrasted with the determinism of his own relativity theories. He insisted that 'God does not play dice'. Likewise David Bohm disparaged the "irreducible lawlessness" (1983, p.75) of the Copenhagen interpretation. He urged that random effects – for example, the random fall of a die – arise from lack of knowledge of, or inability to calculate, causes that are actually deterministic. If we knew everything about the status of the die when it was thrown, and the physics of the air currents in the vicinity and the wood of the table on which it landed, we would be able to predict which face it would land on. Likewise, he argued that quantum randomness must arise from factors that are too small for us to observe.

There is a widespread misunderstanding of quantum physics that regards its randomness and uncertainty as arising from the crudeness of our measuring instruments and the way they interfere with the physical objects we are trying to measure. The problem with this is at least twofold. Firstly, in quantum physics it is not only the act of measuring things that affects the result we get in our experiments, but also the non-act of not measuring them! And secondly, the effect of measuring can span huge distances. The famous example of this is the Einstein-Podolsky-Rosen 'experiment' (actually an experiment in thinking, though the implications for physical reality are well attested). Suppose in a very distant star a particle splits into two particles of opposite spin. One of these arrives on earth and is measured for its spin. The measurement 'collapses' the wave-function of the particle into one of two possible spin-states. But then logically the other particle, which is now far away in space, must at the very same instant also have its wave-function collapsed into the opposite spin. The effect of the measurement propagates instantaneously, even though in relativity theory it cannot do so faster than light.

Bohm's radical solution was to embrace the paradox of a world with such instantaneous effects. He believed that quantum physics gives us access to something that is altogether unlike reality as described in classical physics, and equally unlike the reality we think we know, with its material objects moving around in space. The latter is the 'explicate order' we impose by our thought and language on a much more holistic 'implicate order', which is structured rather like a hologram. In a hologram, a three-dimensional image of an object is stored in every part, so that every part of reality contains, in some sense, the whole. Karl Pribram (1993) has mustered evidence that the brain stores memories and ideas like a hologram. Those who

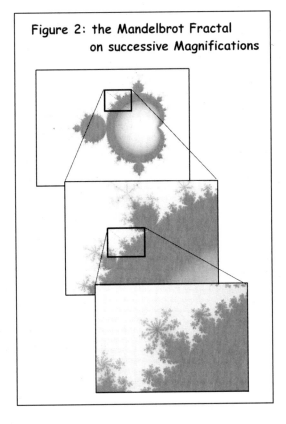

Figure 2: the Mandelbrot Fractal
on successive Magnifications

know Buddhism may be reminded of the *jijimuge* teaching of the Kegon school, which states that everything interpenetrates everything else.

Meanwhile the beautiful work of Benoit Mandelbrot (1982) has made us familiar also with the fractal, which is a geometrical pattern designed in accordance with a mathematical law such that each part resembles the whole pattern. Moreover, there is no bottom layer: as we magnify the fractal (see **Figure 2**) it never reaches a stage where we encounter the ultimate elements it is made of, only smaller versions of the big pattern, often with intriguing variations. Could reality develop like a fractal, in accord with deterministic laws, but laws which create ever new variations on the theme? And could it, like a fractal, be bottomless, having no atomic bottom level out of which all is made, only a law according to which all is made?

The Copenhagen interpretation treats the quantum world as a useful fiction and so allows us to 'save' the reality of our conventional world, while Bohm affirms the strange quantum universe as the real world and regards conventional world as a kind of fiction 'explicated' from it. The third option is to affirm the reality of the quantum world, but to allow our conventional world also to be real, but only as one of the **many worlds** that arise from different 'collapses' of the wave function in the quantum world. The physicists Everett and DeWitt retained determinism in a different way from Bohm, by proposing that when the wave function splits, *all* possibilities are realized in alternative universes. The statistical uncertainty is overcome by suggesting that the way things turn out in our world – seemingly by chance – is only one of many ways in which they actually turn out. The die is thrown, and we in our world see it falling on one side, but in reality it falls on all six sides, creating a different world for each side it lands on!

This view may seem even more fantastic than Bohm's implicate order, and seems to create infinitely more universes than we need! But it has a respectable scientific following, and as we shall see, forms the basis of one of the main contenders in modern cosmology.

Groundless Lawfulness

On the face of it, all three interpretations are much more devastating for classical physics than for Buddhist or Christian world views. Classical physics presented a world that is *unified* (a single interconnected whole), *objective* (existing 'outside' us and independently of our observations of it), *reductionistic* (made of independent parts which ultimately explain everything about it) and *deterministic* (every event having a cause such that we could in principle have predicted it). Different interpretations sacrifice different features in the interests of preserving others. Broadly, the Copenhagen interpretation safeguards scientific method and results at the expense of any pretence of describing objective reality, deterministic or otherwise, though in practice reductionistic explanations are allowed to remain because they prove so useful. Bohm emphasizes unity, objectivity and determinism but profoundly opposes reductionism. And the many-worlds view safeguards determinism and objectivity but sacrifices the unity of the cosmos in favor of a radical fragmentation into parts that cannot know of each other at all.

The alliance of Christianity and its doctrine of Creation with Greek rationalism have given it a traditional liking for an objective world of discrete law-abiding objects. While Christianity has rejected wholesale determinism and reductionism, because they undermine human freedom and the soul, the Christian world view was, as noted above, one in which scientific enquiry made sense. It is Christianity that gave birth to the scientific 'dragon' that now threatens to devour it. But now that dragon, in quantum physics, seems to be consuming instead the determinism and reductionism that are the claws and teeth of its attack!

Buddhism is often vaguely presented, along with other

oriental faiths, as holding to holistic view of the world, making it a natural ally of the quantum revolution in physics. And it is true that each of the three interpretations coheres with some aspects of Buddhism. The refusal of metaphysical speculation in the Copenhagen interpretation is close to the spirit of Buddhism at least in its Theravada and Zen forms. Bohm's implicate order resonates with certain Mahayana teachings, notably *jijimuge*. And the many-worlds idea finds an (imprecise) echo in the Buddhist understanding that the world has been through an infinite number of cycles, so the world we know is only one of an infinity. Finally it is worth noting that the universe as described in quantum physics is nearly all emptiness, but not an empty emptiness. What looks vacant to us is a teeming sea of virtual particles forever appearing and annihilating. It is a 'full emptiness', a prolific womb that suggests something of the Buddhist *Sunyata*, of which more in the next chapter.

However, karma does require a strong, if not deterministic, notion of causality. And Buddhism in its chariot analogy for the self has a strong reductionistic dimension. Some varieties of Buddhism hold to materialism, and though other forms have waxed metaphysical, it is possible to state the core truths of Buddhism in an atheist and materialist perspective, without reference to the soul or the supernatural, in a way that is not easy for Christianity.

But what we mean by reductionism and determinism needs teasing out. Too often the issues are polarized, such that the deterministic and reductionistic world of classical physics is opposed to the more 'spiritual,' holistic and free world of the religions (and on some interpretations, quantum physics). But reductionism versus holism, and determinism versus freedom, are independent variables, giving us four possibilities.

1. Reductionism and determinism: everything is made of utterly predictable particles. This is classical **materialism**.

2. Reductionism and freedom: ultimately everything is made of particles and nothing else, but when they combine into larger wholes: these wholes exhibit new relationships that allow for awareness and freedom. This process is often described as **emergence,** a concept that allows for degrees such that human beings can be seen as continuous with the more complex animals.

3. Non-reductionism and freedom: the idea that human freedom and consciousness derive from something irreducible to matter, often called the soul. One version of this is the **dualism** in which Christianity, at least since its adoption of the thought of Plato, has tended to express itself. Historically dualism has tended to place a sharper division between humans and the animals than the alternative views do, because animals have been assumed to lack the divinely implanted soul.

4. Non-reductionism and determinism. This is perhaps the understanding that is least often explored, though it is what Bohm's theory implies. The fractal gives us a model for a reality that is utterly deterministic, all of it following a mathematical law, yet capable of producing unpredictable new forms. I have used the term "transcendent monism" (1990, p.207) to describe a world view based on such a model. But I now prefer the more down-to-earth phrase '**groundless lawfulness**' to describe the uncanny combination of lawfulness and unpredictable spontaneity, regular pattern and irreducible bottomlessness, that seems to characterize the world we live in. As the next chapter will explore, the Emptiness and *Dharmakaya* of Mahayana Buddhism, express such a groundless lawfulness, which also seems to be the essence of the Tao (Way) of Taoism. What unifies the world is not *what* it is made of but *how* it moves and evolves.

Quantum physics undermines the notions of particles with precisely identifiable position and momentum, but describes a wave-function which evolves according to deterministic law. This seems to exemplify the groundless lawfulness I am describing.

Because it does not reduce the world to 'things' of any kind, the world of groundless lawfulness is not made up of material things or mental sensations or ideas. It is not made of anything at all; it is like a tune played on the hollow flute of nothingness, or a "divinely stirred something happening to nothing" (Thompson, 1990, p.254). So as we shall see, Buddhists speak of 'emptiness' and Christians (in a different vein) of 'creation out of nothing'.

Now just as quantum reality can be seen as bearing wave-like or particle-like qualities, so the event stream of groundless lawfulness can be seen as bearing a mental or a material aspect. According to David Pears (1967, p.142), the philosopher Bertrand Russell at one stage moved from a view that reduced everything to sensations in the mind to a "neutral monism":

> [Russell's] theory of sense-data had flattened the world against the window-pane of perception; but at least it had left a detached observer within. But now the observer too vanished into the glass, and the world became a transparent wafer.

What Buddhist meditation seeks to realize seems very like such a 'flattening' of my opaque observing ego on the one hand, and the world of solid desirable objects on the other, into a transparent wafer in which the ungraspable flow of life is realized beyond the dualism of mind and matter, subject and object. To refer back to the butterfly dream, I cease to dream the world into 'things' that 'I' can possess, and cease to know if I am dreaming the world or the world is dreaming me.

The familiar 'emergence' approach describes matter, as it evolves into ever more complex wholes, coming to manifest the activities of mind and consciousness. But scientists and philosophers have shown no clear way of correlating these activities to material happenings (cf Chalmers, 1996; Wallace, 2009) Perhaps the 'groundless lawfulness' approach should be preferred. This would describe an evolving pattern which can be known or 'realized' in different ways. Measured quantitively it would be manifest as matter, but enjoyed for its qualities it would be realized as sensation and consciousness. We can look at a person and see only carbon, hydrogen and other elements, or we can see an embodied soul like our own. We can look at a gene and see only a spiral molecule, or we can see (see below) one more solution found in the thought of God.

Are We Responsible?

But what is the force of 'law' in 'groundless lawfulness'? Here we encounter perhaps the deepest divide between science and religion. Science wants a deterministic universe, because it seeks to discover laws that govern the world and does not want exceptions. But both Buddhism and Christianity want to make people free and responsible for their actions. If everything is determined, and evolves 'lawfully' the way it has to, what room is there for freedom and responsibility?

Part of the answer here lies in the just-mentioned spontaneity and newness that seems to be compatible with 'bottomless' laws like those we find in fractals. Though the fractal follows fixed laws, it may still posses what mathematicians call 'computational universality'. This means that its behavior cannot be predicted in advance by any model simpler than the fractal itself. The universe could be lawful in the same way. The only way we could work out what was going to happen next would be to build an exact replica of the whole universe, run that vast replica, and observe the results! Of course there is another, rather less demanding way of getting the same results. We might just observe the universe itself and see what happens in it! The universe, in this case, is deterministic but unpredictable and for practical purposes full of freedom. You could say that from a God's-eye view the future development of the world is determined, but from our point of view it is free.

> In your book were written all the days that were formed for me when none of them as yet existed. (Ps.139.16)

But that book, which God has written from eternity, is not one we humans can read.

The rejection of reductionism in 'groundless lawfulness' is vital to this understanding. Reductionism allows us to build simpler models of atoms and so forth to which the world is 'reduced'. By observing what happens to that simpler model, we can predict what will happen in the real world. But in our 'bottomless' world, though there may be simpler models that work in particular circumstances, there is no general model from which we can predict the world's behavior that is simpler than the world itself.

The kind of determinism involved in this view does not subject us to anything alien like the 'iron laws of matter'. Unlike some classical accounts of physics, in which the laws of matter were seen as ultimately the laws that governed the brain and hence the mind, the determinism of quantum physics refers only to the wave-function; it actually generates unpredictability in terms of what we observe. So it is not a case of 'matter over mind'! In classical physics, as noted, the observing mind is separate from the world it measures, but in quantum physics observer and observed form a single interactive whole. So the determinism of quantum physics involves our contribution. What will happen in the future is wholly determined by what is going on now. But this is not in spite of anything I can do about it, but on the contrary, partly because of what I am doing about it now.

And this determinism that includes my free involvement is

surely just what responsibility requires. We cannot responsibly decide on any course of action if the future effects of our actions are very unpredictable. And responsibility also involves an understanding and acknowledgement of the past influences that have made us who we are. Of course, responsibility means that we are one of the factors that determine the outcome of our acts, but we can only be one factor, and we ourselves are partly determined. Nothing more endangers genuine responsibility than thinking of ourselves as totally free and autonomous agents. If we think that, we are all the more likely to act according to psychological factors to which we have made ourselves blind.

It may seem threatening to think that my actions follow the laws that govern the whole universe. But if what is threatened is my sense of having a self-constituting, independent ego, that threat is altogether a good thing. If I have to surrender some of my sense of self-reliance, and see myself as part of a cosmic whole, both Buddhists and Christians ought to welcome that. In fact both Buddhist karma and Christian predestination call into question the kind of total autonomy of the self, which as Chapter 4 noted is such a central article of faith in the modern world view.

The doctrine of karma views our actions as enmeshed in an immensely long and complex web of previous causes and future effects. D. T. Suzuki criticizes the individualistic version of karma which speaks as if I were the only one to suffer for my bad actions, so that karma works with perfect justice. He advocates the authentically Buddhist understanding that "deeds, once committed, leave permanent effects on the general system of sentient beings... and it is not the actor himself, but everybody constituting a grand psychic community ... that suffers or enjoys the outcome of a moral deed" (1963, p.193). He goes on to use the familiar Buddhist analogy of the stone that causes circles of ripples to travel throughout a pond, and then return back to the stone again. And he states that "as far as a general theory of determinism is concerned, Buddhism has no objection to it" (p.197).

Quite how I and the world around me together determine outcomes is, of course, a mystery this chapter has not the space to explore. But the intertwining of self and other is a fundamental feature of groundless lawfulness. And it is just what makes for genuine responsibility in our actions. One analogy might be the playing of a part in a play or a symphony. The words I am to speak or the note I am to play are part of the fixed script. But I can play my part well or badly, and how I perform my individual part can radically affect whether the whole goes well or badly. I need to listen to the symphony as it unfolds, be ready with my contribution and play it with all my skill and sense of responsibility, and then allow the remainder to unfold.

On this analogy, a strong degree of determinism actually increases our freedom. We might compare modern individualism with a situation where each person in the orchestra is free to play whatever note on whatever instrument she likes. The result is a cacophony where each note relates to nothing else; once it is played, it is forgotten. In strong user-involved determinism, on the other hand, though the variation in what I can play is tightly constrained, my subtle variations will have great impact on how the symphony sounds. Karma is very realistic about the constraints the past places on my present freedom, but by the very same token, variations within that small area of freedom ripple out into truly cosmic significance.

Area 2: Evolution, Karma and Creation
But does this mean that Buddhism and Christianity can fully embrace the perspective which sees the human as part of a seamless train of causality that traces it back to the animal and the animal in turn back to the primeval slime? Is mind just a predetermined outcome of the laws of matter? And can the moral law be derived from the laws of nature 'red in tooth and claw'? These questions take us from the quandaries of quantum physics to those evolutionary theories that have often been viewed as most

directly in conflict with religious, or at least Christian, belief.

Darwin's Wasp

Central to Christianity is belief in a God who created the world and "saw that it was good", and who continues to love, order and provide for it. Buddhism lacks this belief but does believe that the world follows the law of karma that rewards good actions and punishes bad ones. It has been argued, from the point of view of traditional theology (Schmidt-Leukel, 2006) and from the point of view of process theology (Aasulv Lande in the same volume) that the doctrine of karma implies a basic goodness and justice in creation and is therefore equivalent to the creation doctrine. The arguments are not entirely convincing, since two ideas can have similar implications without being equivalent. But the differences fade by comparison with the world of evolution, in which divine providence and karmic justice are equally lacking.

Sometimes the conflict between Darwinism and religion is seen as a specific conflict between the stories offered in Genesis and in modern science. If this were so the conflict would only involve Judaism and Christianity, in whose Bible the creation story occurs. But the real problem with Darwin's account is that it describes how all the different species can be explained without any reference to divine providence, solely in terms of the blind casual processes whereby species pass on their characteristics with minor variations. Nature ruthlessly weeds out the less well-adapted variations, and the best adapted survive.

Since Darwin's time scientists have discovered and analyzed the mechanism by which traits are passed on from one generation to the next, namely the gene, or more precisely the large and complex DNA molecule that lies at the heart of each cell. This has opened up the possibility of explaining the whole evolution of life, up to and including humanity, in terms of the deterministic and chance factors discussed in the previous section. We move away from a perspective in which 'man' is the hero, the pinnacle of life on earth, to one in which *Homo sapiens* is just one more mutation in an ongoing process that will in time produce more complex and better adapted forms. If there is a hero of the story of life, it is the gene itself. Richard Dawkins has famously coined the term 'selfish gene' to describe a world in which the bodies of the living species we see are just the structures genes organize in order to propagate as many copies of themselves as possible, at the expense of others.

This dethroning of 'man' does not fit well with the traditional Christian perspective. The ruthlessness of competition between species – epitomized for Darwin in many species of wasp that lay their eggs in the bodies of caterpillars and other insects, to hatch and slowly eat their way out through the bodies of their hosts – does not fit well with the providence of a God who knows and cares every time a sparrow falls (Matt. 10.29). And the lion who, on defeating his rival and taking charge of the pride, kills all his rival's cubs to make way for siring his own, may well be doing what best advances the likelihood of his genes being spread. But the world which rewards this kind of competition and aggression – hardly Buddhist virtues – sits ill with karmic justice.

The Creative Gene
However, to attribute 'competition' to species, and still more 'selfishness' to genes, may be rather anthropomorphic. Neither species nor genes nor (most) individual animals and plants have intentions, so they cannot be 'selfish', nor are they machines purposely designed to do anything. They just are what they are, and they do what follows from their structure and nature. And as well as competing, they co-operate and weave intricate ecological webs. Survival in such webs is as much about interdependence as it is about outperforming rivals. But this is no more altruistic than the competition is selfish.

Now in this context a world with pain and struggle may

actually be better than one without them. At least, that is what evolution has decided. "Pain is eminently useful in survival, and it will be naturally selected, on average, as functional pain. Natural selection requires pain as much as pleasure in its construction of concern and caring; pain is an alarm system in a world where there are helps and hurts through which a sentient organism must move," (Rolston, 1999, p.304). A world of rocks and trees could be painless, but perhaps it would not be possible to create a painless world of sentient, self-moving beings, especially ones that look after each other.

But let us follow through the logic of Dawkins' selfish gene. This concept rests on a very fruitful comparison with the 'meme'. Dawkins speaks of the DNA as comprising "protein sentences" complete with grammar, syntax and meaning. And just as genes propagate themselves as much as they can in competition with others, and the best adapted survive, so it is, Dawkins says, with the human ideas, symbols and practices that propagate in culture through mimesis, imitation (much as we noted in connection with mimetic desire). So by analogy with 'genes' he describes these propagating ideas and practices as 'memes'.

Now this analogy might be developed further, by noting how large-scale structures like cultures and religions and sciences are in some ways analogous to the bodies that genes construct to propagate themselves. But some such bodies have survival value, among them the religions, which seem to outlast the cultures that for a time host them. Religions are like successful animal species, complex creatures well adapted to the very niches they have helped to create, and I do not quite understand why Dawkins respects them less than he respects the successful species.

But my main point is this. If there is an analogy between the gene and the meme, it can work both ways. If the wonders of humanity and the 'higher' animals have evolved seamlessly from the primeval slime, then that need not be seen as demeaning the human as if humans were just slime. Rather we ought to honor the slime for its (long-term) human potential. And if our ideas propagate like genes, then genes propagate like ideas. They represent what Simon Conway Morris describes as "life's solutions" (2003), testing out different ways of inhabiting the world. Only relatively few structures and patterns of behavior 'solve' well the problems life poses, which is why evolution converges on inevitable 'solutions' – of which consciousness itself is one – much as thought converges on the right answers to its questions.

In religious terms it would even be possible to understand the species as the thoughts of God or *Dharmakaya* as he, she or it explores ever new ways of inhabiting the world, ways of living which, by creating forms to house them, transform the environment and make a new living space for new genetic 'thoughts'. So evolution might be an abundant outpouring of God's creative activity, as he gropes his way towards true insight!

What is involved here is actually more than mere analogy between DNA and language. It is not at all a case of reading human meanings into the animal world, as happened in the Middle Ages when for example the pelican – alleged to feed its young with blood from its breast – was seen as a symbol of Christ's passion. Rather, meaning in a definable sense is 'out there' in the living world, and at a certain stage meaning takes human form. For human meaning can be defined – along with DNA sequence, computer code and many other elements of our universe – as instances of 'information'.

Information is a boring sounding but very rich concept that has been precisely defined in mathematics, and is fundamental to the whole 'information revolution' that characterizes our times. Information arises when a pattern is one of a number of possible alternatives that is explicable not only by what gave rise to it, but to what it generates or communicates by means of its difference from the alternatives. If I see a great boulder that resembles a human face it may be that way through the chance operation of natural causes, in which case it communicates nothing and is not information. But it may be that a human being has made it that way to communicate. For example, it may be designed to remind me of Abraham Lincoln. In that case it possesses information; it is communicating something. Genes possess information; they are 'designed' through the evolutionary process to be capable of generating a new organism of the same kind as the source of the DNA. They are information carried from one organism to another

Now in many cases we can distinguish between the matter which carries the information and the information itself. In a computer we distinguish the information – the software – from the hardware – the silicon chips and so forth that carry and manipulate the information. What is very unique and wonderful about the genes is that they themselves generate the organisms that carry them. The 'software' program generates the 'hardware' on which it runs. The DNA is therefore both a physical thing arising from natural causes, and a language or set of signs that communicates a message about how to build a new organism, including itself. It is a special case of 'interbeing', a structure 'designed' for interrelating with other structures to produce further structures. In the case of life, but not computers, "the medium is the message" (Thompson, 1990, p.197). Life is both 'significant matter' and 'embodied mind'.

With memes this is less obvious, but language and culture are physical things embodied in words on a page, sounds in the air, physical sculptures, buildings and all manner of things. Memes, like genes, create the (human) environment that carries them. Christianity is a meme transmitted through cathedrals, Church buildings, crucifixes, bibles, the chanting of monks, the sounds of hymns, bread and wine: material and spiritual at once, or what it would term sacramental. Buddhism embraces the sacramental less readily than most forms of Christianity, but emphasizes more its embodiment in human practices like meditation. To say this is not to 'reduce' religions to physical things, but to exalt the spirituality inherent in matter.

Science and Violence

We ought then to welcome the deep link Dawkins has developed between gene and meme, nature and culture, matter and meaning. But all too often this link is used only in the reductionistic way. In television nature programs, two contrasting tendencies can be noticed: utilitarian explanations of animal structure and behavior in terms of the old language of design, or what things are *for*; and a sense of awe, reverence and amazement at the sheer beauty and interdependent mystery of the living world. The latter sense is very evident in the writings of biologists like Dawkins, but does not and perhaps cannot form part of the scientific theory, in which the utilitarian tendency dominates.

But in this case we need to ask why the awe drops out of the theory, and why we end up attributing to the living world the worst of our human condition, namely those aspects of our life which, we have seen, are attributable to characteristically human desires: greed, competition and violence? Is there – we wonder – something violent in the method of science itself?

In Matthew Kneale's novel *English Passengers* the Tasmanian aborigine Peevay learns that his mother's dead body has been brutally torn apart for scientific research, so that he cannot give her the proper cremation that his own religion requires. He laments,

All those shootings and chasings and babies dropped in the fire, all that waiting on death islands with sand blowing in your eyes, and getting cheated with God, none of this was so bad, you see, as what they did to Mother... This cutting and playing was just a scornful thing, odious as could be. That was making her small, into nothing at all, not even dirt.

(2000, p.341-2)

The fiction here is based on factual happenings. Some have argued that the dismemberment of the wholeness of nature and human tradition is at the core of scientific method. The feminist writer Carolyn Merchant (1982) argues that in a letter to King James I the pioneer of scientific method Francis Bacon compared scientific investigation with the interrogation of witches under torture, urging "neither ought a man to make scruple of entering and penetrating into these holes and corners, when the inquisition of truth is his whole object" (*De Argumentis*).

The letter is unclear and this interpretation has been contested, but pursuing the metaphor we note that like the witch under torture, nature will give away some truths, but it will be conditioned by what the 'torturer' wants to hear. The world of science is not false, but is pictured in the way desire wants. The 'clothes' of beauty and delight are torn aside and disregarded in favor of naked quantities we can measure. This is because science seeks to generate technology, that is, ways of 'hounding' nature (to use Bacon's term) so she will yield the things we desire to have. Science has been very successful at doing this, but the success comes precisely from a narrow and focused perspective. The lack of meaning in nature is not a discovery or outcome of science, but its premise, its starting point. But if we open our eyes more widely, we can see all sorts of ways of understanding the wonderful world science has opened up for us.

We all benefit from science and technology, and I would be hypocritical if, typing into a technological marvel on which I rely, my computer, I were to condemn them out of hand. But if we want a full view, the scientific approach – which brackets out meaning – needs complementing with the images of poetry and religion, which focus on just that.

[Scientific] models bring to light patterns ever more remote from our own [like stars and black holes and subatomic particles and prehistoric life forms] bringing the unfamiliar into the orbit of the familiar and calculable. They suggest what questions to ask of, and what experiments to perform on, realities with which we would not otherwise be able to interact in order to perceive... But rather than gathering the remote into the familiar, the [poetic] image seems to project the familiar quality of our life into the strange and unfathomable... Images involve what [the poet John] Keats termed 'negative capability'. The ability to stop conceptualizing and start seeing. Instead of helping us cope, images stop us coping and start us looking and wondering. (Thompson, 1990, p.148-9)

The scientist who proclaims the world meaningless is rather like someone who has put on dark glasses – because they tune out the glare of the sun and enable him to see some things much more clearly – declaring that he finds the world to be shady and colorless. Poetry and religion may be needed to restore the true colors of the world.

The Indifferent Web of Love

It remains true that the world of evolution is not compatible with simplistic notions of karma and providence. The notion of a karma that perfectly rewards and punishes the individual, and the notion of a perfectly working divine providence, are equally unscientific. In response to the many, many cases where people seem to suffer from the effect of *other* people's sins, not their own, the Buddhist points to an unknowable past in which that person supposedly did bad things, perhaps in a previous life, while the Christian points to an equally unknowable future, in which the sufferings of the present will be outweighed by the person's just reward and the perpetrator's just punishment. In either case the sense of injustice is taken away by reference to things that cannot be tested. Surely it would be better to retain the pain of the sense of injustice as a motive for action that might create a more just situation. The Russian theologian Nicholas Berdyaev wrote that "God is not in the world, that is, not in its given factuality and its necessity, but in its setting of a task and in its freedom" (1952, p.152).

Evolution invites us to relinquish the last shreds of the idea that God is looking after us personally, and also the last shreds of any idea that karma is always perfectly apportioned to someone's good and bad deeds. It reveals a world that is not just, but indifferent and wild, and contains a terrible pathos. This was brought home to me recently in the television image I saw of a mother seal repeatedly licking the corpse of its cub, which had been killed in the stormy seas. It seemed to be denying the death, persisting in caring, in a way that we can easily recognize from our own response to bereavement.

The spiritual writer Belden Lane (1998) speaks of the way the creation, especially in desert places, imparts a sense of the vast indifference of God; the love is there in the indifference. It was only the vision of the prolific and terrifying and often cruel creativity of God (Job 38ff) that satisfied Job in his questioning. But nature is also prolific, complex, innovative, wonderful and beautiful. We are seamless parts of it, which is why empathy with the higher animals is surely no delusion. Nature is where we belong, with the God who is also Emptiness; with the love that does not *run* things but *is* them.

Not Providence, but Poetry

A great deal of Chinese and Japanese poetry expresses *yugen*, a term which names a bittersweet longing evoked by the combination of beauty and pathos, delightfulness and transience, which we see to be characteristic of the natural world to which we belong. It is evoked, for example, in this poem by Saigyo, a 12th century Japanese poet-priest.

Even a person free of passion
would be moved
to sadness:

autumn evening
in a marsh where snipes fly up (tr. Watson, 1991)

Caroline Brazier comments (2007, p.14) that "the reader of the poem is drawn, through the quiet tone of the writing, into an experience akin to sitting in stillness [in meditation], whilst the images of the poem arise, like the mental objects in the mind of the meditator. The reader observes each image but does not follow. The objects are not grasped, but nevertheless touch the heart. The imagery of a *yugen* poem tends to draw one's attention into the far distance." The images cannot be held and possessed (*tanha*) – that would be a futile response – but desire in the sense of longing remains, a source of joy and sadness at once.

As I look at my garden I see the cherry tree I planted four years ago smothered in pale pink flowers. Normally this tree flowers through the winter, but this winter has been harsh and the tree seems to have saved all its efforts for a late profusion of flowers I have never seen before. I will never see it flower again, because we are soon to move home; that adds not to the bloom but to the intense *yugen* with which I see it now.

I am taken back to the poem I wrote about seeing a pear tree in another garden where I lived many years ago. The written version too is lost, but fragments remain in my memory, and they seem to express the essence of *yugen*: the fruitless beauty of memory, and the clinging that finds only emptiness.

Tall tree
and yet tearless... the dews
of memories gone long gone ago,
gone great
– fruitless
accumulation, like hoarfrost.
The bird's claw on the winter tree:
Cling brilliant. Emptiness that passes through.

A huge amount of poetry from all languages rests ultimately on this tension between love and impermanence. That is why I think Lin Yutang is right to observe that

> though religion gives peace by having a ready-made answer to all... problems, it decidedly detracts from the sense of the unfathomable mystery and poignant sadness of this life, which we call poetry. *Christian optimism kills all poetry.*
> (Cited in Leong p.27)

Certainly there is a ready-answer kind of religion that kills all poetry. Buddhism does so when it urges retreat from the world of Samsara into Nirvana imagined as a kind of permanent state of uninvolved bliss. Christianity does so when it gratifies our egos with the kind of providence that is an 'egoism-via-God', or comforts me about the loss of my flowering cherry or my loved one by telling me how I will find them again in heaven, or else find the infinitely more lovable God. There is something indissolubly particular about our loves, so that though we may come in time to greater and fuller loves, they cannot in any way compensate for the loss of this particular cherry tree, or friend, or whatever. Our love is for someone's or something's 'just-so-ness', their unique way of being, not for some quality that could conceivably be outweighed by something better.

In evolution we confront the fact that we do not live in a tidy world that is neatly designed to achieve clear ends. Rather we encounter a world of mysterious and savage beauty, forever creating forms and destroying them. It is not a world of providence, but it is a world of poetry (a term that means 'making'). If we can bear its painful poetry we may become poets ourselves, and share something of the divine poetry.

Area 3: Cosmology and Time

A narrowly conceived providence is overthrown by evolution,

and both evolution and quantum theory suggest many resonances with the bottomlessness and impermanence of the Buddhist world view. Neither could be said to be incompatible with a Christian understanding of creation; they do not challenge the idea *that* God created the cosmos, but they do force us to revise our understanding of *how* he has done so. With tongue in cheek, we might say that God seems to be more of a Buddhist than he is often conceived by Christians to be.

When, however, we turn to cosmology the reverse seems to hold. Though traditional creation is not the only way of accounting for things, if the world exists by co-arising rather than creation, it accomplishes a remarkable degree of purpose and direction, and an amazing inbuilt thrust towards consciousness and mind.

The Anthropic Principle

Only relatively recently have scientists come to realize the 'anthropic' dimension of the cosmos, that is, the degree to which laws and constants that could have been otherwise seem to be tuned just right for the evolution of a conscious beings like ourselves. The many factors that are 'just right' for us to exist include the three-dimensionality of space (at least on our 'macro' level); the balance between the four basic forces (gravity, electro-magnetism, the 'strong' force that binds the nucleus of each atom, and the mysterious 'weak' force); and the distribution of matter in the early universe. All in all the chances of getting just *one* of these factors (the balance of forces) right for life to form have been calculated as 1 in 10-followed-by-60-zeroes. Thus represents the chance that a blindfolded archer would hit a one-inch across point on a target set up at the opposite end of the known universe, twenty billion light years away! (Davies, 1992, p.178 – for a longer summary of these factors and the disastrous effects of not getting them just right, see Thompson, 1990, p.215-19, and for a full account, Barrow and Tippler, 1988.)

And this is just the beginning. Once the universe has been tuned so very carefully to be capable of producing life, and not just, say, clouds of vapor or rocks of iron, there has to be a sun that burns for just the right length of time and intensity, with a planet of just the right size and distance from it, capable of receiving and retaining water and other crucial elements, with a moon created in just the right conditions, and a big planet the size of Jupiter to scoop away dangerous meteorites, and so on and so forth (Morris, 2003). Even then the chances of life evolving seem infinitesimally small; for in laboratories where just the right materials are present in carefully optimized conditions, at the time of writing, no scientist has ever seen anything like life emerging. Life requires something very strange to happen on a very strange planet with a very strange sun and a very strange moon in a universe that is strangely 'right'. But strangely, life exists. And once it does exist, its evolution into the conscious beings we are is not so strange. Stephen Conway Morris argues that it is almost inevitable, because there are only a limited number of ways in which life can 'solve' the problems it faces, and we are one.

The simplest explanation of why the cosmos proves so remarkably right for the evolution of life and consciousness – on both the grand and the local scales – is the familiar notion that it is designed with that purpose in mind by God. But this explanation does have a big disadvantage, as Dawkins and others are quick to point out. It explains consciousness by an original consciousness, the arising of mind by the working of a primordial mind. What we want to explain is invoked in the explanation. The case is rather like explaining the color of a red apple by tiny red particles in its skin; the redness itself is not explained at all.

However, if our idea of God is not that of an anthropomorphic super-Mind, but a reality that transcends the concepts of mind, consciousness, matter and so forth, then God might be capable of explaining mind and so forth. But in that case we lose a lot of what Christians ascribe to God. And in particular it becomes hard to say what we mean by saying that God 'intends' to create consciousness, and fine-tunes the cosmos accordingly. Intention is surely a conscious mental state or act.

There is an alternative that is very popular among scientists, which is to say that if the cosmos were not this way we would not be here to observe it. The cosmos could be one of a vast or infinite number of possible universes with different initial conditions and forces. On the 'many world' interpretation of quantum physics, this would indeed be the case. But nearly all the universes would slumber away unobserved. On one view they would not exist at all. Our consciousness would collapse the wave function and select precisely this universe, and the non-observation of the other possible universes would entail their non-existence. What makes this universe exist, then, would not be the big bang that originated it, but the consciousness that emerges from within it. It would be created from its end or goal, so to speak, rather than from its beginning.

In this case we are not using *another* kind of mind to explain the existence of our minds. We are making mind its own cause. There is a circularity in such an explanation. But explanation has to stop with something that explains itself. God is thought of in Christian theology as the only self-explanatory being, but Buddhists might prefer to see the universe itself as self-explanatory through the operation of mind. They might ask Christians, why delegate the inexplicably 'just so' to a God who is inexplicably 'just so'? Why not let the universe be inexplicably just the way it is. They have a point.

Creation by purpose, that is by a final rather than originating cause, may sound unscientific. However, natural selection explains how purpose can emerge in nature. It is not that organs like eyes were designed in order to see, rather that organisms that had eyes to see with were naturally selected to survive. Biologists are always explaining animal structure and behavior in terms of purpose, but this purposiveness emerges through natural causes rather than a divine plan. In the case of the universe it is impossible to tell whether its 'just rightness' is a matter of divine design or a kind of 'natural selection' by human consciousnesses, in which the other possible universes fail to achieve existence because there is no consciousness to know they are there!

In either case, we no longer have grounds for being afraid of the vast dark spaces of the cosmos, as the mathematician Blaise Pascal was, or for feeling the universe is hostile or indifferent to us. The cosmos is now known to be remarkably consciousness-friendly. A smaller, shorter-lived, cozier cosmos would not have been able to generate life, and the vastness of the cosmos is one of the factors that appears to be needed for us to be here looking at it. Christians (along with other monotheists) are entitled to delight in the possibility opened up that our home was designed with us in mind; but Buddhists may prefer the explanation that the consciousness that has called this home into being is our own.

Time

One big difference between the world views of Christianity and Buddhism is that Christianity (like the other monotheistic faiths) presents us with a linear, historical world that develops in time from a point of creation to a point of ultimate fulfillment. Buddhism on the other hand (like Hinduism) sees time as consisting of endless interminable *kalpas*, cycles in which the cosmos is destroyed and created again. For Buddhism, if we reversed time and played it backwards there would not be a great difference, whereas for Christianity this would make an overwhelming difference.

At every level it has it be said that scientific discovery now favors the historical and directional understanding of time. Only on the medium-large scale of the revolutions and orbits of the earth and the planets does cyclical time appear to prevail. Of course those regular planetary movements form the basis of the hugely dominant cycles of the day, month and year by which we have measured time since the ancient world. But even these cycles are regular in appearance only; we now know that the day is imperceptibly slowing down, and the orbit of the earth getting imperceptibly faster and closer to the sun, like water spinning down a plughole.

If we move to a larger scale, we know that the stars that once seemed eternal themselves have a history; they had a beginning, and will have an end. Larger still, and the cosmos itself which was once thought eternal by cosmologists is now know to have a beginning and to be destined – after unimaginable eons – to die out. Move smaller, and we know the species are not permanent but evolved from other species and often die out, and that overall there is a trend towards ever greater complexity. Finally, even in the minute world of the quantum, where scientists thought time was reversible and the future indistinguishable from the past, we now know that, because of the 'left-handedness' of the universe, even the elementary particles would be subtly different if time were run backwards. Just as in a mirror my right hand becomes my left hand, so if particles traveled back in time they would be mirror images of their normal selves, similar but not quite the same (Gardner, 2005). We live in a universe of change in which, in the present on earth at least, development has overall outweighed decline for at least a million millennia. As noted, this has not led all scientists to belief in God, but many resonate with the remark attributed to cosmologist Paul Davies that "there is something going on".

Christians are sometimes criticized for seeing the history of human beings as the only tiny aspect of the universe that really matters to God, the only arena of his salvation. Clearly this can weaken and has often weakened concern for ecological integrity. In Tsuchiya's terms (Chapter 4) Christians have focused on the relational self at the expense of the cosmological self. But recent cosmology challenges any crude distinction between history and nature or cosmos. The whole cosmos is now seen to be historical, in the sense of being an irreversible process that involves the coming to be of the human. Rather than reject the accounts offered by evolution and cosmology, Christians surely ought to be re-writing their salvation history in a way that includes not only the history of the Jews and early Christians (specially significant though that must be for Christians) and not even only the whole human race, but the whole cosmos from the big bang onward.

Moreover, since Einstein's General Theory of Relativity, time has come to be seen not as an immutable container in which the universe drifts, but as co-evolving with space and matter – in other words, with the universe itself. This has the logical advantage that, since time and before and after are features within the universe, we cannot ask what happened 'before' the universe existed. Nor should Christians think of God as hanging around for infinite stretches of time 'before' creating the universe. According to St. Augustine, time was created along with space, matter, spirit and everything else out of nothing. Like space, then, time is no inert receptacle; it has a direction and meaning. In words ascribed to Augustine, "life is only for loving; time is only that we may find God."

Buddhists would not put it quite that way, of course. But it does seem to me that, though Buddhism inherited from Hinduism an eternal cosmos, this sits ill with the Buddhist teaching of the impermanence of *everything*, from which the impermanence of time (and hence, since things can come and go only in time, the impermanence of impermanence itself) seems to follow. Moreover, in Mahayana Buddhism the *Dharmakaya* suggests a direction and purpose in time, namely the bringing of all beings to salvation in Nirvana. That implies time must have an end and goal, however distant.

Summary

This chapter was never intended to be a gladiatorial contest between Buddhism and Christianity to see which survives best when the lions of science are set upon them! Rather I hope we have seen that no single account of things is dictated by science. An array of possibilities has opened up which you, the reader, must ponder for yourself. Nevertheless in terms of the five questions with which this chapter was introduced, the answers are now clear, and they are broadly positive for both faiths.

1. **Is it reducible?** No. The world is bottomless. We will never fully understand it, and it cannot be reduced to a basic substance or elements. It is empty, a something happening to nothing. So are we. This is good news for Buddhists and Christians, in that it allows us to delight in the play of the world without it being possible to cling on to anything firm. We will never be in a position to say we have got life 'sussed'.

2. **What is real, mind or matter or both?** There is no dualism between mind and matter. Meaning arises not because a soul is planted in a limited number of bodies – the human ones – but because bodies themselves and the genetic code that gives rise to them are full of meaning; they communicate. Life is shot through with and woven out of inter-being. Most of the meaning of life is inaccessible to human consciousness; for genes are not designed to 'talk' to 'memes' or minds, only to other proteins. In the beautiful forms of life and the intricate behavior of animals we sense great meaning even though we cannot participate in it ourselves. The cries of the whales seem to be communicating messages our minds cannot decipher. This is good news too, for it prevents humans feeling too 'special' and proud, yet makes human meaning-making, as in the great religions, an important part of the cosmic process.

3. **What holds it together?** There is no simple karma or provi-

dence. The cosmos does not reward the good person or look after the individual. But we are located in a vast web of interacting causes which has to be grasped before we can act freely. However, if we can grasp this – understanding what we follow from and what follows on from our acts – the small degree of freedom we possess can make an immense difference, like playing the right or the wrong note in a cosmic symphony. This is good news for Christianity and Buddhism, as it prevents any egocentric understanding of God or karma, but teaches responsibility and care.

4. **Is it hostile or friendly?** The world is not alien or indifferent to us, but the carefully adjusted nursery of consciousness. We belong to it and it to us. This, again, is good news. In the twentieth century many philosophers – the existentialists, the novelist and philosopher Iris Murdoch, theologian Don Cupitt in one of his phases, to name but a few – took it for granted that the cosmos was empty of any significance, and the only source for meaning is our own minds. That feeds the human ego. But the vast, impartial, in some ways ruthless, and yet homely cosmos we are now beginning to discern enables both humility and a sense of belonging.

5. **Does it develop through time?** The universe is not eternal but historical. Time has an irreversible direction in which 'something is going on'. In particular, the complexity required for consciousness arises seamlessly within the causal history of the cosmos. Though the cyclical time of Buddhism may have to be rejected, the news is basically good for Buddhists as well as Christians. We have seen that grasping is not some eternal cosmic catastrophe but essentially a historical development, such that liberation has to be sought also through historical and political as well as personal struggle. The historically growing cosmos

we know of is an appropriate arena for this struggle: time is there for us to find God, or perhaps, achieve Nirvana.

But what will we find? God? Nirvana? Or what? Some of the different options in this chapter – creation out of nothing versus emptiness, and design in the universe versus 'natural selection' by the human mind – depend on the answer to this ultimate question, which, it would seem, will have to be different for Buddhists and Christians. So let us turn to this question now.

Chapter 8

Grasping the Nettle: God – or Emptiness?

In the beginning
was wine, poured out
from some dark wound
in your sacred heart.

The falling world
has burned to chaos'
ash, out of which
arose life's vine.

Now reflected on
the river at dusk,
your images speak
like fruits of fire.

This book has suggested that if we allow Buddhism and Christianity to mingle more, we might gain a rich understanding – of suffering, sin and desire, of how they may be transcended, and of the universe itself – as well as a much deepened practice of personal transformation. But there is a nettle of divergence that we have yet firmly to grasp, which seems to force a separation in several areas. Regarding the overcoming of desire, it was left unresolved whether all desire and all relationship need to be transcended, or whether desire in the bad sense can be transformed by desiring love. In terms of religious practice the relationship with God that is the ultimate end of Christian worship finds no echo in Buddhism, in which the goal is rather the insight into emptiness realized in meditation. And finally, the

231

Buddhist emphasis on the dependent-co-arising of all things contrasts with the Christian doctrine of creation of time and all things by a loving God. The stereotype – that Christians believe in a loving and personal Creator who created a real and fundamentally good world, while for Buddhists all is illusion and emptiness – appears to be confirmed, and this would seem to set a severe limit to any cross-fertilization between the two faiths. Whatever concepts and practice they might borrow from each other would seem to be harnessed to the service of radically different and irreconcilable aims.

So this chapter endeavors to grasp the nettle of this divergence. It begins by tracing the development of the Jewish and Christian God from the YHWH of the Hebrew Bible through to the subtler God of philosophers and mystics, and asks whether the trajectory whereby the violence of YHWH is overcome does not demand a further step. Then it looks at how Mahayana Buddhism has conceived the ultimate in terms of *Dharmakaya* and *Sunyata* or Emptiness. The Zen Buddhist Masao Abe's remarkable synthesis of the Buddhist idea of emptiness and the Christian idea of a self-emptying God is explored and some criticisms are offered, enabling us to move further towards a reconciliation of the bottomless, cosmic, and altogether immanent Buddhist conception of *Sunyata* with the historical, personal and transcendent Christian understanding of the self-emptied Trinity.

'The One True God': Loving or Violent?

Thus Says the Lord of hosts, 'I will punish the Amalekites for what they did in opposing the Israelites when they came up out of Egypt. Now go and attack Amalek, and utterly destroy all that they have; do not spare them, but kill both man and woman, child and infant, ox and sheep, camel and donkey. (1 Sam. 15.2-3)

So the prophet Samuel addresses King Saul with God's command to commit genocide. It is not unique in the Bible; many times God is described as commanding genocide against the 'People of the Land', the Canaanites whose land Israel was to colonize. On this occasion Saul actually spares the cattle and sheep and takes them as spoil, and is then rebuked by the prophet for his disobedience. It is one of many occasions when human beings seem to temper the outright fanaticism of their God with a degree of common-sense self-interest.

We are forced to ask the question posed at the beginning: is there something intrinsically violent about monotheism, or at least the kind of monotheism inherited from the Hebrews? Of course few Christians and Jews today would take passages like the one just quoted as definitively describing the nature of their God. But is any 'jealous God' who tolerates no other divinity not inherently likely to encourage acts of destruction against rival creeds and those who follow them? Is the history of Christianity and Islam (and Judaism, at least before the diaspora which made the Jews major victims of the persecutions of the other two faiths) not littered with jihad and crusade, with genocide, colonialism and the burnings of heretics?

John D'Arcy May (2003) has considered the argument that there may be a connection between the transcendent God and violence, while polytheism may be more peaceful. He quotes the aborigine Peevay, whom we met in Chapter 7:

> Truly Robson's God was one puzzle to confound. Everybody knew where our real ones were as they could see them every night shining in the sky, but when I asked Robson where God was, he just said, "He is everywhere"... Also he told us that if we didn't believe God was everywhere then God would get angry and send us to some piss-poor place to get burnt... Our real ones never did care if we knew they were in the sky. They were just in the sky. (Kneale, 2000, p.226)

The many gods of the polytheist just are there in the natural world. They do not 'care' whether we acknowledge them; they demand no allegiance, and are not jealous of any rivals. By contrast the Christian God seems angry, demanding and punitive.

However, May argues faiths like Buddhism and Hinduism, in which the one God is absent or non-transcendent, have often been violent too. Buddhism has not always lived up to its peaceful reputation. The Japanese persecution of Christians in the 17th century was probably the most violent that Christians ever faced. In medieval Tibet the different sects, and in Japan the monasteries (often practicing martial arts) were involved in frequently violent struggles for political supremacy. A whole Buddhist mythology regards Sri Lanka as an exclusively Buddhist isle, resulting in militancy against the Tamils and other minority groups (Faure, 2009, p.93ff). However, Buddhism has become violent, on the whole, when identified with partisan or national feeling. Of course, this has often happened to Christianity too – for example, in Northern Ireland, and in former Yugoslavia.

But monotheism transcends nationality. The crusades, like *jihad*, are international phenomena fired not by patriotism but zeal for the one true God. Monotheism takes the conflict between Israelis and Palestinians beyond a local conflict between colonizers and colonized, drawing in militant Islamic and Christian fundamentalists, allied to one side or the other through theological rather than national or racial solidarity. Monotheism does seem to incite violent loyalties and passions. It is an idea that will always have potential to do that because the oneness of the one God tends to exclude the otherness of the other, and demands total allegiance. Monotheism always risks being, in Girard's terms, sacrificial, scapegoating the alien and making an enemy of the other. This is, of course, not the fault of God but of the way groups often use the idea of the one God to build a sense of corporate identity. To overcome violence it seems to me that the one God has to be freed from this tangle with human identity, embracing difference and otherness, and internalizing sacrifice. In the process the one God may have to become the Trinity – of which more later.

Of course, if monotheism tends to violence, atheism seems to be worse. The lack of God enables a leader like Stalin or Hitler or Mao to take on God's worst aspects – the demand for sincere allegiance, and paranoia regarding potential rivals –without any allegiance of their own to a divine justice and compassion that transcends them.

YHWH - Exclusive yet Multifaceted

Paradoxically, for all his exclusiveness, the character of YHWH – the unpronounceable God translated variously as 'the LORD', Yahweh and Jehovah – is as Biblical scholar Jack Miles has argued (1995) an amalgam generated by the absorption of many local polytheistic gods. His violence stems mainly from the Canaanite warrior Lord and Master Baal, who dwelt on mountain tops in unapproachable fire. But Yahweh also took on the duties of the household gods, becoming the 'God of our fathers', the friend of the family who tenderly provided for the needs of patriarchs like Jacob and Joseph. And in a reverse movement he became El, the inscrutable Creator of heaven and earth.

> The Lord God has always been intermittently baffling or irritating or inconsistent or arbitrary... Scholarship simply helps to make the conflicts patent, turning muddy shades of grey in the Lord's interior life into clearly distinguishable tints. Here the sky blue of El, there the earth tones of 'the God of your father', over there the blood red of Baal or Tiamat or the evergreen memory of Asherah. (p.21)

For all this, Miles argues, YHWH is a brilliant corporate creation of many generations of writers, a clearly recognizable character who has shaped human self-understanding in the Western world. Loving and jealous, angry and tender, serene and warlike, just and capricious, impartial and favoring, determinedly individual and faithful to his beloved, to a degree every Western man models himself on YHWH despite himself, and sometimes despite his own unbelief.

YHWH is in an obvious sense a creation of the Biblical writers. But that does not mean he is not real. When cultural creations in turn exercise a formative influence on their cultures, such that a real 'interbeing' is generated between them and the people, there is a sense in which they become real, and certainly enable us to discover and engage with realities in ourselves and our world which we otherwise might not be able to

The character of YHWH is quite alien, and often alienating, to the oriental mind, including the Buddhist. Yet Buddhism offers a way of understanding the culture-created reality we are dealing with. Could YHWH be a wonderful *yidam*, like the benevolent and wrathful deities of Tibet, who are not ultimately real, but enable us to realize and relate to realities within ourselves and the cosmos? Rita Gross sees Christ as ultimately more like a *yidam* than a Bodhisattva or the (historical) Buddha (Gross and Muck, 1999, p.48). But Jesus Christ, unlike a *yidam*, has concrete historical reality; he is not purely (though aspects of him as worshipped in the Church may well be) a construct of corporate imagination. In YHWH we seem to see wrathful and benevolent, serene and engaged deities rolled into one supreme figure. Ultimate reality, which has to encompass everything, may be hard to express in an abstract concept, and maybe only a complex but unified character like YHWH can do justice to its paradoxes, and enable us really to relate to the real.

The God Philosophers and Mystics

When Jewish and Christian faiths encountered the sophisticated philosophies of the Greco-Roman world, many were a little embarrassed about YHWH's all too human nature. To make their faiths more respectable and less primitive-seeming, the Jewish contemporary of Jesus, Philo of Alexandria (c.10BCE-c.50CE) strove to reconcile his Jewish monotheism with the tradition of philosophy that stemmed from Plato. Christian theologians based in the same Egyptian city of Alexandria – like Clement (150-215) and Origen (c.185-254) – followed suit. This development was helped by the fact that Platonism itself was coming to resemble more and more a mystical monotheism. Plotinus (204-270CE), and Proclus (412-85) created a mystical cosmology of emanations, which descended from the original One, down through the Logos (the rational order of the world) and the World Soul, to the cosmos. The mystic sought to ascend by corresponding stages from contemplation of the cosmos to unity with the One.

The resemblance between this mystical philosophy and certain strands of Hinduism, notably the Vedanta, has led writers like Aldous Huxley (1945) to regard it as a "perennial philosophy" constituting the common mystical core of all religions. However, unless we crudely identify the One with a concept as different as Buddhist Nirvana, Buddhist spirituality cannot be regarded as a variant of such a philosophy. And Christian theologians after Origen made profound changes to the neo-Platonic understanding of the One, amounting in some cases to a reversal of Plato's concepts in order to accommodate their experience of God-in-Christ.

God as Nothingness

Plato likened the Good – his nearest equivalent of the Christian God – to the sun: clear, bright and self-contained, bringing light and clarity to our world. But Christian theologians like Gregory of Nyssa (c.335-94) pointed out that Moses found God in the great darkness of the cloud on Mount Sinai. For Gregory, God was *apeiron* (boundless, infinite), more like the sea or empty space than the sun. And our knowledge of him is a reaching out (*epektasis*) of love into the dark in which, according to another theologian, "being neither oneself nor someone else, one is completely united by a completely unknowing inactivity of all knowledge, and knows beyond the mind by knowing nothing" (Dionysius, 1993, 1.3, p.137). This divine nothingness seems closer to Buddhist Emptiness than the Platonic light of the Good.

For Plato, our souls belonged to the eternal world, while our bodies belonged to the material world, to which, at death, they returned. But the developing Christian doctrine of creation – noted in the preceding chapter – affirmed our created-ness, over against the uncreated God. Far from being spirits exiled in this earthly realm, our affinity was with the earth, and St. Francis of Assisi was able to call the sun, moon, stars, earth and animals his brothers and sisters.

Chapter 1 noted the way the Christian theologians transformed the neo-Platonic Trinity. The latter had served as a kind of drawbridge (a bridge but also a protective barrier) between the material and temporal cosmos and the spiritual and eternal One. The One could not have contact with the gross material world, but could emanate a hierarchy of three successively coarser manifestations between itself and matter, rather like the Buddhist Trikaya. But the Christian Trinity is not a hierarchical bridge, but a community of equals. It is expressed in the table meals of Jesus, where all, sinners and saints, were invited to share indiscriminately. This non-discrimination is also an essential aspect of Buddhist Emptiness or *Sunyata*.

But how is this non-discriminating sharing possible? How can our "dust grown tall" (as the war poet Wilfrid Owen so memorably put it) respond to God on the 'other side' of the Creator-creature divide? In Christian terms it is not by any natural spiritual affinity, but by the *relationship* Jesus has made possible. God is not like us, but from his otherness comes to meet and engage with us. God is not like anything that is, but comes to meet us through everything that is. That is why idols – supposed resemblances to the divine often made in gold or fine stone – are worse than useless in all monotheistic traditions, but some Christian traditions use icons, pieces or ordinary wood with pictures painted on them through which – it is believed – Christ and his saints address us and draw us into communion with themselves.

So Christianity relaxed the command against idolatry as far as material images were concerned, but at the same time tightened it regarding mental images and ideas of God. God came to be regarded as far above any ideas we could frame, and far above anything in existence. Indeed in one theological tradition he was above existence itself. The writer who describes himself as Dionysus the Areopagite – but was probably a Syrian monk of the 5th or 6th century – regarded the Christian God as beyond existence and non-existence. Though every being expressed its Creator, nothing in created being, by definition, was the Creator. Everything was a shadowy resemblance to the Creator, and could stand as an analogy for God. But nothing in being, not even the totality of being, was God.

In the tradition of Dionysius, then, God transcends being and non-being , and to say 'God exists' is as misleading as to say 'God does not exist'. And this tradition – the apophatic or negative tradition – has been a very important one, both in the Orthodox East, and in theologians like the Celtic theologian John Scotus Eriugena (c.800-877), for whom God "neither was nor shall be nor has become nor shall become nor indeed is" (1987, 3 (628B)). Quoting this, McGinn goes on to comment "fairly negative, that!" (1994, p.100) – and it is probably more negative than Buddhist Emptiness, which as we shall see is also a fullness with many positive features.

Eriugena translated and brought negative theology to the West, where it was very influential in the mystical tradition that includes Meister Eckhart and St. John of the Cross, in whose thought "detachment requires the dismantling of every sense of created selfhood in the breakthrough of the soul into its own ground; there, where its character of being a 'something' is lost, it finds its own 'nothingness' in identity with the 'nothingness' of the ground of God" (Turner, 1995, p.244-5).

God as Supreme Being

However, this tradition is not predominant in modern Christianity in the West. Whether you are an atheist or a firm believer today, probably the God you acknowledge or reject is a much more definite Supreme Being, of one or two kinds.

One is the great Designer whom we met in Chapter 7, whom theologians of a philosophical bent have thought to deduce from the order of nature, leading them into the familiar confrontation with those scientists who reject God but hold the very same idea of who God is. This God is the very opposite of the immanent but elusive Trinity I shall be proposing. He is very knowable; by reasoning about the universe we can deduce he must exist, and what is in his Mind, just as if we found a watch (to use the familiar example from the 18th century philosopher William Paley) we could deduce that someone must have made it, and what he made it for. But God is no more present in the universe than a watchmaker is present in his watch.

The other kind of God familiar today is much more the exclusive possession of his followers, be they Jewish, Christian or Islamic. He is not the kind of being philosophers and other wise users of reason can know, but the God of Abraham, Isaac and Jacob, the God of those who have faith. Rather than attracting our love like the mysterious apophatic God, this God seems to demand it like the jealous YHWH of old. The Protestant theologian Karl Barth has actually made this jealous aspect explicit, arguing that the concept of creation involves election or choosing what is to be, and hence also rejection the jealous exclusion of 'nothingness', which takes on a murky kind of existence of its own, like a shadow cast by the act of creation.

Grounded always in election, the activity of God is invariably one of jealousy, wrath and judgment. God is also holy, and this means that his being and his activity take place in a definite opposition, in a real negation, both defensive and aggressive... God elects, and therefore rejects what he does not elect. God wills, and therefore opposes what he does not will. He says Yes, and therefore says No to that to which he has not said Yes.

(2004, III/3, p.311)

Modern atheists are as hostile to this aggressive kind of God as they are to the blander designer God. Yet they often retain a typically Protestant hostility to dogma, ritual, and institutional religion. Would it be wide of the mark to see modern atheism as the militant way the apophatic tendency reasserts itself in a Protestant environment that is hostile to it?

God as Being Itself

A middle way between God as Nothing and God as Supreme Being can be found in the copious writings of St Thomas Aquinas, for whom God is existence itself, completely realized. There is nothing in God, according to Thomas, that is unfulfilled potential, which might have been or yet might be but is not. God is 'pure act', total self-realization, or as we might put it, the absolutely successful being. In many ways Thomas' concept of God is like a translation of the Hebrew YHWH into the abstract philosophical terms of the Greek philosopher Aristotle. Thomas himself makes much use of God's revelation of his name YHWH to Moses in the episode of the burning bush (Exod. 3.14). He interprets the obscure Hebrew name as meaning "I am who I am" and hence "I am being itself".

Though for Thomas God is supremely Being; he is not 'The Supreme Being' – an individual being who competes successfully for being with other individuals. As Creator, his being is intrinsically on the side of, rather than opposed to, the flourishing of every being; for God is what makes every being be what it is. In his work of creation God is the supreme Agent, the one who acts in all that is. This is a concept on which this chapter will draw.

The Buddhist Ultimate

The inter-faith theologian James Fredericks (2004, p.82) comments on the immense contrast between a Gothic cathedral and a Zen monastery garden. In the former, an intricate variety of statues, stained glass windows and arches are held together in an overwhelming vertical thrust. In the latter, a few stones are scattered, seemingly randomly, like islands in a 'sea' of sand, and that is all. The one is complex, the other simple; the one is full of images, the other imageless; the one emphasizes the vertical, the other the horizontal; the one tells of a tightly organized hierarchy of creation dependent on God, the other places things 'just so' in their egalitarian interdependence; the one shows us the transcendent addressing us in the immanent, the other a sheer immanence that transcends our understanding; the one inspires us with longing for God above; the other settles us peaceably into emptiness here and now.

It is not, crudely, that Christianity affirms transcendence while Buddhism rejects it; rather that Christianity affirms a transcendent God as the incomprehensible ground of everything there is, while Buddhism affirms the mystery of things in their very groundlessness. That mystery is expressed in the zany humour of Zen and the pathos of *yugen* poetry. It leads Buddhists to Emptiness, just as Christians are led to the Trinity.

On an abstract level, the fundamental difference here is that for theologians like Dionysius everything both is and is not God. Everything is an imperfect analogy of God. Translated into the terms developed by the Kegon school of Buddhism, Dionysius teaches *rijimuge*, the non-identical identity between each thing (*ji*) with the ultimate (roughly, *ri*). But in the Madhyamaka tradition – one of the major Mahayana schools – this kind of non identical identity is ruled out. In the strange logic of Indian founder of this tradition Nagarjuna (6th century CE) – as incidentally for the theologian and mathematic Nicholas of Cusa (1401-64) – all four of these propositions about any existent thing are denied:

It is ultimate reality.
It is not ultimate reality.
It both is and is not ultimate reality.
It neither is nor is not ultimate reality.

The denial of the third proposition rules out the possibility that is central for the likes of Dionysus and Thomas Aquinas, that the thing might be an analogy for the ultimate.

The Kegon school of Buddhism taught *jijimuge*, the non-identical identity of each thing with everything else. In contrast with the Christian hierarchy of beings ascending and towards the ineffable God – which is expressed in the medieval cathedral – this generates a horizontal world full of interilluminations. "The Dionysian vision leads to seeing God in all things and all things in God; the Mahayana journey leads to seeing all things in each and each in all things" (Lefebure p.88).

Linji Yixuan, who founded one of the main Zen Schools in the ninth century, explained Nagarjuna's fourfold denial by means of a poem:

Warm sun shines forth, spreading the earth with brocade.
The little girl's hair hangs down, white as silk thread.
(Cited in Faure, 2009, p.32)

243

Sunshine and a girl's hair do not reflect the divine so much as each other, in a way that takes us deep into *Sunyata*. The Japanese verses quoted in the 'Yugen' section of Chapter 7, and those cited here and below, juxtapose images in this same typically Chinese and Japanese way, to create an emptiness full of yearning. In *jijimuge* – the non-identical fusion of everything – the 'Ultimate' is short-circuited, and gives way to the just-so-ness of the Zen garden, where a few rocks, profoundly equal, mirror one another without being the same.

A Western poet might have made a metaphor here: something like 'the warm sun hangs down her silky hair'. In place of the Chinese interillumination between equal images we would have a hierarchy in which the girl and her hair stand as an image describing the appearance of the real sun. We would be in a different world, in which instead of casting light on each other, things stand for and transmit light from the greater realities, and ultimately the divine.

I must say that I love both Gothic cathedrals and Zen gardens. If forced to choose, I would opt for the latter. I can certainly see no point and probably no possibility of combining the two styles into a 'Zen Gothic'! But I can see a lot of point and some possibility of developing a shared understanding of God and Emptiness. The Zen scholar Masao Abe has paved the way to that, but before we look at his ideas, it is worth asking...

Why is there no God in Buddhism?

Buddhists are not atheists in the same way as Lenin and Richard Dawkins. Atheism is not an article of Buddhists' faith, as it is an article of materialists' faith. That is not to say that arguments against the existence of a Creator God do not appear from time to time in Buddhist tradition. The most sustained and noteworthy are those set out by the seventh or eighth century Indian writer Santideva in the *Bodhicaryavatara*. But as Paul Williams points out (2004), though Santideva demolishes many a popular understanding of God as Nature or the Self or a supernatural causality filling the gaps in natural explanations, his arguments do not really touch the subtle understanding to be found in the likes of Thomas Aquinas. They are all arguments a Christian ought to welcome as disposing of idolatrous understandings of the Creator. Like many atheists, Santideva disbelieves in a God in whom Christians too ought to disbelieve.

This is not to say that Buddhists and Christians 'really agree' about God; according to Williams they certainly do not. But the disagreement is really not about whether God exists so much as whether God matters. The Buddha is described as regarding God or the gods, along with other cosmological and metaphysical issues, as unimportant or distracting from the task of liberation. In dialogue, therefore, it is often emphasized that Buddhists do not dogmatically reject what Christians affirm regarding God, but are making a purely practical or tactical move. For "the Buddha was not against God. He was only against notions that are mere mental constructs that do not correspond to reality, notions that prevent us developing ourselves and touching ultimate reality" (Nhat Hanh, 1996, p.151).

However, in Christians terms it could not be regarded as 'practical' to avoid the question of God, since relationship with and worship of God are at the heart of Christian practice and understanding of salvation. And for Buddhists, conversely, going beyond God is more than just a tactical move; it is integral to how Buddhists understand liberation.

We do not need the Buddha to tell us that ultimate reality is ineffable... Nearly all humanity's religious and philosophical traditions contain this same emphasis, albeit in varying degrees. No, what seems to be revealing in Buddhism is its effectuation of this reduction... in respect not only of the object of the quest for the ultimate, but of the subject too.

(Panikkar, 1989, p.102-3)

In other words, whereas most religions place ultimate reality beyond the reach of the human knower, Buddhism teaches a non-dualism in which, in enlightenment, both the ultimate and the human knower disappear into a thoroughgoing immanence (like that of the Zen garden).

This total immanence is precisely the ultimate reality Buddhism seeks to realize. But this ultimate immanence is sometimes described in terms like those that Christians use to describe the uncreated God. In a famous passage the Buddha declares

> Monks, there is a not-born, a not-become, a not-made, a not-compounded. If that unborn, not-become, not-made, not-compounded were not, there would be apparent no escape from this here that is born, become, made, compounded.
>
> (*Pataligama Vagga*, in *Khuddaka Nikaya* I. 3:8)

Nirvana, as here described, is of course not an unconditioned being, still less a person. Yet in Mahayana Buddhism the ultimate reality does seem to bear aspects that are personal at least in the sense of being active and self-manifesting, as is clear from the discussion of *Dharmakaya* in Chapter 1.

> Buddhism does not use the word God. The word is rather offensive to most of its followers, especially when it is intimately associated... with the idea of a creator who produced the world out of nothing, caused the downfall of humankind, and, touched by pangs of remorse, sent down his only son to save the depraved. But... Buddhism must not be judged an atheism which acknowledges an agnostic, materialistic interpretation of the universe... Buddhism outspokenly acknowledges the presence in the world of a reality which transcends the limitations of phenomenality, but which is nevertheless immanent everywhere and manifests itself in its

full glory, and in which we live and move and have our being. God or the religious object of Buddhism is generally called *Dharmakaya*-Buddha.

(Suzuki, 1963, p.219.)

A crucial difference seems to remain. "Buddhism does not take the personalistic divine-human relationship (I-thou relationship) as the *basis* of salvation, thereby regarding impersonal nature as something peripheral, but instead takes as the basis of salvation the transpersonal, universal dimension common to human beings and nature" (Abe, in Cobb and Ives, 1994, p.29).

In Christianity, personhood, relationship and desire are integral to the very ideas of salvation and of God. But however 'personal' the Buddhist descriptions of the ultimate may become, we are not *saved* by a personal relationship with it. We are liberated not by relationship but by insight, not by love but by truth.

Emptiness and Emptying

Despite this difference, a ground-breaking debate has taken place between Buddhist and Christian scholars, initiated by Masao Abe's essay *Kenotic God and Dynamic Sunyata* (in Cobb and Ives, 1994, p.3ff). Abe argues for an understanding of Mahayana Buddhist Emptiness and an understanding of the Christian idea of Self-emptying or 'kenotic' God in which they are one and the same.

Sunyata is generally translated 'emptiness' but does not have the negative connotations of sheer nothingness. Lefebure (p. 63-4) derives it from the root *shvi*, to swell, conveying the image of a round, ripe fruit hollow inside; and he links it to the Indian symbol for 0, zero. In Buddhist thought it is related to the doctrine of dependent co-arising, according to which nothing is *svabhava*, self-existent, and there is no ultimate reason for anything existing. (Christians of course agree with the first point

247

and disagree with the second.) Everything is 'just so', the way it is for no reason at all, so *Sunyata* is identified with *Tathata*, just-so-ness or Suchness.

Abe also relates it to *jinen*, the natural spontaneity, innocence and warmth that comes from accepting the beautiful foundationless world as it is, so that we act well without complicated reasoning about foundations and principles of morality. The same idea is suggested in Eckhart's "living without a why".

And *Sunyata* is also identified with *Dharmakaya*, a concept that as we have seen implies order and rightness in things, and generates wisdom and compassion. *Sunyata* then does not denote the sense of lack, absurdity or meaninglessness we find in modern nihilism and existentialism, but on the contrary, an acceptance of the world in its transient, fragmentary and inexplicable nature as 'just right, just as it is'. Abe quotes (p.45) a verse from the *Futoroku* often used to exemplify Suchness and *jinen*:

Bamboo shadows sweep the stairs,
Yet not a mote of dust is stirred;
Moonbeams pierce to the bottom of the pool
yet in the water not a trace remains.

The Christian term 'kenotic' meanwhile comes from the Greek *kenosis*, the 'emptying' described in Philippians 2.5-8:

Christ Jesus... though he was in the form of God, did not regard equality with God as something to be exploited, but emptied himself, taking the form of a slave, being born in human likeness. And being found in human form, he humbled himself and became obedient to the point of death – even death on a cross.

Many theologians have used the idea of *kenosis* to interpret the incarnation of God in Christ. In becoming fully human, it is argued, Christ could not have held onto his total divine knowledge and power, as classical theology had thought, but surrendered them. And some modern theologians, notably Jürgen Moltmann, controversially argue that *kenosis* involves not just the divine Son but the whole Trinity: on the Cross the Son despairs of the Father, but the Father is bereaved of his Son. And it is possible to argue that, if God suffers and dies in Christ on the cross, but God is also eternal and cannot change God's own nature, then God must eternally include non-being as well as being. Dionysius must be right. God must be essentially kenotic, always pouring Godself out in ecstasy.

Now in a nutshell, Abe's argument is that if *Sunyata* is understood in a *dynamic* way, and if God is seen as *essentially* kenotic, the Christian God and Buddhist Emptiness can be seen as one and the same. Abe was not the first to argue for this identification; as noted, the Nestorian Christians did so in seventh century China. But Abe does so with a subtlety that has provoked wide discussion.

'Dynamic' *Sunyata* is *Sunyata* not 'clung to' as a static concept. *Sunyata* is to be conceived neither as a bare 'not something' nor as a 'thing' that is empty, but as a continual emptying that finally empties emptiness of its own emptiness, and so has positive and saving aspects. These include Suchness and *jinen*, just discussed, and also boundless openness, the reversibility of time, and the classical Buddhist virtues of wisdom and compassion. These last arise because of the profound equality of all things in *Sunyata*. Because all are interdependent, none (myself included) is to be exalted in power over another. On the contrary, the suffering (or happiness) of any being becomes my own suffering (or happiness).

Meanwhile, Abe runs with those theologians who extend *kenosis* to the whole Trinity, and goes one radical step further. If God is eternal, *kenosis* cannot mean that God is first full, and then becomes empty (and then, if we follow the Philippians passage through to the subsequent verses (2.9-11) full again in Christ's resurrection, ascension and return to the Father). Rather it must mean that God is eternally full and eternally empty; that God is insofar as he is not, and is not insofar as he is.

Questions and Responses

Abe's argument is exhilarating, rarefied, paradoxical and at times obscure. His identification of God with *Sunyata* has been called into question in three main ways.

Firstly, **does *kenosis* empty God wholly into the creation**, or does it imply a distinction between Creator and creature that God's *kenosis* overcomes without obliterating? Theologian David Tracy rejects the idea that God's *kenosis* must be so total that God is completely poured out into and identified with the cosmos. God must not, he argues, become so thoroughly immanent that no Trinity is left as it were on the other side of the divide between Creator and created. For Tracy "precisely the divine transcendence of all reality renders the divine reality immanent to all reality (and vice verse)" (Cobb and Ives, 1994, p.168). I note that at the most basic level, if I pour water into a pail, water has to be one thing and the pail another – and the act of pouring a third. A kind of Trinity is involved in any 'kenosis'. And if all the water was always in the pail, it has not been poured.

However, in response to this it seems to me that the divine transcendence is *one* way of making the divine immanent – the way of Dionysius and the Gothic cathedral, which offers us a world full of stained glass windows through which the divine energy and light permeate the material world, and turn it into sacrament. But we also noted that Buddhism in its notion of *Sunyata* – and in the Zen garden – seem to be offering a different way. It does not offer, like modern-day materialism, a midst without a beyond, but rather a midst that is beyond, and a beyond that is in the midst, without any gulfs between the midst and the beyond, or for that matter, anywhere else. Does this not suggest that creation and co-arising are different concepts, between which we have to choose?

Secondly, as the Protestant theologian Jürgen Moltmann asks, **"Can *Sunyata* be understood "dynamically" without expanding the naturalist categories through personalist categories?"** (p.124). Are the (mainly) impersonal categories of Buddhism the best for understanding the ultimate, or do we need the personal and perhaps multi-personal, communitarian concepts of Christianity? Related to this is the question that has been with us for a long time: does liberation involve insight or relationship? Does it involve the dying of all desire, or is there a kenotic desire that empties us of self and so can ground our liberation in God? And if so, does this offer a clue to the nature of *kenosis* that Abe has missed? Again, do we have to choose between incompatible ideas?

Moltmann and John Cobb both suggest that the personal aspects of *Sunyata* cannot really bear fruit unless we abandon Abe's emphasis on the impersonal and cosmic and allow the personal and interpersonal to figure in our understanding of liberation and ultimate reality. Christianity offers a mixture of images of the ultimate, some impersonal (wind, fire, wellspring, light, bread, vine, word), some personal (father, son, mother) and some multi-personal (Trinity, communion of saints, people as all images of God). Those who speak of the 'personal God' of Christianity often forget that the Christian doctrine of God is not only mono-personal, but also impersonal and multi-personal. By tapping this rich variety of approaches, it may be possible to construct a vision of the ultimate that can embrace both Buddhist and Christian insights.

Finally, another question that has been with us a long time: **is liberation mainly a personal struggle or a corporate, political and historical project?** This question has two interrelated aspects. One concerns time – whether liberation takes us into an eternal now from which standpoint past and future are symmetrical, and change a matter of indifference, or whether it will always involve an element of striving to create a future that is radically different from the past. Moltmann asks, "Can *Sunyata* be interpreted 'dynamically' without paying heed to the uniqueness of each occurrence and the finality of the redeeming future?" (p.124). The other aspect of the question concerns society – whether each person has to find her own liberation, or whether liberation is always something received from and given to others in a corporate process. Are the particularities of my situation – whether I am male or female, white or black, colonizer or colonized, employer or employee, living in the 21st century or the first – essentially irrelevant to the primary ethical task, the overcoming of ego and the realization of emptiness? Or am I liberated in and through my particular history? In this context, Catherine Keller – quoted in Chapter 4 – takes Abe to task for ignoring the difference gender in particular makes (p.102 ff).

These questions have been themes of much of this book. They are far from being theoretical issues; they concern how we practice our religion, in terms of worship and/or meditation, in terms of whether self-sufficiency is seen as positive or negative, and in terms of the status of political struggle in our spirituality. The question Abe has raised in the abstract brings these very practical issues to a head. Either we will now find a deep affinity between the two faiths that places the differences in a new context, or we will find that the differences are deep oppositions that render the irenic aims of this book ill-conceived.

I will take the three questions in order, so opening the path to the reconciliation I advocate in the final section of the chapter.

1. Being as Doing

Creation and dependent co-arising look like sheer alternatives. Both, to be sure, entail that existence is shot through with nothingness, having nothing in it that is self-explanatory and self-contained. Everything is impermanent, arising and ceasing to be through causes outside itself. However, "for the Mahayana tradition, impermanence is ultimate reality; for Augustine, impermanence is absolutely dependent on ultimate reality for its very being" (Lefebure, 1993, p. 127).

But is this dependence on ultimate reality distinguishable in practice – or even as a theory, when properly analyzed – from the interdependence of everything on everything else that is the basis of Emptiness? The more we ponder the notion of creation out of nothing, the more, it seems to me, the notion of a 'gulf' between creature and Creator vanishes.

Creation out of nothing is, quite obviously, the alternative to creation out of something, and creation out of something has two alternatives: creation out of something other than God, and creation out of God's own being. The latter case suggests the world comes to be in a kind of emanation or a maternal birth out of the womb of God, and the result is pantheism, a world whose substance is divine. In terms of ethics, such a vision calls us to worship of, harmony with and perhaps submission to the divine natural order. In the former case God creates the world either like a man begetting his seed in an 'alien' womb', or else through struggling with forces that are alien to and co-eternal with God – rather as in the Babylonian myth the hero Marduk creates the world by cutting up the flesh of the feminine monster Tiamat. Such a view encourages a cosmic dualism in which we are all involved in a titanic Manichean clash between God and Evil or God and Matter. Of course we will all be fighting on God's side!

As it spread, Christianity encountered both pagan pantheism and Manichean dualism, and the idea of creation out of nothing was forged by Augustine, himself a former Manichean, as an alternative to both. But while I find many Christians are very wary of the pantheism of the New Age movement, their opposition to modern day cosmic dualism is much more muted. The idea of the world as locked in conflict between Good and

Evil is at least as pervasive as New Age pantheism, and probably more dangerous. It lay behind George Bush's rhetoric of the war on terror and the 'axis of evil', with cataclysmic results, and can be detected in the thought patterns of many a conservative Christian, Muslim or Jew.

Now creation out of nothing avoids both these alternatives. What joins God and the world is as significant as any 'gulf' that might divide them, and God and the world cannot be described either as one as in pantheism, or as two as in dualism. For if two, we have to ask, two what? And answer to that there is none. There is nothing that God and the world are two different instances or kinds of.

Indeed in the apophatic tradition of theologians such as Gregory of Nyssa and John Scotus Eriugena, "*creatio ex nihilo* fundamentally means creation from the *nihil* that is God; it is nothing else than the affirmation of the divine negation... by means of which God reveals 'himself' both to himself and to what he makes" (McGinn, 1994, p.101). On this understanding God is primordially nothing. In creation this infinite nothingness as it were negates itself into a finite fullness, in which moreover – according to Eriugena – God becomes something. For Eriugena, God is created and discovers himself through what he creates.

In the more affirmative traditions of Augustine and Aquinas, creation out of nothing simply denotes the act of God making something happen freely and spontaneously. God relates to the world as agent to act. The world is God's action, God's doing. Science, as noted, shows us a world of lawful activity without ultimate substance; it is a doing, not a being. And if that leads us to ask, "Whose doing?" the Christian answers "God's doing". On the analogy of the sentence "The sun is shining" we could say "God is worlding". The world is neither a substance that emanates from God nor a substance that stands over against God. It is not substantial at all, but an action that is done by God.

Both understandings of creation out of nothing makes God

completely immanent in the world – because everything is God's act, his doing – and completely transcendent – because literally nothing is God. Though we can tell something of the agent from an act, the agent remains unknown. God is revealed in the world, but the world is not God, but merely one way in which God has chosen to express Godself. In the same way a painter is immanent in his painting – every bit of it comes from his creative activity – but also transcends the painting, because we cannot know the painter himself simply from his painting. But that transcendence does not mean there is a 'gulf' between the painter and the painting.

However, to the question 'whose doing is the world?' a Mahayana Buddhist would give a different answer. She would agree that the world has no permanent substance of its own, and it is merely a doing or a becoming, but she would say the world is its own doing. She might say, "The world is worlding" or simply "worlding is going on". But would this be any different from the Christian answer in practice?

'Dependent co-arising' describes the world as being like a house of cards that holds up because every card leans on and supports every other card in perfect balance. The structure holds together of its own. Creation out of nothing says there is no thing – no key card, and no table underneath – that supports the house of cards, but the whole house is there as an act or expression of the divine. These ideas are not identical but they are not incompatible. It could be in and through dependent co-arising that God is worlding.

If God – as Augustine insists – makes space and time as well as everything else out of nothing, then there is no elsewhere 'outside' the universe and no time 'before' the universe, where God exists 'in Godself' as it were. So if we want to speak of creating as a self-emptying by God, we cannot say that first God was full, so to speak, and then emptied into creation. We can only say that without the act of creation there is a boundless infinity that is everything, and therefore nothing in particular. And with the act of creation there is a particular world with a particular history in time. And though the act of creation itself is a free self-emptying, God, if wholly kenotic, must be totally committed to this created order. God cannot keep a part of Godself back, as it were, still infinite and eternal in some other space and time alongside ours. There is no other space and time alongside ours, and even if there were, God could not be infinite and eternal in it.

So in one way Abe is right: God's *kenosis* makes God thoroughly immanent. On the other hand, we cannot articulate the idea of creation as a *kenosis* unless we have a concept of what God would be, so to speak, without the act of creation: the infinity and eternity which God surrenders in creating, and which we cannot know, because we can only really know what is in space and time. This is what Buddhists express as Suchness: the way the world is just as it is and not one of the infinite other ways it might have been, and not for that matter not existing at all. But the experience of Suchness involves a sense of the infinite range of 'might have beens'. The focus is precisely on how things are, but against the background of how they might have been otherwise. That background of alternative possibilities makes of the fact that things are just as they are a wonder to marvel at; it is the shadow that creates the remarkable light of Suchness. The term 'God' names the infinite might-have-been, but again, only to focus sharply on what is as God's self-limiting choice, God's loving act. The naming of God makes the given a gift. In practice these seem to be two ways – the 'emptiness and Suchness' way of Buddhism, and the 'creation out of nothing' way of Christianity – of focusing on the same reality.

Imagine the whole universe as a waterfall, ever changing, ever following its own laws. This waterfall comes from the unknown and falls into the unknown. A Buddhist would describe it as just being so, without explanation. But we notice that this just-so-ness has certain qualities. We can describe the waterfall as wonderful, as a mystery, as a free gift we had no right to expect. But these thoughts draw us into thoughts about the nature of the 'nothing' out of and into which the waterfall flows. It does not seem to be a 'bare' nothing, but a 'generous' nothing, a nothing we may feel we want to know and love, though it is beyond all comprehension. We are drawn into a different description, in which personal language about God and creation out of nothing becomes attractive.

In terms of what they describe as being there, it is hard to specify the difference between the Buddhist and Christian descriptions of the cosmic 'waterfall'. But there may seem to be an immense difference in terms of how we respond to it in practice.

2. Kenotic Yearning

At first sight the practical difference between the emptying God and Buddhist Emptiness seems immense. Creation out of nothing holds onto God as a goal of our desire and yearning, whereas Emptiness and Suchness are where we rest without desire and without goals.

We have seen that a fundamental divergence between Christianity and Buddhism is whether liberation comes finally from overcoming all desire, or whether there is a kind of emptying desire (*eros*) that can liberate us from 'plerotic' self-gratifying desire (*epithumia* in Greek, *concupiscentia* in Latin). In the former case liberation means enlightenment, an insight into Emptiness that makes all desire redundant; in the latter it comes through relationship with God in an ecstasy of desire that takes us beyond all desire for anything in particular, or anything for ourselves alone.

The Latin translation of Psalm 42.4 – an important text for St. Augustine – says the equivalent of "I pour out my soul beyond [or above, *super*] myself". Love – both in the form of *eros* and in generous self-sacrificial charity or *agapé* – involves a forgetting of the self in the other. If the other is God, then love means a total loss of self in what is altogether beyond my grasp; it becomes unrestricted love without any object I can define or describe, transcending created being altogether. According to the Canadian theologian Bernard Lonergan (1973) such unrestricted love forms the basis of conversion and the Christian life.

Buddhism, we have seen, tells us to let go of all desire so as to reach an Emptiness overflowing with wisdom and compassion. Christianity teaches us a love that overflows beyond all objects and renders everything but the ungraspable object, God, empty. The way may be different but is the final state any different? Simone Weil says

> The extinction of Desire (Buddhism) – or detachment – or amor fati – or desire for the absolute good – these amount to the same thing: to empty desire... of all content, to desire in the void, to desire without any wishes. To detach ourselves from all good things and to wait... It is then we touch the absolute good. (2002, p.13)

But in view of what has just been argued about creation and what Abe affirms about dynamic *Sunyata*, a difference remains. The 'good' we touch in this kind of self-emptying love is itself self-emptying love. Dionysus affirms that "God's creating love is ecstatic, that is, it draws God out of Godself and leads God to center God's being on the object of divine love" (*Divine Names*, in1993, 4.13). If creation is best understood (following Maximus the Confessor, the 7th century theologian who was foundational in the development of Eastern Orthodoxy) as the first incarnation – the pouring out of the infinite and eternal into a finite space-time – and if the incarnation in Jesus Christ is a pouring out of the infinite into a particular human life, then what we touch in this love is not the boundless emptiness but a particular life coming to us in the ecstasy of love.

Louis Lefebure argues that this is very different from the Buddhist view.

> The attribution of desire to God reveals a profound difference between the Dionysian and the Mahayana paths. While Dharmakaya is compassion, the source of the Bodhisattva's skilful means, the Mahayana tradition does not personalize the absolute and attribute desire or yearning to it. While Dharmakaya manifests itself in Shakyamuni Buddha, the notion that ultimate reality 'is enticed away from his transcendent dwelling place and comes to abide within all things' is foreign to Zen or Mahayana thought. (1993, p.96)

However, though Abe does not use the term ecstasy, his dynamic *Sunyata* does negate its own being in the particular and just so. The language has less emotional overtones than the word 'ecstasy', but seems to describe the same notion that the infinite has to go beyond its own infinity into the limited and particular.

And in both Buddhism and Christianity, it seems to me, we end with *yugen*, yearning, *epektasis*, reaching out into the unknowable. But this yearning is not bleak or melancholy but full of joy, for in it everything is seen against the background of an infinite emptying and ecstasy of love, enjoyed for its just-so-uniqueness, its being there for no earthly reason at all, but because of a boundless and indefinable compassion.

3. True Atheism?

Buddhists and Christians would surely agree on the point that liberation cannot mean an escape from the 'just so' world into uncreated emptiness. Such an escape is advocated in several religions. Neo-Platonism describes a kind of return of the many to the primordial One, Gnostic Christianity seeks the release of the spark of the soul from its material prison in the body and its return to its natural divine home, while Vedanta Hinduism speaks of the reabsorbing of the self (*atman*) into the divine (*Brahman*). When Theravada Buddhism speaks of Nirvana it sounds like an escape from the world of becoming (Samsara) to a boundless eternity.

But that would involve, in Christian terms, a reversal of God's choice, a seeking of God where God has opted not to be, so to speak, rather than in the world into which he has emptied himself in creation and incarnation. And in Mahayana Buddhist terms it would mean a rejection of Emptiness and Suchness, and a denial of the oneness of Samsara and Nirvana. Liberation, as suggested before, does not mean the escape from history, but beginning to make it anew together.

If religion is defined in terms of a self-sacrificial allegiance to the infinite and absolute, and a depreciation of all that is finite and relative, then both Buddhism and Christianity are fundamentally anti-religious. Overtly atheistic creeds like communism (and we might add what we called scientism) fail to overcome the basic human need for total allegiance to an absolute. Something – the Party or the Nation or the Leader or Scientific Progress – has to take God's place. Christianity – according to Slavoj Žižek (2009), p.25ff – enables a truer atheism.

He argues that Christianity takes the Jewish thrust against idolatry a radical step further. The idol of a separate, allegiance-demanding God is also smashed. Or rather, God is absorbed into human particularity in Jesus and his death and resurrection. Thereafter solemn sacrifice to the big Other gives way to joyous kenotic love for God incarnate in the sister and brother. Sacrificial religion becomes redundant – which is why Christianity did indeed have a reputation in the ancient world for atheism: it rejected the key duty humans are thought to owe to the gods, namely sacrifice. Buddhism – we might add – overcomes religion and idolatry too, but in a 'cooler', less paradoxical way, by overcoming the self that needs to sacrifice itself. If there is no self to sacrifice and no divine, sacrifice becomes impossible.

Christianity – in this sense – is capable of removing all traces of the envy of YHWH. It can offer – to put it in the most challenging way – a God who does not mind whether he exists or not! The sense in which God still exists is more like the star-gods of the polytheist than the demanding God of Robson. As my father realized as a child, if God does exist, he will not crave our attention, and will not bully us into giving it to him. Our belief adds nothing to his reality, and though God delights in our response, he does not crave or need our sacrifice.

Only if God is profoundly 'nothing' to us can we affirm her in the right way, without denigrating suffering, failure and nothingness. The kenotic God of Christianity is the tender matrix of our becoming, embracing limitation and non-existence in preference to a boundlessness and existence that would overpower us. In the words of St Paul, "God chose what is low and despised in the world, things that are not, to reduce to nothing things that are" (1 Cor. 1.28).

Of course, in practice Christianity has all too often reneged on this kind of understanding. But the Christian Trinity is often seen by theologians as a model for liberated, kenotic interbeing. James Alison argues (1998, p.102-10) that the Trinity represents what becomes of God after the Christian transformation just described; what happens if we empty God of any notions of domination, envy, possessiveness and rivalry, either on his part or our own. But to empty God completely of these qualities, it seems to me not enough that the persons of the Trinity are seen as equal, as a kind of lofty and remote model for how we should behave toward one another down here on earth. The relationship between God and the world must also be emptied of all hierarchy. I suggest that the Trinity – if and only if emptied in this way – may also serve as a template for the key Buddhist insights into *Sunyata*, *Tathata* and *Dharmakaya* and the Wisdom and Compassion that flow from them. We will then be left with what I will call...

The Inscendent Trinity

The three issues we have just dealt with give rise to three clusters of ideas about the ultimate in relation to the world, which might form the basis of an understanding of the Trinity that Buddhists could make their own. In the process, I think we can see the impersonal, the personal, and the interpersonal dimensions of the Ultimate – over which Buddhism and Christianity have seemed to be particularly at odds – finding their proper place. I do not expect that all Christians and Buddhists will find this process acceptable as a model of what they believe, but I think it will fall within the area of 'acceptable variation' for both faiths. It will represent what this book has been seeking: something that is both a legitimate variety of Buddhism and a legitimate variety of Christianity.

God is 0: nothing. God is 1, being. God is ∞, everything. I shall use this as our way into understanding the 'three' that make the Trinity.

0

The first cluster of concepts consists of terms and images like creator out of nothing, source of all being, agent whose act is all that is, father of all, mother of all, Emptiness, Suchness, spontaneous arising, *jinen*, emptying. The root image here is of an infinite 'womb' of possibility emptying itself eternally into particular actuality, which thereby becomes the marvelous 'just so'.

One image for the way an infinite array of possibility can collapse into a specific actuality is choice; it happens every time we choose to do something out of all the things we might do. This is a case of emptying, in that we 'lose' all those other possibilities and are left with only one, which we have chosen and are henceforward committed to. This is irreversible; we can repent of our choices, but – despite what Abe argues in defense of irreversibility (p.193) – we cannot undo them. So we can use 'choosing' as an analogy for the creation of the world: God has chosen just this world, it exists because God has chosen it and is henceforth committed to it in love.

Understanding God's 'choosing' in this way has the benefit of reconciling the idea, found in Aquinas and Augustine, of creation as God's act, making something out of nothing, with the more negative tradition of Gregory of Nyssa and Eriugena, which sees creation as God negating his own nothingness. To say God 'chooses' this world out of the infinity of possibilities is ultimately the same as to say God negates her infinite no-thing-ness to bring forth a finite something. The analogies serve to correct each other and prevent us taking either too literally.

Certainly we should not take the 'agent' analogy so far as to suggest that God is a supreme Mind who has rationally decided to create this universe in a big bang moment. That would take us back to the Designer God. But the tradition that derives from Augustine sees creation as God's eternal act, and from our point of view, as relating equally to every moment of time. Because God relates to the world as agent to act, and not as a being substantially tied to the being of the world, God is an absolute mystery. Though everything in its just-so-ness expresses God, nothing can be identified with God. In that sense the First 'Person' of our Trinity is deeply impersonal and unimaginable. For this reason I will refrain from speaking of the First, Second and Third 'Persons' of the Trinity, and speak simply of the First, Second and Third, so enabling us to do justice to the 'imperson-ality' of the First and the 'multi-personality' of the Third.

1

The second cluster of concepts is more affirmative: Word, Wisdom, *Dharmakaya*, the Body of the Law or the Real. Here we are describing not a second reality, but a different realization of the same Cosmos: its beautiful law-abiding glory and splendor, that which makes reality both accessible to human logos or reason, and an inexhaustible source of joy and delight. If under the First we apprehended mystery, inexplicable just-so-ness, here we look for connections and causes, and universal features like space, time, causality, karma; all those aspects that make of the cosmos a nursery for consciousness and enlightenment. The 'kaya' of Dharmakaya is important; meaning 'body', it refers to the way reality is like a body, not a random sequence of events but an interdependent co-arising whole. Hebrew tradition expresses this by depicting Wisdom not only as the structure of things that rewards the wise and teaches the fool better ways, but also a ravishingly beautiful bride and constant companion of God.

It is with the Second that the truly personal dimension comes into its own, if by 'person' we name 'interbeing', being that inherently relational to its other. At this point the Christian terms 'Child' and 'Son' become relevant. They express the way all being is the dependent 'child' originated by the First. But the word Abba which Jesus used for his 'Father', also suggests a tender loving relationship with that First. So it becomes appropriate to term the First, the unfathomable Zero origin before whose face the dharma-body of Wisdom eternally dances, 'Father' or even 'Mother'. If the First is the source of the life and being of the Second, the Second is the source of the interbeing and personhood of the First: there would be no 'Father' were it not for the 'Son'.

If we use the symbol '0' to express the First as the unfathomable emptiness from which all springs, it seems appropriate to use '1' to express the Second, as the unity of the Body of the real. Unlike '0', '1' has two ends. Reality contains many polarities: mind and matter, subject and object, active and passive, cause and effect, particle and wave, male and female. But dualism – thinking of these poles as substantially distinct – is ruled out, since the ends are connected by a vertical line, suggesting relationship and interbeing. And '1' means unity. Even the polarity between Creator and created is subsequent to the act of creation: the Creator comes into being – or as Eriugena radically put it, God is created as Creator – through the act of creating,

But the term 'body' suggests something else too: that the Second is what incarnates or embodies itself, first in the Body of the Cosmos, but then in the person of Jesus Christ, who incarnates the divine Word and Wisdom of God, and the Buddha, who embodies the Dharma: incarnations that are the same and not the same, as described in Chapter 1. The Trikaya teaching represents, not a kind of Buddhist Trinity, but a careful grasp of the different levels of incarnation of the Second: as the Cosmos, as the historical Jesus Christ and Gautama Buddha, and as the Christ and Buddha of faith and joy which forms the body of the universal Church and the universal *Sangha*.

But this third, community 'body' takes us from the Second toward the Third.

∞

The third cluster of terms is the least developed, I think, in both traditions, and particularly embryonic in Buddhism. Buddhist 'Compassion' names it, as does perhaps '*Bodhicitta*'. The *Sangha* of all Buddhism, the Bodhisattvas of the Mahayana and the *Yidams* of the Vajrayana express it. In Christianity the Holy Spirit, the Kingdom and the Church express different aspects of it. Though in Christian tradition there are several dominant impersonal images for the Third – wind, fire, water – other images are strikingly multi-personal. The Kingdom, the Church and the communion of saints are, like the *Sangha*, communities or 'peoples' rather than persons. Bodhisattvas and *yidams*, like saints, are of course plural.

I suggest this is because the Third represents the gathering of many into community and relationship. It is, if you like, the historical directionality of the cosmos, in a movement that is at one and the same time a movement towards ever greater chaos – the 'entropy' of science, which implies an ultimate 'heat death' of the universe in the unimaginable future – and the emergence of ever more complex order; the assembly of molecules into genes and life, and of these in turn into consciousness and memes and cultures.

How can the directionality of time be defined by two such opposing factors, increasing order and increasing chaos? There is no doubt that in science these two aspects do characterize time and give it irreversible direction. And Darwin's theory of natural selection gives a scientific explanation of part of the connection: it is precisely the randomizing, chaotic elements of mutation and competition that cause new and more complex species to arise.

But we can look to a spiritual connection too. The Third represents a 'redemptive' aspect that brings new order out of chaos, 'good' out of 'evil'. (I use quotes here to ward off a simplistic equation of good with order and evil with chaos; one thing that redemption tells us is how chaos can be 'good'.) If Jesus incarnates the beauty of the Word, his death represents the shattering of that beauty by the chaos and antipathy of the world, and the resurrection its remaking into something finer than anything before seen, a beauty and *jinen* that are radically new.

So as well as embodying the Second, Jesus manifests the movement of the Third, the Spirit, beginning a process of healing the disordered and assembling the outcasts, making Church, creating Kingdom out of chaos. This is not the neo-Platonic and Gnostic return of the many to the one, the temporal to the eternal, but an ever-richer and ever-more-interrelated manyness, the arrival in time of what is ever new. It is also the basis of a cosmic *yugen*, the longing of the whole creation for this new birth. As St. Paul writes:

The creation waits with eager longing for the revealing of the children of God; for the creation was subjected to futility, not of its own will but by the will of the one who subjected it, in hope that the creation itself will be set free from its bondage to decay and will obtain the freedom of the glory of the children of God. We know that the whole creation has been groaning in labor pains until now; and not only the creation, but we ourselves, who have the first fruits of the Spirit, groan inwardly while we wait for adoption, the redemption of our bodies. (Rom. 8.19-23)

If we want a symbol for the Third, it might be the spiral, which combines the circularity of the First with the linear progression of the Second. Time contains its circularities, but because of the linear movement, the spiral on every return brings us to a new place. In life and in history we are always coming back to ourselves and revisiting our past, and thereby finding ourselves somewhere new. If we want a numerical symbol, then this spiral translates into the sign for infinity, '∞', the loop that is forever crossing itself. This sign also suggests that Third is well expressed by a musical fugue in which a theme interweaves and interacts with itself in ever new ways. It is conveyed not by the impersonal or the personal but by the never-finished infinity of persons reflecting *Bodhicitta* (see Chapter 5) or the image of God.

Generalizing we could say that the First represents the spontaneous arising of being out of nothing, the Second the arising of interbeing – including personhood and meaning – out of being, and the Third the arising of becoming and community and yearning out of the interplay between the First and the Second, the original nothing and meaningful being. In the terms of Western Theology, the Third proceeds from the First and the Second. However, with the Eastern Orthodox I wish to emphasize that the Third is not merely the relationship between the First and the Second, but is always 'something else', something freshly given.

Each of the Three is kenotic, self-emptying, but in a different way. The First shows the *kenosis* of surrender which negates its own infinite nothingness, and pours itself out into a specific act of creation. The Second shows the *kenosis* of embodiment, and especially the bearing of suffering and dis-grace by the grace-full Body of the Real, which is seen most clearly in the passion of Christ. The Third shows the *kenosis* of *yugen*, the yearning of all creation in its emptiness for a fullness yet to be.

All three kinds of emptying are expressed in the poem of mine at the start of this chapter: the original emptying that is creation, the vine of *Dharmakaya* Christ arising in the midst of it, and the dispersal of Christ in countless images scattered like reflections of the setting sun.

It seems that our Trinity is more than a series of three names for different aspects or 'modes' of reality, for it has something of the inner structure of relations that Christians have traditionally ascribed to the three persons. At the same time it is an immanent Trinity in the sense demanded by Abe. The three persons are not imaginatively located, so to speak, 'beyond' or over against the universe (in what is often confusingly termed the 'immanent' Trinity!) Just as we cannot count the One, Two and Three and make anything but one God, so we cannot count the Trinity and the world and make two (or would it be four?)! As Denys Turner puts it, discussing Eckhart, "God is in no way numerable" (1995, p.248).

It is true that the First takes us so to speak to a boundless ground logically 'before' – or to put it better, 'otherwise than' – being, and the Third to a future beyond anything we can imagine. But the *kenosis* of God is complete in that there is, so to speak, no going back on the divine commitment to a universe that is the whole divine act, the whole divine body and the whole divine desire.

There is a strong transcendent dimension of the Trinity on this interpretation. But traditional theology started from the transcendent Trinity before and beyond Creation, which then as it were made itself immanent in the coming of Christ and the Spirit 'into' the world. I would rather start from the immanence of the Trinity in the world, and see how the Trinity so discovered reaches back and forward and beyond the world, transcending the grasp of our understanding. It is this total immanence in the here and now of what transcends understanding that I like to call 'inscendence'.

Finally, however, the universe to which the Trinity is thus intimately related is no chunk of closed causality to which God is bound. The Trinity is rather the openness of the universe in three ways: to the ground or source 'below' from which it eternally springs; to the order 'in its midst', which it incarnates and embodies; and to its future 'beyond', a realm we cannot grasp or anticipate, but only imagine in the joyful outreaching of self-forgetting love.

Summary

1. The huge unsettled issue between Christianity and Buddhism is whether there is a God, and whether it matters.

2. YHWH the God of Hebrew monotheism possesses a wondrous mixture of qualities, but is best thought of as an image through which we may relate to the ultimate, rather than identified with ultimate reality itself.

3. One tradition of Christian thought regards God as beyond being and non-being, while another emphasizes his jealous exclusion of all non-being and of all rivals to his own being. In the latter we see a spiritualized version of the jealous YHWH.

4. While Christianity sees all things as analogies for God, Buddhism tends to see all things as reflecting each other. The former vision is behind the Gothic Cathedral, the latter behind the Zen Garden.

5. Buddhists are not dogmatic atheists but reject talk of God,

partly for practical reasons – it distracts us from the task of liberation – but partly because of the difference of deep vision just mentioned.

6. However, if God is understood as self-emptying rather than as Supreme Being, and Buddhist Emptiness is understood in a dynamic way that includes wisdom and compassion, God and Emptiness may be identified.

7. Christianity speaks of a God whom we can love and who loves and yearns for us. But the desire-consuming love of Christianity, and the overcoming of all desire in Buddhism, which generates total compassion, may actually lead to the same place.

8. Both Buddhism and Christianity represent major alternatives to the kind of God who needs sacrifice. They achieve an 'atheism' that modern atheism cannot.

9. The book argues for an 'inscendent' Trinity – immanent in all things, yet transcending understanding – embracing:

   1) the 'non-personal' emptiness of nothing out of which all things spring in their delightful just-so-ness;

   2) the *Dharmakaya* or Logos or Wisdom or beautiful order of all that is, incarnating itself as the body of the divine – in whom it becomes 'personal' as it relates back to the beloved Source – Christ and the Buddha being such embodiments;

   3) the Spirit, the 'multi-personal' multifaceted kingdom, Church or *Sangha*, the gathering of all things historically into a future community beyond our imagining.

Chapter 9

A Buddhist Way to Follow Christ?

There are those who think it is possible to be both a Christian and a Buddhist at the same time. I doubt it!... [There are] a number of areas where Christianity would need considerable reinterpretation if it were ever to be truly compatible with Buddhism as Buddhism has existed in doctrine, practice and history.

(Williams, 2006, p.75)

Thus concludes the excellent little booklet on Buddhism which Paul Williams wrote for the Catholic Truth Society. I stand accused of attempting the impossible. My plea in this book is firstly that Buddhism and Christianity have been in doctrine, practice and history many things. Most of the Christian variations, including doubtless Williams' own Roman Catholicism, are certainly incompatible with most Buddhist variations. But not all. One outcome of the book is that I am not a vaguer Buddhist or Christian than I was; I can actually be more precise about the kind of Buddhist I am and the kind of Christian I am – see later.

And secondly, I would be the last to deny that "considerable reinterpretation" is needed of Christianity, but this book has attempted it and stands and falls on whether the reinterpretations it offers are improvements in terms of enabling the mission of both faiths in the contemporary world.

However, if all the differences between Buddhism and Christianity were satisfactorily overcome, so would all the deep mysteries this book has explored: what if anything is self, God, mind, matter, the nature of the universe, causality, freedom, responsibility, desire, and our final goal? I cannot pretend to have resolved all these issues. To use T.S. Eliot's phrase from *Burnt Norton*, I have only conducted a series of "raids on the inarticulate" with the help of the Buddhist and Christian traditions. Nor was it ever part of my intention to offer a new 'Buddho-Christianity' to which all members of both faiths, once they understand it, will subscribe! A majority of Buddhists and Christians will be sure to disagree with my Buddhist Christianity on a number of issues; but then a majority of Christians, and a majority of Buddhists, disagree among themselves to the same degree.

My aim has been a little less grandiose, namely, first, to see whether it is possible to hold a position that is a legitimate variety of Buddhism and a legitimate variety of Christianity; and secondly, to see what each faith has to gain and lose were it to move towards such a position. It is now time to see how these questions have been answered. Or to put it more personally, since I feel that through writing this book I have come to a position that is both Buddhist and Christian, to see whether my claim to be authentically both can be sustained, and what would be gained and lost if members of both faiths began in some way to take up something like the position I have come to.

This chapter will first summarize the conclusions reached in this book. It will then need to ask, first, whether I am a Buddhist, what I have learned from Buddhism in my journey, and what Christian queries I have brought to bear upon Buddhism in this book. It will then ask whether I am still a Christian, what I have brought with me from Christianity in my journey, and what Buddhist queries I have brought to bear upon Christianity. It will say a little about what it now means to follow Jesus Christ in a Buddhist way, as I now feel I need to do. And then, as a bold and probably foolish venture, it will summarize the kind of Buddhist Christian commitment that has emerged from these pages.

Conclusions of the Chapters

I list these chapter by chapter.

1. The Buddha is often depicted in the West as a human teacher in contrast with Jesus the divine Savior. But in the practice of their religions both are revered as incarnations – in their different ways – of ultimate Wisdom or the Dharma Body. Christians who regard Jesus as a unique incarnation misunderstand the original doctrine, which teaches that Christ takes all humanity into the divine.

2. We can only approach the 'original' Jesus and Buddha through the traditions that have sprung from them. The sayings ascribed to them show a remarkable convergence in their teaching, which in many ways goes against the grain of common sense morality. This justifies using the same term, 'liberation', to describe what both were advocating. Though the Buddha is mostly depicted as a serene wisdom teacher, and Christ as a prophetic man of challenge and sorrow, we can discern a prophetic and struggling 'Christic shadow' in the Buddha and a witty, Zen-like 'Buddhic shadow' in Jesus.

3. Buddhism and Christianity depict a huge negative 'hole' in life in order to offer something overwhelmingly positive. Buddhism sees the hole in terms of the universal experience of suffering, while Christianity sees it in terms of our tendency to cause it, namely sin. Both trace the causes of these to egocentricity and desire, but while Buddhism teaches us to quieten desire, Christianity teaches us to find the true goal of our desire in God.

4. Both accounts have underestimated the social and political causes of desire. Desire needs to be distinguished from instinctive natural drive. Desire has its causes in the economic 'scarcity' society creates and the 'mimetic rivalry' which creates the envious, craving ego. The

Enneagram combines Christian and Buddhists insights into a model whereby each of us is conditioned at the root of our ego by one or another form of desire; but this root desire can become a means of liberation from desire.

5. Buddhism as a religion of self effort is often contrasted with Christianity as a religion of salvation by faith in what another (Christ) has done for us. But Buddhism in all its forms – especially Shin – acknowledges the need for some kind of 'other power'; both faiths vary in the emphasis they place on self help versus grace; entire self-reliance cannot save us if the self is what we need saving from; and ultimately, once egocentricity is overcome, the dichotomy between self and other power disappears. Jesus in his death and resurrection is best seen a radical Bodhisattva who resolves the sin at the root of the delusion of self, setting us free to help one another towards salvation.

6. Both traditions offer a variety of practices – of mind, sight and imagination, speech and hearing, heart and feeling, and body – to help us toward liberation. Though a pick and mix approach would ruin the integration and balance that exists within each tradition, each has much to learn from the practices of the other regarding the way it follows its own path.

7. Buddhist Christianity integrates well with the insights of modern science. The world of modern science exhibits a groundless lawfulness – it is not reducible to atoms but does follow laws, in an unpredictable determinism that includes our free agency. We belong seamlessly to the universe, which is all at once entirely material and entirely spiritual and meaningful. The world is not ruled by a providence or karma that punishes and rewards individuals. But in terms of natural causality our actions have a big past and a big future, so that as part of the one cosmic 'symphony' it matters immensely that we sound

our 'note' well. The universe is not alien but a nursery of consciousness that develops historically. Rather than opposing evolutionary accounts, we should be widening the story of liberation to encompass the history and destiny of the universe.

8. Christians and Buddhists seem most divided over the issue of God. The Christian God derives from Hebrew stories of YHWH, who is best seen as an imaginative creation who can help people relate to ultimate reality. Mainstream Christians see all things as manifesting the unknowable God and as presenting analogies for God, whereas Buddhism sees them as arising interdependently and mirroring one another within a deep 'Emptiness'. This Emptiness, however, manifests personal aspects of Wisdom and Compassion, and can be compared with the Self-Emptying Trinity of Christianity. Buddhism and Christianity converge in a Trinity which is everywhere present but transcends understanding. This Trinity brings together in mutual relationship an impersonal Emptiness from which everything springs, a more personal *Dharmakaya* or embodied Wisdom (incarnated in Buddha and Christ), and a multi-personal Spirit that historically gathers all beings together into a diverse unity we cannot yet conceive.

Am I a Buddhist?

In the introduction I proposed that if one affirms the Four Noble Truths, the three characteristics of being, and the Eightfold Path, one is a Buddhist. So am I a Buddhist by my own criteria?

Regarding the three characteristics, I do regard all 'formations' – which sounds roughly what a Christian would call 'created beings' – as impermanent. All things change and pass away. If the Trinity does not, it is because it is not a created thing, not a 'formation' but the very source of time and change.

Buddhists themselves regard Nirvana as beyond change, but this is because Nirvana is unconditioned, not formed, and again, an exception to the rule of impermanence. The characteristic of 'no-self' follows: there is no permanent entity in me I could call a self. There was a time when I was not, and there will be a time when I will not be. That may be different from what most Christians believe, but the eternal soul is an inheritance from Platonism, I think, not integral to Christianity. I have argued that it arises from grasping desire, and when such desire ceases, so will any separate self. I do think our 'interbeing' with the Trinity and with others may 'remain', but this is not a separate something that remains, and whether the concept of 'remaining' is appropriate here I am not sure, and need to explore some more. The universal characteristic of *dukkha* – suffering, lack, unsatisfactoriness – is also, I think, quite obvious.

It is this *dukkha* that forms the basis of the first noble truth, and I have suggested that one of the strengths of Buddhism is that it sees suffering, not sin, as the basic problem. No Buddhist would deny that sin is a problem, but there is clearly much problematic suffering that is not caused by sin, whereas a great deal of sin – perhaps all sin ultimately – is caused by suffering or lack. To see sin as the core problem is in a sense to take an egocentric view of suffering. Whether I can take pride in my resistance to sin or am humiliated by my capitulation, my good or evil status takes center stage, and the victim's point of view is occluded by that of the sinner. To start from the suffering and discontent I am afflicted with is more honest, less pretentious, more genuinely humbling, as it unites me with the rest of humanity in my power-lessness.

The cause of this suffering in our *tanha*, grasping desire, is also something I know to be true. We suffer, and feel things to be unsatisfactory, because we cling to and want to posses them; and we do so because our egos are invested in them. As noted in the autobiographical introduction, this hits my nail on the head.

What I have been wrestling with is my need to inflate and sustain an ego, and desires I was not able to control, but which controlled me because I had excluded them from the ego I wanted to have. Christianity, by placing the emphasis on sin and atonement, hit my nail obliquely, creating a guilt that gnawed at but also preserved my ego structure. In this sense Buddhism has been necessary to my path of liberation.

But from Christianity I have learned the distinction between *epithumia* and *eros*, between the desire that is inherently envious, competitive and ego-boosting and the love that is self-emptying and absorbed in a self-forgetful delight, whether in an equation, in a beloved person, or in the divine. And I have also argued that the source of the former kind of desire is not cosmic but historical and social. So I depart from the Buddhist mainstream in three big ways. The first is that I seek a social, corporate and historical overcoming of desire. Solitary meditation is essential, but not sufficient. The second departure follows from this: I cannot liberate myself on my own but need what Pure Land Buddhists call 'other-power' and what Christians term *charis* – meaning 'free gift' and usually translated 'grace'. These departures mean that I am not a typical Buddhist, but I remain, I think, within the orbit of a Buddhism that includes the Shin form, and in many quarters today, a growing sense of the social and historical dimension of the struggle for liberation.

The third departure relates to the third noble truth, that of Nirvana. I certainly believe in the possibility and desirability of a state in which mimetic desire is overcome, and the separate self is no more. I believe too that this must be possible in this life; I do not think Jesus was asking us to strive for a Kingdom of heaven 'in the sky when we die' – a Kingdom I am quite unsure about and am not prepared to defer to – but rather urged that the Kingdom is 'at hand' so we must change our state of mind right now. This became clear in Chapter 2. But I believe this state is compatible with, and enabled by, the self-forgetful kind of kenotic longing, or *yugen*. So it cannot mean a detachment from all love. Though this is in tension with the heart of Theravada Buddhism, even the Theravada involves a lot of loving devotion in practice, while the Mahayana embraces the ideal of the Bodhisattva whose love of all beings takes precedence over her personal liberation. In practice in the Mahayana tradition the Bodhisattva ideal replaces what it regards as the lonely *Arhat* ideal of the Theravada. So again, I think I represent a legitimate variation of Buddhism.

As for the fourth noble truth – the way to Nirvana – this is the Eightfold Path: right view, right intention, right speech, right action, right livelihood, right effort, right mindfulness, and right concentration or meditation. I have no quarrel with these, and would certainly emphasize how much the last two, mindfulness and meditation, have brought an understanding and discipline to my mind which I have come to regard as an essential part of my path to liberation. I would probably wish to elucidate the ethical aspects of the Eightfold Path both by means of the six Mahayana perfections – giving, morality, patience, energy, meditation and wisdom – and through what I have learned from the parables and teachings of Jesus. But we have seen how the teachings ascribed to the Buddha and Jesus have so much in common that, this can only be an enrichment, not a contradiction.

I have said very little about the 'afterlife' – whether in terms of reincarnation, resurrection or immortality. The book might have benefited from a chapter on death and beyond, but I am not yet ready to write it, and need to reflect some more. At present I am 'agnostic' about what lies beyond death, except I am confident that if I follow Jesus and the Buddha as faithfully as I can, I will come to whatever future is best for me. And that is enough for now.

All in all I am surely a kind of Buddhist. I need to affirm this now, by deepening my Buddhist practice, by finding a Buddhist community to belong to, and by taking – when the time is right –

the triple refuge.

It is very significant that Buddhism as it has developed has moved – albeit not universally – in the directions of the three 'departures' I have described. Many parts of Buddhism have accepted the need for a dimension of political liberation, and in many places – as in Vietnam, Myanmar and Tibet – a dimension of political struggle has been forced on it through hostile rule. The Pure Land – the most numerous form of Buddhism in Japan, and influential on many forms of Mahayana Buddhism – has stressed the importance of 'other power'. And the Bodhisattva ideal has developed.

None of these three developments could have been predicted from the teachings of the Buddha or early Buddhism. Nor is it plausible to explain them (except perhaps the first) by way of Christian influence. Is it arrogant to suggest that the developments are explained by the fact that Wisdom was indeed incarnate in the Buddha and in the development of Buddhism? We might even say that the 'Christic shadow' of the Buddha (the aspect of Wisdom that was not explicit in his life and teaching, but is explicit in Jesus) has operated in the history of Buddhism.

Christoyana Buddhism?

Perhaps what is happening now is a further development in this direction – the arising of something we might even call 'Christoyana' Buddhism. The Theravada vision of Nirvana as a remote future state developed into the Mahayana vision of Nirvana as an ever-present reality at one with Samsara, the world of becoming. Nirvana grew from being a state of mind and a final goal to an ever-present cosmic principle, *Sunyata*, an ineffable full emptiness somewhat akin to the Tao of Taoism. But with the Christoyana it might also become the Resurrection, erupting from within history and working within it. The Theravada emphasis on the final and the Mahayana emphasis on the universal might be completed by a new emphasis on the historical. And just as Mahayana and Vajrayana forms of Buddhism did not replace the Theravada, but exist alongside it, so I suggest a 'Christoyana' Buddhism is becoming possible in our time that will not replace but enrich those other forms.

Am I a Christian?

Christianity has been as varied as Buddhism, but in the Introduction I proposed that if anyone who assented to the baptismal commitment – with its affirmation of God as Trinity, and Christ as incarnate Lord who has saved humankind by his cross and resurrection – could be safely regarded as a Christian. In this sense I remain as Christian as I ever was.

The Trinity is a teaching I have definitely affirmed. My emphasis on the immanent Trinity rather than a Trinity 'outside' or 'beyond' the universe may contradict emphases that began to arise in the fourth century. But it is thoroughly in line with many early and recent understandings.

As for incarnation, we have seen how the understanding of Jesus as the incarnate Word of God is closer than is commonly realized to the understanding of the Buddha in terms of the three bodies. And I find the Chalcedonian Creed of 451, which presents divine and human nature coming together – while remaining distinct – in the person of Jesus Christ, to be a beautiful expression of what the incarnation means. That makes me a lot more orthodox than many contemporary Christians.

But that definition describes the whole of human nature being united with the whole Word of God in Jesus Christ. This incarnation is not a rival to other possible incarnations, but a full historical expression of what is irrevocably true of all humanity. Far from forcing us to reject incarnation in other traditions, we should be led to expect it. And speaking personally, I have not found that believing Jesus Christ is not the one and only incarnation of the divine has in any ways undermined my love and devotion to him. On the contrary, by looking to Buddha as another embodiment of the one and only Logos or Dharma, I have been led to see all sorts of interilluminations that have enhanced my amazement in Jesus Christ as such an incarnation.

And I also find myself able to affirm the uniqueness of what Jesus has done for me and for the world. The Buddha too is of course unique, he has done different things for me and for the world, and it would be foolish to claim that the roles of Jesus and the Buddha are interchangeable. In particular, by his cross and resurrection Jesus has delivered us from the necessity of remaining in the grip of the desire that separates us as rival egos. It is not that there is an offended feudal God up there needing someone to be punished before he can be at peace with us. But because we are so deeply formed by desire, deliverance requires something more radical than the self-effort that (mainstream) Buddhism teaches. The desire that forms us is not first and foremost 'our' desire, so 'we' cannot overcome it on our own, but only through new ways of relating passed down from generation to generation. So literally a new society, a new way of relating, and hence a new 'us' has to be given. And these are what the death and resurrection of Jesus, I believe, has given to history. Once given these things, we do not remain infantile and dependent but become free to 'work out our own salvation'; once given a canoe and a paddle, we have what we need to get one another to the shore.

Mahayana Buddhism, I argued, has in the ideal of the Bodhisattva and the transfer of merit the basis of a better theory of atonement than the feudal theory that still dominates large parts of Western Christianity. But though I am sure there are Christians who will anathematize me for saying this, this is still a recognizable understanding of atonement that places me within the range of traditional Christian variation. It still enables me to say that Jesus was "handed over to death for our trespasses and was raised for our justification" (Rom.4.24).

So I am a kind of Christian, more precisely a Christian who

wants to combine the 'apophatic' darkness of God with an affirmation of God's self-emptying in creation and in Christ. In this combination Orthodox theologians like Maximus the Confessor (580-662) might be my natural allies. But Anglicanism – if it holds out against current pressures to go beyond its traditional reliance on the basic creeds – will probably remain my Christian home.

Now the arising of the 'apophatic' tradition could not be predicted from early Christian teaching, or from neo-Platonic Greek tradition, but arose as we saw out of the interaction of the two. Buddhist influence, at best, would have been a minor factor. Meanwhile after centuries of domination in the West by Anselm's theory, the atonement is widely being rethought in relation to the darkness and self-emptying love of God. I suggested that we can see the coming to light of the 'Christic shadow' of the Buddha. Can we not likewise see in these Christian developments the coming into the light of the 'Buddhic shadow' of Jesus – the aspect of Wisdom that was incarnate but not explicit in his life and teaching and that of the early Church? Finally, in Western Christianity the political emphasis has become steadily stronger, starting with papal and monastic reforms of 12th century, gathering pace in the radical wing of Reformation, and becoming more radical and urgent in recent Liberation Theology.

And I would argue that the 'Buddhist Christianity' that I advocate only continues these trajectories toward apophatic understanding of God on the one hand, and a seemingly contrasting liberation theology on the other. Like 'Christoyana Buddhism' in relation to the other vehicles of Buddhism, Buddhist Christianity will not replace the other forms of Christianity – Orthodox, Catholic and Protestant – but I hope it will enrich them. And the point of this book is not that Christianity and Buddhism are ultimately the same, but that 'Christoyana' Buddhism – if we can call it that – is the same as Buddhist Christianity in its main beliefs.

Christian in a Buddhist Way

Now in terms of practice it would be extraordinarily hard for me to give up my Christian ways, even if I wanted to. To the core of my being I have been spiritually shaped and formed by the pattern of worship and sacrament through the year and the day (see Thompson, 2008). I understand and imagine the world through Christian eyes, in a way that goes deeper with every year of my life. I have found my Christian practice deepened by Buddhist ones, notably meditation. But there would be nothing to be gained by abandoning all my Christian experience and starting again with Buddhist practices alone.

But what Buddhism has mainly given me is not new content, new beliefs that might add to, or might contradict, this Christian content. A comparison of the texts I used in the Introduction to define adherence to the two faiths reveals a vast difference. The Buddhist texts are a mixture of philosophical descriptions of how the world is – which can be tested against experience – and practical and ethical directives. The Christian texts are creeds, a series of mythical and historical statements I am asked to believe. But how these statements relate to the world – where for example the right hand of the Father is located, and who or what the devil and the deceit and corruption of evil are – is left open. Christianity gives us rich content for our faith, but Buddhism gives us a way of engaging with that content and relating it to the world in actual practice. Christianity is full of dramatic objective presentations of the goal of our search, but Buddhism seems to be richer in engaging with and transforming our subjective consciousness.

For this reason it is possible to believe in the Christian faith in a Buddhist way. Christianity offers objects for our imaginations to ponder and our hearts to delight in. Buddhism tells us how to entertain those objects without becoming over-attached to them, so that they can be beneficial and not destructive to ourselves and humanity. I believe that if Christians go on holding their beliefs and attending their worship, but in a Buddhist frame of mind, much will be gained.

Buddhism in essence is quite simple and honest. It does not demand statements of faith that cannot be tested and proven in heart and mind. Compared with Christianity it is not 'talkative' (as the E.M. Forster character so aptly put it). It does not use emotional rhetoric as a substitute for rational argument. In an age when 'mission' is all the rage, being Christian in a Buddhist way will make us quieter, less ready to talk, more eager to explore what we really feel and what difference our belief really makes, and more able, therefore, to influence the world for good.

Buddhism is concerned with practice more than metaphysics. Even its metaphysical flights have practice in view. It resists the hard objectifications that are in the end projections of a needy ego. Being Christian in a Buddhist way will help us see that what we believe has no 'objective reality' unless it makes an objective difference in our practice. It will make us more 'liquid', less dogmatically sure we are right, and less focused on set courses of action we believe to be a panacea for the world's needs.

It occurs to me that I always have interpreted my Christian concepts and faith in this Buddhist way. In some ways it has been my Buddhism that has enabled me to remain Christian. (These words echo the title of an excellent book by Paul Knitter (2009) that – without my realizing it – was being written even as I wrote this!) The standard Christian ways of understanding Christianity have not been something I could really believe, but a latent Buddhism has enabled me to understand them in a believable way. This may have meant that often I meant different things by Christian concepts from what my hearers or readers understood. In this respect my belief has not changed as I wrote this book, but I hope it may have become a bit clearer and more honest.

All in all, it seems to me there are plenty of good reasons, whether our practicing allegiance is primarily Christian or Buddhist, for our Christianity to be held with a Buddhist openness, or our Buddhism to take on board Christian imagination and passion. A Buddhist Christianity, as explored in this book, offers an openness to which we can be passionately committed, and a passion that is not grasping and narrowly focused, but opens us out to all that there is. It places the free and open sky which both Christ and the Buddha offer within our reach.

A Buddhist Christian Commitment

It was not my initial intention to develop a Buddhist Christian form of commitment. But the following seemed to emerge from the logic of the book. It is not intended as the creed of a new faith. But some Buddhists and Christians may find it sheds new light on their own commitment. And those who can commit themselves wholly to neither faith may find it helps them to understand better those who can, and perhaps take one step closer to a commitment of their own.

I have tried as far as possible to use ideas explored in the book rather than specifically Christian or Buddhist terms. The structure is that of the Christian baptismal renunciation and creed quoted in the Introduction, but into this I have woven the Buddhist triple refuge and the Three Marks of Being, the Eightfold Path and the Four Noble Truths.

In detail, (1)–(3) express the Christian baptismal renunciation of "the world, the flesh and the devil" in terms that incorporate the three Buddhist 'poisons': delusion, craving and violence. (5) represents the baptismal turning to Christ, combined with (4) the triple refuge. (6)–(8) represent the trinitarian baptismal creed, but using the imagery developed in Chapter 8 in place of the traditional Christian images. (A)–(D) are the Four Noble Truths expressed in the terms developed in Chapters 3–5. The adjectives in (D) describing the parts of the Eightfold Path (to which I have been so bold as to add a ninth) are taken from St. Paul's list of the fruits of the Spirit (Gal. 5.22-3). The final sentence (9) unites the last words of the Buddha with part of the Bodhisattva vow.

Make of it what you will. To me, all that is essential to Christian and Buddhist commitment is in this creed, though not necessarily in the familiar order or terms. But it may not be so for you.

The Renunciation

1) I renounce the web of delusions and ideologies that lure and entangle us in society.
2) I renounce all grasping and desire to possess people and things for myself alone.
3) I renounce the proud belief in myself as a self-sufficient being, and all envy, violence and injustice against others and the earth.

The Refuge

4) For rescue I turn to the Buddha, the Dharma, and the *Sangha*.
5) For rescue I turn to Christ, his teaching, his living, dying and rising, and his Church.

The Resolve

6) I affirm in the infinite Openness beyond all that we can know or imagine, the Emptiness that is emptied out in everything;

despite all the harm that goes on, I embrace all beings just as they are, as the only basis of our future;

daily I restore myself in the innocent Freshness from which they spring.

A) Despite this abundance we have become full of dissatisfaction and unhappiness.

B) This is caused by our grasping, our delusion and our proud egocentricity, as in a world which is always new, we crave a fixity which can never be realized, and would mean spiritual death if it ever were.

7) I affirm the Body of Wisdom: the ordered beauty of the Cosmos revealed in the sciences and arts; the Bride in whom the Source of all delights; the Child to which it is a tender Father;

who is fully poured out in the fully human Gautama Buddha, whose life and teaching have shown us the path of liberation;

and fully poured out in the fully human Jesus Christ, whose teaching, life, death and resurrection have overcome all that prevents liberation.

C) Liberation is therefore possible. We can live without delusion, craving and violence here and now, and the way to do so is known. Therefore we are accountable for how we choose to live.

D) If we hold to generous views, faithful intentions, judicious speech, loving actions, humble lifestyle, great-hearted effort, good mindfulness, peaceful meditation and joyful worship, liberation will come.

8) I affirm the Spirit, the sudden wind and fire, which overcomes our fears and fixity and moves life on;

the Compassion that fills all with yearning for a new world of justice and liberation;

the Way of Reconciliation that gathers people into the community of those committed to its coming.

9) I commit myself to seeking liberation with all diligence, for myself and for all beings.

Bibliography

This lists under chapter headings books referred to in that chapter, or relevant to it, or which helped the writing of the chapter. Inevitably this involves some duplication.

Prelude

Heinrich Dumoulin; tr. John Maraldo, 1974, *Christianity Meets Buddhism*, La Salle, IL: Open Court.

Anthony de Mello, 1983, *The Song of the Bird* Anand, Gujerat: Gujarat Sahitya Prakash.

Aloysius Pieris, 1988, *Love Meets Wisdom: A Christian Experience of Buddhism*, Maryknoll, NY: Orbis,

Ross Thompson with Gareth Williams, 2008, *SCM Studyguide: Christian Spirituality*, London: SCM.

Introduction

Masao Abe, 1995, *Buddhism and Interfaith Dialogue*, Honolulu: University of Hawaii Press.

R.C. Amore, 1978, *Two Masters, One Message*, Nashville: Abingdon Press.

Karen Armstrong, 1999, *A History of God*, London: Vintage.

Stephen Batchelor, 1997, *Buddhism Without Beliefs*, New York: Riverhead and London: Bloomsbury,

Bhikkhu Bodhi, (tr.), 2000, *The Connected Discourses of the Buddha: A New Translation of the Samyutta Nikaya*. Boston: Wisdom Publications.

J.E. Bruns, 1971, *The Christian Buddhism of St John: New Insights into the Fourth Gospel*, Maryknoll, NY: Orbis Press.

John Cobb, 1982, *Beyond Dialogue: Towards a Mutual Transformation of Christianity and Buddhism*, Philadelphia: Fortress.

Gavin D'Costa, 1990, *Christian Uniqueness Reconsidered: The Myth of a Pluralistic Theology of Religions*, Maryknoll, NY: Orbis.

Gavin D'Costa, 2000, *The Meeting of Religions and the Trinity*, Maryknoll, NY: Orbis.

Don Cupitt, 1980, *Taking Leave of God*, London: SCM.

Don Cupitt, 1986, *A Sense of History*. Theology, September 1986.

Bernard Faure, 2009, *Unmasking Buddhism*, Hoboken, NJ: Wiley Blackwell.

Richard Garbe,1914, *Indien und das Cristendom: eine Untersuchung religiongeschichtlicher Zuzammenhänge*, Tübingen: J.C.B. Mohr.

Lama Anagarika Govinda, 1969, *Foundations of Tibetan Mysticism*, London: Rider.

Dom Aelred Graham, 1963, *Zen Catholicism*, New York: Harcourt, Brace and World.

Tenzin Gyatzo, the Dalai Lama, 1996, *The Good Heart*, London, Sydney, Auckland, Johannesburg: Rider.

Christmas Humphreys, ed., 1960, *The Wisdom of Buddhism*, London: Rider; also 1995, London: Routledge.

John Keenan, 1989, *The Meaning of Christ: a Mahayana Christology*, Maryknoll, NY: Orbis.

Robert Kennedy, 1995, *Zen Spirit, Christian Spirit: The Place of Zen in Christian life*, New York: Continuum.

Whalen Lai, Whalen and Michael von Bruck, 2001, *Christianity and Buddhism: A Multicultural History of Their Dialogue*, Maryknoll NY: Orbis.

Kenneth Leong, 1995, 2001, *The Zen Teachings of Jesus*, New York: Crossroad.

Donald Lopez, ed., 1995, *Curators of the Buddha: The Story of Buddhism Under Colonialism*, Chicago: Chicago University Press.

Thomas Merton, 1961, *Mystics and Zen Masters*, New York: Noonday Press

Keiji Nishitani, 1982, *Religion and Nothingness*, Berkeley, Los Angeles and London: University of California Press.

Aloysius Pieris, 1996, *Fire and Water: Basic Issues in Asian Buddhism and Christianity*, Maryknoll, NY: Orbis.

Ray Riegert and Thomas Moore, 2004, *The Lost Sutras of Jesus: Unlocking the Ancient Wisdom of the Xian Monks,* London: Souvenir Press.

Robert Sharf, 1995, *Buddhist Modernism and the Rhetoric of Meditative Experience,* Numen, Vol.42, 1995, p.228-81.

Perry Schmidt-Leukel. 2005, *Buddhism and Christianity in Dialogue,* London: SCM.

D.T. Suzuki, 1957, *Mysticism, Christian and Buddhist,* New York: Harper and Row.

Ross Thompson, 1989, *What Kind of Relativism?* New Blackfriars, April.

Chogyam Trungpa, 1996, *Shambhala: The Sacred Path of the Warrior,* Boston, MA: Shambhala.

Alan Watts, 1957, *The Way of Zen,* London: Thames and Hudson.

Paul Williams, 2002, *The Unexpected Way: On Converting from Buddhism to Catholicism,* Edinburgh and New York: T & T Clark.

Chapter 1

Fritz Buri, tr. H. H. Oliver, 1997, *The Buddha-Christ as the Lord of the True Self: The Religious Philosophy of the Kyoto School and Christianity,* Macon, GA : Mercer University Press.

Robert Elinor, 2000, *Buddha and Christ: Images of Wholeness,* Cambridge: Lutterworth Press.

Bernard Faure, 2009, *Unmasking Buddhism,* Hoboken, NJ: Wiley Blackwell.

Rita Gross and Terry Muck, 1999, *Buddhists Talk About Jesus, Christians Talk About the Buddha,* London and New York: Continuum.

Tenzin Gyatzo, the Dalai Lama, 1996, *The Good Heart,* London, Sydney, Auckland, Johannesburg: Rider.

Christmas Humphreys, ed., 1960, *The Wisdom of Buddhism,* London: Rider; also 1995, London: Routledge.

Christmas Humphreys, 1990, *Buddhism,* Harmondsworth:

Penguin.

John Keenan, 1989, *The Meaning of Christ: a Mahayana Christology*, Maryknoll, NY: Orbis.

Robert Kennedy, 1995, *Zen Spirit, Christian Spirit: The Place of Zen in Christian Life*, New York: Continuum.

S.J. Samartha, 1991, *One Christ, Many Religions: Towards a Revised Christology*. Maryknoll, NY: Orbis.

Perry Schmidt-Leukel. 2005, *Buddhism and Christianity in Dialogue*, London: SCM.

Philip Sherrard, 1998, *Christianity: Lineaments of a Sacred Tradition*. Edinburgh: T & T Clark and Brookline, AM: Holy Cross Orthodox Press.

D.T. Suzuki, 1963, *Outlines of Mahayana Buddhism*, New York: Schocken Books.

Ross Thompson, 2009, *Spirituality in Season: Growing Through the Christian Year*, Norwich: Canterbury Press.

Paul Williams, 2008, *Mahayana Buddhism: the Doctrinal Foundations*, London: Routledge.

Walter Wink, 2001, *The Human Being: Jesus and the Enigma of the Son of the Man*: Minneapolis: Augsburg Fortress.

Chapter 2

Karen Armstrong, 2000, *Buddha*, London: Weidenfeld and Nicolson.

Marcus Borg, 1997, *Jesus and Buddha: The Parallel Sayings*, Berkeley, Ca: Seastone.

Roger J. Corless, 1989, *The Vision of Buddhism: The Space Under the Tree*, New York: Paragon House.

Bernard Faure, 2009, *Unmasking Buddhism*, Hoboken, NJ: Wiley Blackwell.

Rupert Gethin, tr., 2008, *Sayings of the Buddha: New Translations from the Pali Nikayas*, Oxford: Oxford University Press.

Thich Nhat Hanh, 1995, *Living Buddha, Living Christ*, New York: Riverhead.

Thich Nhat Hanh, 1999, *Going Home: Jesus and Buddha as Brothers*, New York: Riverhead Books.

J.K. Kadowaki, 2002, *Zen and the Bible*, Maryknoll, NY: Orbis.

John Keenan, 2005, *The Wisdom of James: Parallels with Mahayana Buddhism*, New York: Newman Press.

Kenneth Leong, 1995, 2001, *The Zen Teachings of Jesus*, New York: Crossroad.

Ulrich Luz and Axel Michaels ; tr. L. M. Maloney *Encountering Jesus & Buddha: Their Lives and Teachings*, Minneapolis : Fortress Press.

Friedrich Nietzsche, 1968, *The Twilight of the Idols and The Anti-Christ*, Harmondsworth: Penguin.

William Morrice, 1997, *Hidden Sayings of Jesus*, London: SPCK.

Max Muller, ed., 2006, *The Dhammapada: The Essential Teachings of the Buddha*, London: Watkins.

Aloysius Pieris, 1988, *Love Meets Wisdom: A Christian Experience of Buddhism*, Maryknoll, NY: Orbis,

James Robinson, ed., 1990, *The Nag Hammadi Library*, San Francisco: HarperCollins.

Chapter 3

Masao Abe, 1985, *Zen and Western Thought*, Honolulu: University of Hawaii Press.

Robert Bellah, 1970, *Beyond Belief: Essays on Religion in a Post-Traditional World*, New York: Harper and Row.

Ruben Habito, 2004, *Living Zen, Loving God*. Wisdom Publications, Boston.

Christmas Humphreys, ed., 1960, *The Wisdom of Buddhism*, London: Rider; also 1995, London: Routledge.

Leo Lefebure, 1993, *The Buddha and the Christ: Explorations in Buddhist and Christian Dialogue*, Maryknoll, NY: Orbis.

Friedrich Nietzsche, 1968, *The Twilight of the Idols and The Anti-Christ*, Harmondsworth: Penguin.

Perry Schmidt-Leukel. 2005, *Buddhism and Christianity in*

Dialogue, London: SCM.

Mark Siderits, 2007, *Buddhism as Philosophy: An Introduction*, Aldershot: Ashgate.

Paul Williams, 2002, *The Unexpected Way: On Converting from Buddhism to Catholicism*, Edinburgh and New York: T & T Clark.

Chapter 4

James Alison, 1998, *The Joy of Being Wrong: Original Sin through Easter Eyes*, New York: Crossroad.

Morris Berman, 1990, *Coming to our Senses: Body and Spirit in the hidden History of the West*, London, Sydney, Wellington: Unwin.

Robert Carter, God, 1990, *The Self and Nothingness: Reflections: Eastern and Western*, New York: Paragon House.

Chuang-tzu, 1964, *Basic Writings*, New York, Columbia University Press.

John Cobb and Christopher Ives, 1990, *The Emptying God: a Buddhist-Jewish-Christian Conversation*, Maryknoll, NY: Orbis.

Edward Conze, ed., 1969, *Buddhist Scriptures*, Harmondsworth: Penguin.

John Fowles, 1968, *The Aristos*, London: Pan.

Rita Gross and Rosemary Radford Ruether, 2001, *Religious Feminism and the Future of the Planet: a Buddhist-Christian Conversation*, London: Continuum.

Thich Nhat Hanh, 2007, *The Art of Power*, New York: HarperCollins.

Franz Kafka, 1961, *Metamorphosis and other Stories*, Harmondsworth: Penguin.

Søren Kierkegaard, 1980, *The Sickness unto Death*, Princeton: Princeton University Press.

David Loy, 2002, *A Buddhist History of the West: Studies in Lack*, New York: State University Press.

Karl Marx, ed. F. Engels, 1954, *Capital*, London: Lawrence and

Wishart.

Gabrielle Roth, 1998, *Maps to Ecstasy: A Healing Journey for the Untamed Spirit*, Novato, CA: New World Library.

Perry Schmidt-Leukel. 2005, *Buddhism and Christianity in Dialogue*, London: SCM.

Lynn de Silva, 1979, *The Problem of the Self in Buddhism and Christianity*, London: Macmillan.

Ross Thompson, 1990, *Holy Ground: The Spirituality of Matter*, London: SPCK.

Seiichi Yagi and Leonard Swidler, 1990, *A Bridge to Buddhist-Christian Dialogue*, New York: Paulist Press.

Slavoj Žižek, 2009, *Violence*, London: Profile Books.

Chapter 5

Caroline Brazier, 2007, *The Other Buddhism: Amida comes West*, Winchester and Washington: O Books.

Fritz Buri, tr. H. H. Oliver, 1997, *The Buddha-Christ as the Lord of the True Self: The Religious Philosophy of the Kyoto School and Christianity*, Macon, GA : Mercer University Press.

Frederick Franck, ed., 1982, *The Buddha Eye: An Anthology of the Kyoto School*, New York, Crossroad.

Rita Gross and Terry Muck, eds., 1999, *Buddhists talk about Jesus, Christians talk about the Buddha*, London and New York: Continuum.

Rita Gross and Terry Muck, eds., 2003, *Christians talk about Buddhist Meditation, Buddhists talk about Christian Prayer*, London: Continuum, 2003.

Tenzin Gyatzo, the Dalai Lama, 1996, *The Good Heart*, London, Sydney, Auckland, Johannesburg: Rider.

Leo Lefebure, 1993, *The Buddha and the Christ: explorations in Buddhist and Christian Dialogue*, Maryknoll, NY: Orbis.

Donald Lopez, and Steven Rockefeller, 1987, *The Christ and the Bodhisattva*, Albany, NY: State University of New York Press.

Gendo Nakai, 1946, *Shinran and his Religion of Pure Faith*, Kyoto:

Kanao Bunendo.

Walpola Rahula, 1978, *What the Buddha Taught*, London: Gordon Fraser Gallery.

Peter Rollins, 2006, *How (Not) to Speak of God*, London: SPCK.

Sangharakshita, 1994, *Who is the Buddha?*, Glasgow: Windhorse Publications.

Perry Schmidt-Leukel. 2005, *Buddhism and Christianity in Dialogue*, London: SCM.

Shinran, tr. Denis Hirota, 1997, *The Collected Works of Shinran*, Kyoto: Jodo Shinsu Hongwanji-ha. 2 Vols.

Perry Schmidt-Leukel. 2005, *Buddhism and Christianity in Dialogue*, London: SCM.

Lucien Stryk, ed., 1968, *The World of the Buddha: A Reader*, New York: Doubleday.

D.T. Suzuki, 1957, *Mysticism, Christian and Buddhist*, New York: Harper and Row.

D.T. Suzuki, 1963, *Outlines of Mahayana Buddhism*, New York: Schocken Books.

D.T. Suzuki, 1974, *Essays in Zen Buddhism*, 2nd ser 5th edition, London: Rider.

Lillian Too, 2003, *The Buddha Book: Buddhas, Blessings, Prayers and Rituals to Grant You Love, Wisdom and Healing*, New York: Crossroad.

Alan Wallace, 2009, *Mind in the Balance: Meditation in Science, Buddhism and Christianity*, New York: Columbia University Press.

Maurice Walshe, 1995, *The Long Discourses of the Buddha: a Translation of the Digha Nikaya*, Somerville, Mass: Wisdom.

Paul Williams, 2002, *The Unexpected Way: on converting from Buddhism to Catholicism*, Edinburgh and New York: T & T Clark.

Slavoj Žižek, 2009, *Violence*, London: Profile Books.

Chapter 6

Bruno Barnhart and Joseph Wong, 2001, *Purity of Heart and Contemplation: A Monastic Dialogue Between Christian and Asian Traditions*, London and New York: Continuum.

Caroline Brazier, 2007, *The Other Buddhism: Amida comes West*, Winchester and Washington: O Books.

Fritz Buri, tr. H. H. Oliver, 1997, *The Buddha-Christ as the Lord of the True Self: The Religious Philosophy of the Kyoto School and Christianity*, Macon, GA : Mercer University Press.

Gabriel Bunge, 1996, *Earthen Vessels: the Practice of Personal Prayer*, San Francisco: Ignatius Press.

John Cowan, 2004, *Taking Jesus Seriously: Buddhist Mediation for Christians*, Collegeville MN: Liturgical Press.

Tom Chetwynd, 2001, *Zen and the Kingdom of Heaven: Reflections on the Tradition of Meditation in Christianity and Zen Buddhism*, Boston: Wisdom Publications.

Bernard Faure, 2009, *Unmasking Buddhism*, Hoboken, NJ: Wiley Blackwell.

Laurence Freeman, 1999, *Common Ground: Letters to a World Community of Meditators*, New York: Continuum.

Lama Anagarika Govinda, 1969, *Foundations of Tibetan Mysticism*, London: Rider.

Rita Gross and Terry Muck, eds., 2003, *Christians Talk about Buddhist Meditation, Buddhists Talk about Christian Prayer*, London: Continuum, 2003.

William Johnston, 1981, *The Mirror Mind: Spirituality and Transformation*, San Francisco: Harper & Row.

James Jones, 2003, *The Mirror of God: Christian Faith as Spiritual Practice – Lessons from Buddhism and Psychotherapy*, New York: Palgrave Macmillan.

Martin Laird, 2006, *Into the Silent Land: The Practice of Contemplation*, London: DLT and New York: Oxford University Press.

Kenneth Leong, 1995, 2001, *The Zen Teachings of Jesus*, New York:

Crossroad.

Donald Lopez, ed., 1995, *Curators of the Buddha: The Story of Buddhism Under Colonialism*, Chicago: Chicago University Press.

Mary Jo Meadow, Kevin Culligan and Daniel Chowning, 2007, *Christian Insight Meditation: Following in the Footsteps of John of the Cross*, Boston: Wisdom Publications.

William Morrice, 1997, *Hidden Sayings of Jesus*, London: SPCK.

Pi-yen Chen, 2001-2, *Sound and Emptiness: Music, Philosophy and the Monastic Practice of Buddhist Doctrine*, History of Religions 41, pp.24-48.

Paul Reps, ed., 1971, *Zen Flesh, Zen Bones*, Harmondsworth: Penguin.

Michael Sells, 1994, *Mystical Languages of Unsaying*, Chicago and London: University of Chicago Press.

Ross Thompson, 2006: *SCM Studyguide: the Sacraments*, London: SCM.

Ross Thompson, 2008, *Spirituality in Season: Growing through the Christian Year*, Norwich: Canterbury Press.

Lillian Too, 2003, *The Buddha Book,* New York: Crossroad.

Kosho Uchiyama, 1993, *Opening the Hand of Thought: approach to Zen*, New York: Penguin.

Alan Wallace, 2009, *Mind in the Balance: Meditation in Science, Buddhism and Christianity*, New York: Columbia University Press.

Paul Williams, 2002, *The Unexpected Way: on converting from Buddhism to Catholicism,* Edinburgh and New York: T & T Clark.

Chapter 7

J.D. Barrow and F.J. Tipler, 1988, *The Anthropic Cosmological Principle*, Oxford: Oxford University Press.

Nicholas Berdyaev, 1952, *The Beginning and the End*, London: Geoffrey Bles.

David Bohm, 1983, *Wholeness and the Implicate Order*, New York: Routledge.

Caroline Brazier, 2007, *The Other Buddhism: Amida comes West*, Winchester and Washington: O Books.

Fritjof Capra, 1975, *The Tao of Physics*, New York: Shambhala.

David Chalmers, 1996, *The Conscious Mind: in Search of a Fundamental Theory*, Oxford: Oxford University Press.

John Davies, 1992, *The Mind of God: Science and the Search for Ultimate Meaning*, Harmondsworth: Penguin.

Alexei Filippenko and Jay Pasachoff, 2002, *A Universe from Nothing*, Mercury, Mar/Apr, on web page http://www.astrosociety.org/pubs/mercury/31_02/nothing.html

Martin Gardner, 2005, *The New Ambidextrous Universe: Symmetry and Asymmetry from Mirror Reflections to Superstrings*, New York: Dover.

T.H. Huxley, 1876, *Lectures on Evolution* (many modern editions, including 2004, Whitefish, MT: Kessinger.)

Stanley Jaki, 1986, *Science and Creation*, Edinburgh: Scottish Academic Press.

Matthew Kneale, 2000, *English Passengers*, Harmondsworth: Penguin.

Belden Lane, 1998, *The Solace of Fierce Landscapes*, Oxford and New York: Oxford University Press.

Kenneth Leong, 1995, 2001, *The Zen Teachings of Jesus*, New York: Crossroad.

Benoit Mandelbrot, 1982, *The Fractal Geometry of Nature*, San Francisco: Freeman.

Carolyn Merchant, 1982, *The Death of Nature: Women, Ecology, and the Scientific Revolution*, Aldershot: Wildwood House.

Simon Conway Morris, 2003, *Life's Solution: Inevitable Humans in a Lonely Universe*, Cambridge: Cambridge University Press.

David Pears, 1967, *Bertrand Russell and the British Tradition in Philosophy*, London: Collins.

Karl Pribram and Ervin Laszlo, 1993, *The Creative Cosmos: Towards a Unified Science of Matter, Life and Mind,* Edinburgh: Floris Books.

Holmes Rolston III, 1999, *Genes, Genesis and God: Values and Their Origins in Natural and Human History,* Cambridge: Cambridge University Press.

Perry Schmidt-Leukel, 2006, *Buddhism, Christianity and the Question of Creation,* Aldershot: Ashgate.

D.T. Suzuki, 1963, *Outlines of Mahayana Buddhism,* New York: Schocken Books.

Ross Thompson, 1990, *Holy Ground: the Spirituality of Matter,* London: SPCK.

Trinh Xuan Thuan, 2004, *The Quantum and the Lotus: a Journey to the Frontiers where Science and Buddhism meet,* New York: Three Rivers Press.

Alan Wallace, 2009, *Mind in the Balance: Meditation in Science, Buddhism and Christianity,* New York: Columbia University Press.

Burton Watson, tr., 1991, *Saigyo: Poems of a Mountain Home,* Columbia: Columbia University Press.

Chapter 8

James Alison, 1998, *The Joy of Being Wrong: Original Sin through Easter Eyes,* New York: Crossroad.

Karl Barth, tr. G.W. Bromiley and T.F. Torrance, 2004, *Church Dogmatics,* Edinburgh: T. & T. Clark.

John Cobb and Christopher Ives, eds., 1990, *The Emptying God : A Buddhist-Jewish-Christian Conversation,* Maryknoll, NY: Orbis. Essays by Masao Abe with Christian responses.

Dionysius, 1993, *Pseudo-Dionysius: the Complete Works,* Mahwah, NJ: Paulist Press.

Bernard Faure, 2009, *Unmasking Buddhism,* Hoboken, NJ: Wiley Blackwell.

James Fredericks, 2004, *Buddhists and Christians: Through Comparative Theology to Solidarity,* Maryknoll, NY: Orbis.

Rita Gross and Terry Muck, 1999, *Buddhists talk about Jesus, Christians talk about the Buddha*, London and New York: Continuum.

Aldous Huxley, 1945, *The Perennial Philosophy*, New York: Harper.

John Scotus Eriugena, tr, I.P. Sheldon-Williams and J.J. O'Meara, 1987, *Periphyseon (the Division of Nature)*, Montreal and Paris: Bellarmin.

Matthew Kneale, 2000, *English Passengers*, Harmondsworth: Penguin.

Leo Lefebure, 1993, *The Buddha and the Christ: Explorations in Buddhist and Christian Dialogue*, Maryknoll, NY: Orbis.

Bernard Lonergan, 1973, *Method in Theology*, London: DLT.

Robert Magliola, 1997, *On Deconstructing Life-Worlds: Buddhism, Christianity, Culture*, Atlanta: Scholars Press.

John D'Arcy May, 2003, *Transcendence and Violence – The Encounter of Buddhism, Christianity, and Primal Traditions*, London and New York: Continuum.

Bernard McGinn, 1994, *The Growth of Mysticism*, New York: Crossroad.

Jack Miles, 1995, *God, a Biography*, London et al.: Simon and Shuster.

Donald Mitchell, 1991, *Spirituality and Emptiness: The Dynamics of Spiritual Life in Buddhism and Christianity*. New York: Paulist Press.

Paul Mommaers and Jan Van Bragt, 1995, *Mysticism, Buddhist and Christian: Encounters with Jan Van Ruusbroec*, New York: Crossroad.

Raimundo Panikkar, 1989, *The Silence of God: The Answer of the Buddha*, Maryknoll, NY: Orbis.

D.T. Suzuki, 1963, *Outlines of Mahayana Buddhism*, New York: Schocken Books.

Denys Turner, 1995, *The Darkness of God: Negativity in Christian Mysticism*, Cambridge: Cambridge University Press.

Hans Waldenfels, tr. J. W. Heisig, 1980, *Absolute Nothingness:*

Foundations for a Buddhist-Christian Dialogue, New York: Paulist Press.

Simone Weil, 2002, *Gravity and Grace*, London: Routledge.

Paul Williams, 2004, *Aquinas Meets the Buddhists: Prolegomenon to an Authentically Thomas-ist Basis for Dialogue*, Modern Theology Vol.20 no.1, January 2004.

Slavoj Žižek and John Milbank, Creston Davis (ed.), *The Monstrosity of Christ: Paradox or Dialectic?*, Cambridge, MA and London: MIT Press.

Chapter 9

Paul Knitter, 2009, *Without Buddha I could not be Christian*, New York: Oneworld Press.

Paul Williams, 2002, *The Unexpected Way: on converting from Buddhism to Catholicism*, Edinburgh and New York: T & T Clark.

Index

Only the main text is indexed, not the chapter summaries or bibliography.

BOOKS

MySpiritRadio